MUHAMMAD ALI

MUHAMMAD ALI

A Humanitarian Life

MARGUERITTE SHELTON

ROWMAN & LITTLEFIELD
Lanham • Boulder • New York • London

Published by Rowman & Littlefield
An imprint of The Rowman & Littlefield Publishing Group, Inc.
4501 Forbes Boulevard, Suite 200, Lanham, Maryland 20706
www.rowman.com

86-90 Paul Street, London EC2A 4NE, United Kingdom

British Library Cataloguing in Publication Information Available

Library of Congress Cataloging-in-Publication Data

Names: Shelton, Margueritte, 1958– author.
Title: Muhammad Ali : a humanitarian life / Margueritte Shelton.
Description: Lanham, Maryland : Rowman & Littlefield, 2023. | Includes
    bibliographical references and index. | Summary: "Muhammad Ali: A
    Humanitarian Life is a unique biography of this iconic champion to chronicle
    his rise as a great humanitarian alongside his rise as a fighter, revealing the
    profound influence Ali had both in and out of the ring and that will endure for
    ages to come"—Provided by publisher.
Identifiers: LCCN 2022027424 (print) | LCCN 2022027425 (ebook) | ISBN
    9781538171547 (cloth) | ISBN 9781538171554 (epub)
Subjects: LCSH: Ali, Muhammad, 1942–2016. | Boxers (Sports)—United
    States—Biography.
Classification: LCC GV1132.A44 S44 2023 (print) | LCC GV1132.A44 (ebook)
    | DDC 796.83092 [B] —dc23/eng/20220712
LC record available at https://lccn.loc.gov/2022027424
LC ebook record available at https://lccn.loc.gov/2022027425

*For my dear parents Lili and Marquis who shine a
brilliant guiding light with love and compassion.*

An unseasonal storm raged against a rare Black Butterfly,
midair where it dared rending crosswinds, with fighting will to prevail.
Agilely transcending by winning spirit unending, through violent
rounds defending the perilous ascent.

Still magnificent as breaking sunrise electrified rainbows on
wounded wings, fluttering freely once more for all the world to see,
mighty flight to higher heights in the bright azure sky, raising sights on
its guiding light to boundless horizons.

Undefeated
The Greatest of All Time
By Margueritte Shelton

CONTENTS

ACKNOWLEDGMENTS

I would like to gratefully acknowledge the help, advice, and encouragement I received during the completion of this book.

Special thanks to Christen Karniski at Rowman & Littlefield for publishing guidance and encouragement.

Many thanks to Andrew Yoder at Rowman & Littlefield for artfully guiding me through the production process.

My deepest appreciation to author Norman Giller who introduced me to special paths along Muhammad Ali's journey outside the ring.

My gratitude to Karen Trost for her expert editing guidance through various development stages of the book.

With appreciation to the following:

Sportswriter David Kindred who shared his personal experiences about Muhammad Ali.

Thomas Hauser and Hana Ali who provided consent to use quotes for the book.

Photographers Michael Gaffney and Neil Leifer who provided personal accounts of Muhammad Ali.

Kathy Hertel-Baker, director at Sisters of Charity of Nazareth Archival Center, for providing source material.

Researchers at the Library of Congress, Arlene Balkansky and Darren L. Jones, who tirelessly provided access to a wealth of information.

Leah Cover, librarian at Spalding College in Louisville, Kentucky for access to special collections.

The Muhammad Ali Center for the Humanitarian Exhibit virtual tour.

FOREWORD

by Norman Giller, who knew him better than most[1]

Muhammad Ali would have warmly approved of this meticulously researched and conscientiously compiled study of his extraordinary life and times. I can almost hear him proclaiming: "This is the way I want to be remembered."

There is so much information and detail in the following pages that you would never guess that it is a debut book by Margueritte Shelton, a New York raised, Virginia-based writer who is a stunningly skilled newcomer to the literary world.

There have been scores of books and millions of words written about the great man, yet this addition to the Ali catalogue comes across as fresh, revealing, and illuminating. Even those who, like me, think they know the Ali parable well will have to concede that this book lifts our knowledge to a new level.

I had the pleasure and privilege of working with him as a publicist on several of his European fights. He needed a public relations expert like Einstein needed a calculator. In 2015 I wrote a book *The Ali Files* (Pitch Publishing) which centered on his momentous ring career, but I accept with all the sincerity I can muster that this book knocks mine through the ropes.

It is a perfectly paced dual story of Ali's magical, mesmerizing boxing exploits combined with an expert commentary on his continual battle in support of civil rights. A prizefighter turned humanitarian. He used his fame in the boxing ring to get his heartfelt message across and fought all his life for a fairer society.

The author, clearly sympathetic to her subject's ideals, understands the worth and weight of words, and never wastes them—just like Ali knew how to conserve his energy for the right moments in a fight. If only somebody had been around to stop the headstrong champion going to the well too many times. But that is "if only" territory we cross purely in hindsight.

While Ali drives the story with his phenomenal personality, the book includes great and, in many cases, legendary characters like Martin Luther King Jr., Elijah Muhammad, Malcolm X, John F. Kennedy, and boxing immortals, such as Joe Louis, Rocky Marciano, Jack Dempsey, and Sugar Ray Robinson.

The history and excitement of the boxing world ingeniously unfolds with the fascinating story of Ali's membership with the Nation of Islam and his years of conflict with the United States government over his refusal to take any part in the unjust Vietnam War.

This book accurately and boldly tells how he was prepared to sacrifice millions of dollars on the altar of principle and the desire to earn equal rights and dignity for his brothers and sisters. His bragging and bravado were all an act to draw attention to his message of peace and goodwill to everybody, which was a contradiction of the violent way he made his living.

The story comes to a crescendo with Ali's long, brave battle with Parkinson's, and captures perfectly the international platform and status he had that transcended boxing and made him the most famous man in the world.

I cannot recommend this book strongly enough for anybody who wants an intimate glimpse of a man who was, yes, The Greatest.

INTRODUCTION

The Fight for Equality:
A Champion in the Struggle

The title song from the Oscar-winning documentary *When We Were Kings* captures the impact of Muhammad Ali, an undefeated champion in the fierce fight for equal rights in America. When Ali was the most famous man in the world, he led the way for millions in the African American community to embrace their ethnic pride and remember the heritage of majestic kings in the African fatherland. On the ascent to win the crown, Ali ignited the golden age of boxing with lightning jabs, blinding flurries, and audacious moves in the ring. He was the fastest heavyweight who stole the brilliant spotlight by showcasing his athletic style with unmatched grace in motion from round one. With exceptional talent, he won the competitive edge as a dynamic world-class prizefighter who became a preeminent force in the evolution of the sport. The artistry of his innovative ring science led to many victories that eclipsed rare moments of defeat.

His celebrity persona gained worldwide attention and a talent for lyrical self-promotion attracted an unprecedented wealth of lucrative contracts for championship fights. Heavyweight opponents in the competitive inner circle praised him as a champion who elevated the sport to international acclaim more than others dared to venture. Ali had the gift of astonishing fortitude, often outdistancing contenders through 15 brutal rounds to victory. A phenomenal athlete, world renowned as "The Greatest of All Time," was the first in the history of the sport to capture three world heavyweight titles.

In the 1960s, Ali's bold personality *shook up the world*, while strengthening esteem for his African American identity in ways that challenged demeaning racist terms of engagement that deny inherent rights. His influence withstood the test of time through a violent decade when strong bloodlines of racial hatred seemed to flatline the compassionate heartbeat

1

of America. With a relentless voice promoting social justice, he had a far-reaching impact that defined his place among the vanguard of visionaries who shifted a worldview during the freedom fight. He spoke out courageously against the Vietnam War as a conscientious objector, then faced heavy odds in rounds of appellate court hearings after his conviction for draft evasion. Through life-defining legal battles to defend his religious beliefs, he persevered until his conviction was overturned by Supreme Court decision.

By demonstrating unwavering strength to overcome extreme adversity, he inspired faith that justice would prevail for those imperiled by virulent discrimination. His spirited sense of freedom, which reflected the soul of the civil rights struggle, empowered heirs of a politically dispossessed generation with deep roots in a cruel history of antebellum slavery. The world watched him defiantly cross a dangerous dividing line, beyond the unjust limits imposed on civil liberties, to strike massive blows against oppressive racism. During a revolutionary decade, he became a rebel who threatened the ruthless sentinel at the forbidden gateway to racial equality. Revered as the *People's Champion*, his humanitarian initiatives enriched lives around the world for decades while his impact continued to transcend sports. Muhammad Ali became a legendary champion in the ring and admired as a powerful force of nature who advanced the fight for human rights.

1

ON THE ROAD TO GREATNESS

The Journey Begins with Dreams of Gold

Cassius Clay on the Olympic Podium in Rome, 1960.
Central Press / Getty Images

Muhammad Ali often reminisced about his great aspirations as the young starry-eyed dreamer named Cassius Clay. "Before I won a gold medal at the Olympics, before I became the heavyweight champion of the world, before I stood up to the United States Government for my religious beliefs, before I was named United Nations Ambassador of Peace, and before I became the most recognized person in the world, I was just a kid from Kentucky who had the faith to believe in himself and the courage to follow his heart." From his West End neighborhood, 12-year-old Cassius rode to Downtown Louisville on his new deluxe trim red and white Schwinn bicycle. He felt the wheels spinning across the changing landscape of segregated Kentucky in 1954. It was a dangerous time for race relations in a territory that would resist integration long after the groundbreaking *Brown v. Board of Education* case that same year, when the Supreme Court ruled segregation in public schools unconstitutional. "Whites Only" signs were still prevalent guideposts warning him to follow oppressive Jim Crow dividing lines. The established racist culture taught him a cruel childhood lesson in subjugation when he was refused a drink of water on a sweltering day because of the color of his skin.

Falling rain caused Cassius to change his course to Columbia Auditorium, where he sought shelter from the storm by venturing inside to the local fair. This twist of fate led to an opportunity that would bridge the way to Olympic gold. When ready to leave for home, he discovered that an admiring thief had stolen his prized bike. Sounding the alarm with cries for help, Cassius drew the attention of Officer Joseph E. Martin Sr., an Irishman who was the resident boxing coach at the racially integrated Columbia Gym. He frantically told the policeman that he was ready to fight the culprit who had taken the bike. Officer Martin cautioned him to learn how to fight if he intended to beat someone up. Clay's passion for boxing began when Martin introduced a game plan to prepare the 12-year-old for heated battle. This chance encounter introduced a fitting sport to a young boy whose fighting spirit and natural athletic talent would lead him to extraordinary achievements in the boxing ring. After Clay joined the youth program mentored by Martin, he dedicated hours to the gym learning the craft for his fight debut in six weeks. Proven skills after numerous amateur tournament victories inspired his hope of becoming a world champion. He later gained fame in his hometown after Martin publicized Clay's growing record of national competitive wins on a local television show he produced, *Tomorrow's Champions*. The young dreamer entered the ring as an 89-pound light flyweight, who imagined himself on the throne as an invincible 220-pound world heavyweight champion. Mother Odessa Clay discovered, "His mind was like the March wind, blowing every which way . . . we'd sit at night, and he'd tell me how someday he was going to be champion of the world."

At home on Grand Avenue his family instilled pride, strength, and integrity in Cassius, while supporting his enthusiastic boxing ambition.

Although his mother Odessa asked with a hint of alarm, "You want to be a boxer?," she strengthened his belief in himself when he confided the dream of becoming a crowned champion. Lasting childhood memories were recalled by a grateful son who wrote, "My mother once told me that my confidence in myself made her believe in me. I thought that was funny, because it was her confidence in me that strengthened my belief in myself." His father, Cassius Marcellus Clay Sr., taught him to bravely confront fears while striving to reach his personal best. Young Cassius developed a sense of self-worth, as his father contradicted racist expectations that African Americans accept an invisible marginalized place where dreams of gold are unfulfilled. Cassius would make his place in the world with this strong foundation of support from his loving parents. He reminisced, "Although, at times my father had a quick temper, and my parents had disagreements, I had a happy home life and I knew that I was loved."

In the summer of 1955, Cassius heard the news about a heinous crime involving the murder of Chicago eighth grader Emmett Till. The teenager was close to his own age when brutally murdered while visiting family in Mississippi. National outrage would resonate for decades with the acquittal of defendants in this case about an African American boy killed after a rumored glancing encounter with a Caucasian woman. Later that year in Alabama, Rosa Parks defied segregation laws when she was arrested after refusing to give up a front "Whites Only" designated seat on the bus. While Clay followed youthful dreams of greatness, he fully understood the ferocity of the racist attitudes that threatened lives in these unsafe times.

In the training ring, Clay split his sparring time between coaches Martin and Fred Stoner, who were early influences refining his natural athletic talent. He spent six days a week in the gym, learning the science of boxing from Stoner, while perfecting his featherweight hand speed and graceful footwork to master a unique style. Clay brought an unshakable confidence to the ring, impressing Martin with his ambition to become the greatest heavyweight champion of the world.

Schoolmates at Central High School watched him train on fitness runs across miles of Downtown Louisville. Starting from his West End Parkland neighborhood, he tried to outdistance the school bus driving down Chestnut Street and historic Walnut Street. He imagined himself fighting the greatest professional prizefighters, as he sparred in school hallways with the bravado of a world-class champion, like his idol Sugar Ray Robinson. During school days, he pretended there were loudspeaker announcements identifying him as the crowned heavyweight champion of the world. Each day of disciplined workouts in the gym prepared him for the rounds of

Olympic light-heavyweight competition to come. Martin described him as brashly "popping off before fights from the very beginning," announcing the victory round of his bouts with rare prescience. He was the hardest worker in the gym, who enjoyed his newfound fame knowing the potential to make a fortune in prize winnings to lavish his parents with a new house and car.

As his amateur boxing career began to flourish, the 15-year-old worked at Nazareth College where librarian Sister James Ellen Huff supervised his work through his sophomore year in high school. The college was later renamed Spalding College, after the two had formed a friendship that would last more than 40 years. They shared a sense of compassion for those in need that engaged them in charitable missions. From the start of their relationship in 1957, she noticed his soft-spoken courteous demeanor was seemingly uncharacteristic for a tough-edged Kentucky Golden Gloves champion. She said, "I encouraged him to read, to have a bout with the books . . . he arrived at the library running and left running." Sister James Ellen watched him shadowbox his way through the stacks before he trained with Joe Martin at the Columbia Gym across the street. She recalled, "Once I found him asleep in the corner. We later put up a sign there that said, 'Cassius Slept Here.'" She followed his career, sending congratulatory letters including invitations to return to Louisville for visits to the college. When the sisters were confronted with questions about their continuing support of a boxer, they simply explained, "it has been characteristic of the Sisters of Charity of Nazareth that we continue to support our students when they leave school."

Legendary boxing coach Angelo Dundee noticed 15-year-old Clay's shining self-confidence when they met for the first time in 1957. Cornerman Dundee was in Louisville with professional light-heavyweight champion Willie Pastrano, whom he trained for his 48th bout against John Holman. He was introduced to Clay when the excited amateur boxer phoned their hotel room asking about the best practices for a world champion. Clay presented himself by saying, "Hi, my name is Cassius Marcellus Clay. I'm the Golden Gloves champion from Louisville. I won the Golden Gloves in Chicago. And I'm going to win the Olympics." Dundee met with the ambitious future national Golden Gloves champion, who was seeking expertise from the renowned boxing coach. Dundee returned to Louisville later, when Pastrano was defeated by Alonzo Johnson in his 60th fight in 1959. Clay would be given the chance to spar one round with Pastrano, surprising them both with the speed and agility of his unique natural style. By this time, 17-year-old Clay was a proven Golden Gloves champion primed for Olympic trials, after following Dundee's advice to win a medal first to become an accomplished professional contender. In addition to strict hours in the gym and maintaining a healthy lifestyle free from alcohol or smoking, Clay followed a dietary regimen that included a special elixir of garlic water chased with raw eggs. During the six years of amateur competition leading to the Olympic Trials, he would win over a hundred fights, including wins at six Kentucky Golden Gloves tournaments, two national Golden Gloves tournaments, and two American Athletic Union (AAU) titles.

On his way to qualifying for the Olympics, Clay became the top light-heavyweight contender in national amateur competitions and gained favorable press coverage. As he traveled from Louisville to tournament cities, "Tomorrow's Champion" televised his fights and interviews, making him a hometown celebrity. The local *Louisville Courier-Journal* would publicize his announcement that he was going to be the heavyweight champion of the world. During his prime fighting years, he displayed an unorthodox signature style that delivered punches with remarkable speed. In the ring, he circled opponents with hands low at his sides, relying on quick reflexes that showed off instinctive moves reminiscent of the fastest lightweights in history. He developed the ability to combine legendary stinging jabs and precise powerful hooks and uppercuts while agilely dancing around his opponent. His approach to ring science and unrivaled determination helped him defeat more seasoned amateur fighters for Golden Gloves championship wins.

During his rise to top-ranked Olympic medal hopeful, he never forgot neighborhood friends, whom he visited often to share his dreams of glory. His childhood best friend, Lawrence Montgomery, said, "He was a very energetic and compassionate boy. He just never stopped running. Everywhere he went he would run and shadowbox. . . . Even then he'd say he was going to be the heavyweight champion. . . . He'd say he always wanted to come back to see his friends. He never forgot us." Clay amassed a following of admirers in Louisville on his ascent to Olympian glory, reaching new heights that far surpassed the marginalized experience imposed by an unjust tradition of racial subjugation at home.

Travel for amateur fights introduced Clay to life in cosmopolitan cities like Chicago, the headquarters for the Nation of Islam (NOI) under the leadership of the Prophet Elijah Muhammad, who espoused the virtues of a prestigious African American heritage. NOI members believed in the prophecy of a new world order, with the devoted following a divine destiny to a spiritual path free from the reins of oppression. The Nation affirmed the threat from government operatives would fail to destroy the religious sanctuary of their separatist sect. Controversial Islamic temples preached a revolutionary African American theology, with a view of the world stratified by race, sharply divided into good and evil. The faithful stood united to defend against an ill-fated lineage of evil "white devils" guilty of perpetuating a cruel tradition by acts of inhumanity. In his book *Redemption Song*, author Mike Marqusee described the solidarity of the Nation strengthened by beliefs about an "irredeemable racism" in America. On a continuum of racist offenses, ranging from heinous crimes to passive indifference toward unjust wrongs, the Nation handed down indictments against White America. Core ideologies translated a brutal history in race relations into powerful political oratory resonating within the hallowed walls of the Islamic temples. Precise dividing lines traced by the Messenger, Elijah Muhammad, empowered a social movement deeply rooted in Black Nationalism. NOI teachings offered an alternative way of life to forced integration that incited a spate of deadly resistance from white supremacists.

When Clay was introduced to the Nation of Islam in 1959 during Golden Gloves tournament competition in Chicago, he became aware of a different worldview in the fight for civil rights. The rising champion's vision of greatness was empowered by tenets that espoused devout religious faith, strength in African American pride, and independence with self-determination that defied dominant racist attitudes. The temple's congregations worshiped Allah as Muslims, but were also influenced by a Black Nationalist movement that they believed would reign supreme in a racially stratified America. He defined his destiny from this empowering worldview, knowing that one day he was going to be great. Clay set his sights on winning the coveted heavyweight crown and advancing the fight for equal rights and justice. His confidence, determination, and bold personality impressed many people from the start of his rise to fame. They were not surprised when he would have a significant impact that would change the world as he discovered a greater life purpose.

The Nation's headquarters distributed published messages from Elijah Muhammad on windy street corners across Chicago's South Side. Clay became impressed by the teachings of this revolutionary Islamic sect, which vowed a solution for racial injustice with a powerful Black Nationalist ideal. Successful NOI-owned enterprises invested financially in strengthening inner-city communities. The Messenger delivered assurances that followers would become the best they hoped to be with faith in Allah. Even an aspiring world champion was not safe in certain places because of the color of his skin. Fame as a young Olympic hopeful did not alter the reality that he was a prime target of violent racial hatred in America. Self-determination, solidarity, and religious faith were compelling elements of the Nation's precepts, inspiring a collective vision of greatness. Clay returned to Louisville with a record album of Elijah Muhammad speeches that influenced a change in his beliefs, reinforcing his proud identity and giving him greater life purpose.

By this time, Clay was on course for the Olympics Team Trials in California. He gained attention as a medal hopeful after some 150 amateur fights had proven his relentless drive for excellence in the sport. His two national Golden Gloves titles and two AAU wins had placed Clay on the list for the Olympic Trials. One thing that threatened to sideline him from winning a medal was his fear of flying in an airplane. The qualifying matches held in San Francisco forced him to board a plane for a long-distance trip for the first time. After surviving a turbulent flight, the panic subsided, and he easily won a place on the American Olympic Boxing Team in light-heavyweight competition. Coach Martin observed that, "He was different. Quick as lightning for a big man, the quickest I ever saw."

As the new year of 1960 dawned, the media shifted its attention to the civil rights movement, which in its second decade was gaining momentum after progressive action by college students crossing forbidden boundaries. Parts of the country still defended a political paradigm of racial segregation against freedom fighters of the era. On one side of this pernicious divide were racists in the Deep South, guarding their territory by fiercely resisting an advancing freedom movement. Political turmoil in the 1960s provoked social conflict on many levels, from private outrage to public protests across the nation. Civil rights activists voiced inherent rights for all from a united front to expose the unjust truth about systemic racial discrimination in the "land of the free." Peaceful protests in 1960, during student sit-ins at business establishments, involved more than a hundred students from Nashville's Fisk University, who were arrested as they waited to be served at segregated lunch counters. These protests followed the first campaigns in January 1955, which brought together student activists from Morgan State University and the Congress for Racial Equality (CORE) to form an effective alliance. These sit-ins forced Read's Drugstore in Baltimore to announce the end of segregating customers at every store location within hours. The next decade experienced a resurgence of the movement, despite protesters being confronted with escalating violence reaching unimagined proportions. In February 1960 a student sit-in at a Woolworth's lunch counter in Greensboro, North Carolina, defied segregationist practices and inspired others to engage in peaceful protests across the South. Later that year Reverend Martin Luther King Jr.—a powerful influence rallying support for the widespread movement—was arrested and sentenced to several months in an Atlanta jail for leading defiant sit-ins.

While student activists rallied support for civil rights, the handsome all-American boy next door graduated from Central High School, on the verge of international boxing acclaim. Clay knew he was favored to win an Olympic medal in Rome that summer and set his sights high on next becoming the greatest boxing champion in history. *Sports Illustrated* first featured the 18-year-old high school graduate as "the best American prospect for a gold medal [in boxing]." Sportswriters described an unorthodox boxing style that conveyed supreme confidence. He was in constant motion, dancing on his toes out of reach and landing punches while circling the ring. Coaches encouraged the rising star to tone down his brash overconfidence in the Olympic arena, where a fighter's ring skills customarily do most of the talking. The incessant self-promotion talk would earn him the nickname "Louisville Lip." The world began to take notice of this talented athlete with a unique winning signature style. Kentucky, known for bourbon, bluegrass music hits, and celebrated fortunes in thoroughbred racing at Churchill Downs, would be the focus of an even brighter international spotlight with the fame of hometown boxing champion Cassius Clay.

His seemingly invincible stride toward superstardom nearly ended when fear of flying once more momentarily grounded plans for his Olympic debut. Martin quickly intervened, settling Clay's nerves by emphasizing that this was the opportunity of a lifetime. A temporary solution was to take extreme precautions and wear a parachute as an emergency exit strategy, which somewhat compromised his Superman image during the transatlantic flight to Rome. He arrived at the XVII Olympiad beaming with unrivaled confidence that attracted attention from other athletes at the Olympic Village. The press rallied around the boxing talent with finely tuned instincts, quick reflexes, and agility that he used against tough opponents in the ring. A new season of *Louisville Courier-Journal* articles documented the impressive accolades given to the rising champion as he stepped out onto the world stage.

When Olympic competition began on August 25, 1960, Clay was featured in Italian newspapers taking his place as the popular mayor of the Olympic Village. As he commanded the limelight, new friends rallied around his warm-hearted spirit, personality, and talent for sensational public relations. The press, including the sports media in America, kept pace with his rapidly growing appeal while apprised of his plans for a professional boxing career on his return home. Even before his Olympic matches, Clay announced he was prepared to fight reigning world champion Floyd Patterson. He competed with intimidating confidence, sporting an intense bravado in the ring that would continue into his years as a professional prizefighter. A world of new admirers experienced his innovative boxing style, using fast combinations with skillful marksmanship, moving in the ring on his dancing feet. Wilbert "Skeeter" McClure, his roommate during the Olympics, described the charming side of the famous contender. He observed that he always tried to impress the pretty girls: "he was so shy . . . Cassius was philosophical . . . voluble . . . managed to distract his fears by talking a lot. . . . Even then, you knew he was special; a nice, bright, warm, wonderful person."

Clay took the Games by storm, winning against Belgian Yvon Becot in Round Two before reaching the quarterfinals with a 5–0 decision over 1956 middleweight gold medalist Gennadiy Shatkov of the Soviet Union. Clay continued to advance through his semifinal win by unanimous decision over Tony Madigan of Australia that assured him a medal. His next fight was against 25-year-old Polish champion, Zbigniew "Ziggy" Pietrzykowski, who qualified for the games as a 1956 bronze medal Olympian and three-time amateur European champion. On September 5, Clay rose to the challenge wearing athlete number 272, setting the pace and overwhelming Ziggy with lightning ring speed. Defensive footwork had Clay circling the ring staying out of range, as he displayed devastating rhythmic flurries from all directions to daze his seasoned opponent in the final round. He was on track to be the best light-heavyweight in the world of amateur boxing.

Fight analysts commented on his effective tactics, which allowed him to land right-hand leads and brilliant counterpunches against Ziggy's southpaw style. Clay later explained his strategy: "I knew that I had to take the third round big to win." His in-and-out gliding footwork, the speed of blinding flurries, and a lightning right hand over a left jab dominated the stunned Polish fighter. Clay's bloody opponent sustained mounting damage and the fight almost ended in a knockout, but ultimately the judges would decide the winner on points. In the final moments, the 6'1", 178-pound Clay finished off Pietrzykowski with swift agility and sharply timed punches. Clay was crowned the gold medal champion after the 5–0 unanimous decision. *New York Times* journalist Arthur Daley wrote that Clay was the proudest champion on the Olympic podium that day. He returned as a gold medalist to hometown fanfare and national acclaim. By May of 1961, Daley would be writing about Clay's professional career, documenting his impressive wins during the first six fights against top seasoned heavyweights.

Media attention focused on both his Olympic win and the ongoing civil rights struggle in America. From reports of sit-ins at lunch counters to protests in communities across the nation, interest in the fight for equality extended across international boundaries. When an overseas Russian journalist asked questions about segregation laws, raising the topic of American racism, Clay responded patriotically, "Tell your readers we got qualified people working on that problem, and I'm not worried about the outcome. To me, the USA is the best country in the world, including yours." He would return home with proud honors only to realize that, despite a crowning Olympic achievement, Jim Crow practices remained an in-force threat against him. He believed that if the medal did not mean equality for all it was worthless.

During the Games, Clay became secretly enamored with American track star Wilma Rudolph, who astounded the world as the first American female sprinter to win three gold medals. She was named "La Perle Noire" (The Black Pearl) by the French press, after her Olympic performance surpassed all others with a talent that outdistanced her competition by miles. Before overcoming his shyness to ask for a date, Clay challenged her to a race that would be his only moment of defeat at the Olympic Games. A more personal meeting happened much later during a visit to Louisville, when they drove together around town in Sugar Ray Robinson style, showing off his new pink Cadillac with the top down, an enjoyable moment of celebration they shared before she returned to home state Tennessee. After turning professional later that year, Clay overcame his apprehension once more, driving his Cadillac convertible to visit her at Tennessee State University. The two would share the same understanding about pursuing a greater purpose beyond athletic accolades to better lives in the world. Rudolph said, "I would be very disappointed if I were only remembered as a runner because I feel that my contribution to the youth of America has far exceeded the woman who was the Olympic champion."

As a proud young Olympian, Clay wore his precious gold medal for everyone to admire. Before returning home, he celebrated his victory in high style in New York City, where he spent time at Sugar Ray Robinson's Harlem restaurant, toured Times Square, enjoyed New York cheesecake served at Jack Dempsey's restaurant, and visited jazz mecca Birdland before returning to his plush suite at the Waldorf-Astoria. The itinerary and carte-blanche accommodations were courtesy of millionaire William G. Reynolds, executive vice president of Reynolds Metals Company, looking to manage his career jointly with Joe Martin. Clay then brightened the luster of hometown Louisville while parading in a motorcade celebration down Walnut Street, a landmark dividing line during racial segregation. The road symbolized the fight for equality that escalated in brutal conflict between separate worlds.

Proudly adorned with Olympic gold, he returned home, where jubilant cheers for the victorious champion fell silent to threatening overtones from forbidden segregated grounds. Despite the magnitude of his achievement at the Olympics, here he remained an unwelcome presence who was denied entry at a downtown "Whites-Only" restaurant. His radiant light of self-pride shattered against the refractive lens of a racist culture when the waking reality defied his dreams. Evidence of suffering was starkly visible against a vivid spectrum of iniquitous color boundaries that scarred the landscape. Centuries of reprehensible events stayed the course as sanctioned racial discrimination continued to satisfy a voracious appetite for dehumanizing cruelty. Segregationists still ruled this territory by preserving a brutal legacy of supremacy in the South, when Clay's ascent to glory was defaced by the malicious crosscurrents of hatred in Kentucky.

With each step forward, Clay vied against assailing racist attitudes that emerged with a vengeance to remind him of life with endangered liberties. State politics controlled this jurisdiction of intolerance, turning his homecoming motorcade down Walnut Street to West End Louisville. The master of ceremonies leading the procession through a segregationist tradition protected white supremacist territory with an impassable color line. He reached a riverfront bridge, where unrelenting discontent surged beneath the unforgiving sun. Soul-searching gave rise to revelations that transformed him through the scathing rite of passage into manhood. Innocent dreams were cast away on bloody waters, when his brave spirit was cut down by backlashing currents that immersed him in a brutal fight for freedom. Legend has it that Clay threw his gold medal into the river with the belief it could stem the tide of injustice in an evil world.

Fresh from his Olympic victory, with the help of his father, Clay searched for an experienced management team to handle contracts for his advancing career. The champion widely publicized his dream of winning the crown, claiming the world heavyweight champion title was his destiny. He attracted offers from seasoned, elite professionals with the best deals in the boxing world. Taking the lead on business decisions, his father selected the Louisville Sponsoring Group (LSG) to manage Clay's prizefighting future. Days before his first professional match, Clay signed a generous six-year contract with the LSG, which provided legal expertise and business acumen to launch his career. The group consisted predominantly of heirs to Kentucky business fortunes whose expertise ranged from tobacco and bourbon to professional team sports, including Archibald M. Foster, Patrick Calhoun Jr., William S. Cutchins, J. D. Stetson Coleman, William Faversham Jr., James Ross Todd, Vertner-DeGarmo Smith Sr., George W. Norton IV, William Lee Lyons Brown Sr., Robert Worth Bingham, and Elbert Sutcliffe. Louisville attorney Gordon B. Davidson was a lawyer for the 11 financiers and maintained a lifelong friendship with the charismatic champion. The LSG handled travel and training expenses for the local hero, ensuring funds were set aside in a pension account that vested when he turned 35 or retired. He entered the ring of professional heavyweights with intellectual assets from power-elite sponsors spending venture capital and arranging lucrative deals in the Mob-controlled world of heavyweight prizefighting. Tuning in to fight broadcasts on the radio inspired the stargazing Clay to set a course toward great achievements in professional heavyweight boxing, with new savvy sponsorship.

Clay embarked on his professional career, traveling around the country with expert sportswriters who would discover they were covering the start of a new golden age in boxing. From the beginning of his ascent to the heavyweight throne, he advanced without rave reviews from reporters who had covered many great champions in the ring. Eminent journalist A. J. Liebling complimented Clay's novel boxing style, despite being unconvinced that his ring science would have a powerful impact in the arena of seasoned heavyweights. Writing about Clay's Olympic victory, Liebling stated, "He was good to watch, but he seemed to make only glancing contact. It is true that the Pole finished the three-round bout helpless and out on his feet. . . ." Arthur Daley wrote about "the loudmouth from Louisville" revealing his critical assessment that "He can't fight as well as he can talk. . . ."

Despite skepticism from the media, the aspiring world champion embodied resolute tenacity during his early professional wins and showed great promise. The month following his first professional fight, a win over Tunney Hunsaker, the political landscape changed when John F. Kennedy—determined to secure equal rights for African Americans—was elected president of the United States.

As the rising world heavyweight champion entered the professional spotlight, the LSG protected his interests while watching the fights from ringside seats. Member Elbert Sutcliffe said, "Some of us wouldn't cross the street to see a concert, but we'll go hundreds of miles to see Cassius in the ring." The group optimistically introduced their fighter to everyone as the next heavyweight champion of the world. Clay was a prizefighter with a rare brand of star quality, backed by sponsors who invested time and money in the promising fighter they believed could one day be crowned heavy-weight champion. Clay brashly boasted to everyone that he was destined to overthrow the reigning champion to capture the throne. Renowned boxing coach Angelo Dundee would soon realize that the sport of professional boxing had entered the "Age of Cassius Clay."

2

SCIENTIFIC APTITUDE

Power, Speed, and Grace in Motion

A Scientific Fighter Commands the Ring.
Trinity Mirror / Mirrorpix / Amaly Photograph

The rise of Cassius Clay would return the sport to a golden age of great prizefighting unmatched since the days of Hall of Famers Sugar Ray Robinson, Joe Louis, "Jersey" Joe Walcott, and Rocky Marciano. Clay managed expectations by broadcasting, "I'm young, I'm handsome, I'm fast, I can't possibly be beat." On March 11, 1963, sportswriter Houston Horn featured Clay in a *Sports Illustrated* article as "heir apparent to the throne of heavyweight boxing." After a sweep of amateur wins that led to Olympic gold, a series of early professional career wins would place him as the top-ranked contender to face reigning world champion Charles "Sonny" Liston for the title. Clay's ascent to the summit brought attention to a multi-talented fighter with extraordinary athletic skills from millions of people around the world, while attaining record-breaking attendance unseen since Rocky Marciano vs. Joe Louis in 1951. The sport, until then ruled by a criminal underworld syndicate, was about to experience a dramatic changing of the guard with the rise of a new champion. At a time when government indictments ensured the downfall of Mob bosses, the arena of heavyweight boxing was opened to new, lawful business management.

Of the Hall of Fame champions, Clay idolized Sugar Ray Robinson, who once claimed both the welterweight and middleweight thrones after more than 100 career knockouts. The young champion explained that Sugar Ray was the type of boxer he aspired to become. Impressed by Robinson's ring talent, good looks, and fashionable style, Clay emulated the great champion. He listened to Sugar Ray's fights on the radio, admiring the artistry of the world-class fighter, who would win 174 fights during his 25-year career. Clay referred to the fastest welterweight on the scene in past decades as "the king, the master, my idol." Sugar Ray possessed exceptional speed and knockout power that combined flurries, hooks, and uppercuts in unconventional ways. With a versatile talent for different styles, he interchanged between brawling and boxing techniques. He could launch a flurry of punches between dance moves, taking him beyond reach in rounds of his choice. According to boxing analyst Bert Randolph Sugar, "Robinson could deliver a knockout blow going backward." A 1951 *Time* magazine article stated, "Robinson can always count on a sure sense of rhythm and the ability to cut loose with a stunning flurry of punches with both hands." He understood the value of high-intensity training techniques to build reflexive muscle action in the ring. The great champion explained, "You don't think. It's all instinct. If you stop to think, you're gone." Robinson drove a flamingo-pink Cadillac admired by Clay, who purchased the same model for his mother after landing his first professional contract with the Louisville Sponsoring Group. Clay was heavier and faster than Sugar Ray, achieving an impressive fight record with hallmark jabs flicked on impact with abrasive stings. Years later, Sugar Ray continued to watch him rise to new heights in prizefighting as the fastest heavyweight ever to step in the professional ring. Light-heavyweight champion José Torres observed about Clay, "He didn't bend down. He didn't go to the body. He punched going backwards. He held his hands too low. He pulled straight back from punches. He didn't even throw combinations; he threw punches and flurries. And then he would win for two reasons—speed and magic."

In the early 1960s, some of the most renowned boxing greats were enthusiastic about the talents of the rising contender for the throne. International Hall of Fame legends Jack Dempsey and Joe Louis remarked on Clay's exceptional speed after observing the fighter display his unique moves. World heavyweight champion Floyd Patterson commented on the boxing aptitude that would become Clay's trademark: "It's very hard to hit a moving target, and (Clay) moved all the time, with such grace, three minutes of every round for fifteen rounds. He never stopped. It was extraordinary." International Hall of Fame boxing coach Eddie Futch was among those managing the corner ring when his best fighters faced the versatile range of skills Clay mastered and were defeated. During matches, he used classic right-hand leads, powerful hooks, lightning-fast stinging jabs, Rope-A-Dope defense, Ali Shuffle bravado, the Mirage tactic, and mind-over-matter ring science. Clay caught opponents by surprise with his legendary "Anchor Punch," knocking them to the canvas in the blink of an eye. His approach to psychological warfare provoked an emotional reaction that distracted opponents from their usual game plans. He monopolized the spotlight with lighthearted fight promotion captured by sports media, posturing as if to ask, "See how pretty I am?," directed toward those he thought may not have noticed. Sportswriters acknowledged his natural grace and athletic beauty that brought an innovative new artistry to the brutal sport of boxing.

The skills of this talented fighter balanced elements of bold personality, brutality, grace, and beauty in a unique signature style that dominated his weight class. In addition to his rhapsodized self-confidence, Clay sometimes grabbed the spotlight with prefight lightheartedness, playing practical jokes and doing magic tricks to amaze the eye. The showmanship sometimes continued during the main event, even when he displayed great fortitude in getting down to serious business demanded in the cruel fight ring. He proved to be a skillful tactician, building his stellar record on quick footwork, staying unscathed even as he seemed to have his guard down, circling opponents before he moved in with precision blows. Using damaging psychological warfare, he often accurately predicted the winning round, mercilessly taunting his opponents before the prediction came true. The rising contender for the throne informed the ringside crowd that his opponents would fall in the round of his choice.

Creative tactics earned him a reputation as the most innovative heavyweight of all time. Opponents struggled with the featherweight speed that took him beyond the range of counterpunches milliseconds before impact. His blinding speed outpaced his opponents and threw them off balance when they misjudged the range of impact. The effect of his punches was cumulative, strategically overwhelming opponents through advancing rounds. He was a tricky fighter who feinted punches from all angles, then stepped out of tempo to deliver dizzying flurries or magically timed jabs. With a special aptitude for scientific fighting, he defeated many opponents inside the distance using his greatest asset—*speed*. Like many of the most talented prizefighters, he won by outsmarting his opponents with masterful ring-science skills instead of powerful punches.

Clay's style of showmanship elevated tempers in the opposite corner of the ring and was designed to distract the competition. Name-calling, boasting about his superior beauty, and predicting rounds combined to give him a psychological edge and infuriate his opponents to the point where they would lose focus and make crucial mistakes.

As Clay rose in the professional ranks, journalist A. J. Liebling wrote, the young heavyweight was just a lightweight "butterfly . . ." with "busy hands stinging like bees." His metaphor was a prelude to the famous mantra "Float like a butterfly, sting like a bee" first shouted by assistant trainer Drew "Bundini" Brown Jr. from Clay's corner in 1963. Bundini—who had been introduced to Clay by Sugar Ray Robinson—added a seasoned perspective to Clay's experience in the fight world and the pair developed a bold camaraderie. Clay said that Bundini was a great inspiration heard by millions around the world, sparking his winning spirit in the ring by shouting, "Dance! Dance, Champ! Dance!" Clay lived up to the catchphrase, flaunting his bravado with fast stinging jabs while floating across the ring on gliding footwork. His signature punch was the left jab, believed to be the fastest in history for any weight class. He threw his overhand right with precision, rarely failing to reach the mark. While promoting himself as the uncrowned heavyweight champion of the world destined to become the "Greatest of All Time," the ultra-confident spirit behind his winning mindset created an effective psychological advantage. High-powered fight-talk produced record-setting gates and sellout closed-circuit revenues around the world. In 1961, sporting matches in the ring reached a new level of excitement with Clay's brand of showmanship, fashioned after the outlandish escapades of wrestler "Gorgeous George" Wagner. He listened to fight promotion suggestions from Wagner, who encouraged him to wear white shoes in the ring to accentuate his foot speed.

There were those who disparaged his talents, despite a high athletic aptitude for boxing, effective rapid-fire fists, and undefeated record. Boxing conventionalists refused to accept his unorthodox style that was too much of a departure from the great heavyweights who fought toe-to-toe withstanding massive blows. Critics felt his style left him ill-equipped to win the prized world title. Martin Kane of *Sports Illustrated* observed, "no prizefighter ever has fought entirely by the book." The victory-round predictions, fight-talk self-promotion, and calling himself "The Greatest" were ultimately meant to crowd his opponent's mind with self-doubts. He sailed high on a wave of wins that showed how his sharp reflexive jabs allowed him to move effortlessly across the ring and outpace more experienced heavyweights of his time.

The LSG continued to provide financial backing for the aspiring heavyweight champion and were now invested in all aspects of his promising career. Under their sponsorship, Clay could devote all his time to boxing with enough money to hire first-rate sparring partners, expert trainers, and a ring doctor. Clay realized the premium value of experienced trainers like Cus D'Amato, and legendary fighter Archie Moore who had the professional experience to teach him techniques for winning ring science. The LSG decided to send him to San Diego where he trained under Moore, who would amass a record of more than 200 fights. When Clay fell short of his expectations, Moore complained, "My wife is crazy about him, my kids are crazy about him, and I'm crazy about him, but he won't do what I tell him to do." Clay responded that he wanted to be a "heavyweight Sugar Ray," not a fighter like Moore.

Personality conflicts set the stage for negotiations in Miami for Clay to train with renowned 39-year-old cornerman Angelo Dundee. Before Dundee would accept the contract, Clay had to prove he was meant for the big leagues. The 18-year-old debuted in his hometown in front of 6,000 people at Freedom Hall. With astounding pace, he won the six-round match by unanimous decision against Fayetteville, West Virginia, policeman Tunney Hunsaker. The seasoned Hunsaker offered an assessment to the press after the fight stating, "he could hit from every position without getting hit. . . ." Before heading to his new training grounds with Dundee in Miami, Clay donated the prize winnings to a local hospital for special needs children, which was just the beginning of his lifelong concern for the well-being of other people during his travels across the nation visiting hospitals. Armed with great ambition, the young man from Louisville adapted to segregated Miami, where he was welcomed in the African American community of Overtown. As demonstrators in the South were defying Jim Crow segregation practices, Clay became the top-ranked contender for the heavyweight crown while training in Miami. He worked on physical conditioning for fights on endurance runs across MacArthur Causeway to Miami Beach, often confronting police who were enforcing curfew laws that were a product of a racist tradition, keeping African Americans from freely stepping into forbidden segregated places.

Dundee was the perfect match for Clay, who began training sessions on December 19 at the famous 5th Street Gym owned by Dundee's brother Chris, a well-established fight promoter. The second-story walkup in a rundown building on the corner of 5th Street and Washington Avenue was once a Chinese restaurant. Dundee was in charge of speed bags, heavy bags, and ring action, while sharing his boxing wisdom that inspired many crowned champions. Two months after defeating Hunsaker, Dundee was in Clay's corner for his second career win against Herb Siler by a technical knockout in four rounds. Siler was outclassed by Clay's phenomenal speed, accuracy, and intuitiveness in the ring.

Clay's exceptional work ethic was characterized by a tenacious drive that fit the bill for a future world champion. The intensity of his disciplined approach to training in the gym remained unchanged, while he worked with Dundee to refine a world-class style inside the 5th Street Gym. Dundee recalled, "he'd be the first kid in the gym and the last guy to go home." Clay developed a lifelong bond with the International Boxing Hall of Fame cornerman who trained 15 world champions over six decades. Dundee was a master of ring psychology, adapting his coaching approach to suit his fighters, while encouraging them to build mental toughness against their opponents. Dundee appreciated the value of Clay's showmanship stating, "Those experts who are critical of his clowning don't understand the psychological advantage it gives him over opponents." Dundee wrote the playbook on psychological warfare for his fighters to gain the prefight buildup advantage. Although the press nicknamed Clay the "Louisville Lip" for his incessant fight-talk they captured in news headlines, many fans were surprised to discover he was a quiet man in private life. Dundee's coaching style gave Clay latitude to show off his creative flair and sharp instincts in the ring. He was known as a matchmaking guru who carefully selected journeymen fighters as opponents to set the pace of Clay's ascent into the championship spotlight. Dundee encouraged Clay to learn to play on opponents' emotions as part of his tactical repertoire. He continued to refine Clay's stinging jab, which cut many opponents for wins by technical knockout. Dundee said, "I smoothed Clay out and put snap in his punches . . . I got him down off his dancing toes so he could hit with power." Clay responded emphatically to questions about his style stating, "Dundee gave me the jab. But the rest is me."

Demanding physical workouts, endless sparring rounds, and endurance runs to and from the gym conditioned the gifted boxer for top performance. Over the next four years, Clay's unique style would be perfected at the 5th Street Gym in Miami, leading him to a shot at the title. Easy rhythm, fast footwork, mental toughness, precision marksmanship, sharp instincts, phenomenal speed, physical power, and effortless agility comprised the rare skillset of the young fighter on the rise against the best heavyweights of the era. The rising contender realized, "Champions aren't made in gyms. Champions are made from something deep inside them—a desire, a dream, and a vision. They have to have the skill and the will. But the will must be stronger than the skill."

Clay's star performance was not a solo act but involved a constellation of talented specialists who comprised his winner's circle. Professional commitment, competitive spirit, and lasting friendships ruled this universe of excellence. He learned from the start about the importance of being part of a talented team. Dundee was a valuable tactician who taught Clay a scientific approach to fighting well-suited to his free-spirited unorthodox style. The success envisioned at the 5th Street Gym, where future champions were invited to dream big, inspired fearless imagination and winning spirit in the ring.

Dundee and Clay traveled the world together forming one of the most admired relationships in sports. Clay would rise through challenges of tough competition, as assistant trainer Drew "Bundini" Brown amplified the trademark of an exceptional talent in lyrical catchphrases like "Float like a butterfly; sting like a bee." The shoutouts from the corner of the ring reinforced Clay's positive self-talk, fueling momentum to victory rounds. Luis Sarria was a masseuse and physical trainer with healing hands who helped Clay recover after long painful hours of training and competitive matches. The Fight Doctor on his team, Dr. Ferdie Pacheco, treated injuries, evaluated medical exams, and monitored the health of the rising champ. Assistant trainer Wali Muhammad would join the team later, when Clay was the newly crowned champion defending his throne. The successful collaboration among these specialists lasted through most of the champion's 20-year career, demonstrating an exceptional team chemistry that was rare in the history of professional boxing.

Willie Pastrano, a light-heavyweight champion trained by Dundee, recalled Clay's unorthodox boxing style refined in the gym. "I worked with him once. I watched him do all the wrong things, but they always seemed to come out right, and he is a beautiful judge of distance." Dundee described how Clay easily found the opportunities to win the advantage in creative ways. "Cassius was one of the most innovative imaginative fighters I ever saw," which was high praise from the exceptional coach in boxing.

Well-crafted publicity sound bites with elements of psychological intimidation were used to promote fights around the world. Dundee would admit that he learned lessons about finer life principles from the gifted rising star. "He taught me patience; he taught me decency. I watched how he reacted to everything. I saw things done to him that made me sick to my stomach. And all he'd say was, 'You have to forgive people.'"

Dundee taught his champions that training in the gym "is the most important part of boxing." He said, "It's the laboratory where a fighter's skills and styles are developed. . . . It's polishing a fighter's assets and filing rough edges, teaching a fighter to develop a style to fit his natural abilities . . . then to repeat it over and over again, until it becomes instinctive." Dundee so strongly believed in Clay's "great natural talent" he said, "he would have been a great champion without me."

Clay also engaged in creative self-promotion outside the ring, orchestrating a story for the lens of *Life* magazine photographer Flip Sculke. He invited the journalist to take pictures of a special training technique he used to build speed, agility, and power in the ring. Photographs taken of Clay shadowboxing underwater, featured in the most popular magazine in the nation, were one of many successfully masterminded publicity stunts during his career. The magazine issue hit the stands accompanied by a lingering (true) rumor that Clay could not swim. His athletic beauty, entertaining showmanship, poetic verse, and humor ushered in a golden age with unprecedented style that would bring international attention to a brutal sport. He defied critics who called him a runner without essential heavyweight skills to win the world championship title. Clay would have moments of doubt like everyone else, and his team continued to work with him on sharpening a strong winning attitude. He understood that "It's the repetition of affirmations that leads to belief. And once that belief becomes a deep conviction, things begin to happen." Dundee coached his fighters knowing it is essential to have someone in your corner who believes in your chances for success.

Through miles of endurance roadwork and hours of developing his technique with sparring partners in the ring, his trainers were ever ready to strengthen his winning mindset, which would prove to be his most important asset. Outside the gym in the community of Overtown, he lived near an exciting neighborhood where great jazz and blues musicians like Count Basie, Ella Fitzgerald, Billie Holiday, Duke Ellington, and Louis Armstrong had performed in glittering Northwest Second Avenue nightclubs. In addition to racist curfew laws interrupting his training runs, the 5th Street Gym was surrounded by segregated hotels, drugstores, and business establishments, but these oppressive facts of life never disrupted the pace of the ascent during his coming of age as a great professional fighter.

Clay emerged in the prizefighting spotlight determined to reach the height of his profession just when epic fights in racial politics were taking aim at desegregation. He defied racist expectations for African Americans explained by James Baldwin: "You were born into a society which spelled out with brutal clarity, and in as many ways as possible, that you were a worthless human being. You were not expected to aspire to excellence. . . ." At the same time that praise rained down on the undefeated title contender, troubling news about violence against peaceful protesters rocked his corner of the ring. Civil rights marchers calling for full citizenship and equal access to the American Dream were broadcast around the world, prompting horrific retaliation by segregationists enforcing Jim Crow practices in the Deep South. With faith in Allah, the separatist Nation of Islam advanced the cause in a new direction with Black Nationalist aspirations that inspired African American independence, self-determination, and personal excellence. The dynamic image-maker in pursuit of boxing greatness listened to the Messenger, whose teachings magnified a sense of empowerment that strengthened solidarity and reinforced a proud racial identity. Boycotts organized by Reverend King brought down "Whites Only" signs from local buses. The Freedom Riders continued their desegregation demands aboard buses en route through Jim Crow strongholds from Washington, DC, to the Deep South. They asserted rights determined by a US Supreme Court case banning segregation on interstate buses: *Morgan v. Virginia* (1946). The Freedom Riders faced angry mobs who threw firebombs to block their buses from reaching America's freeways. Angry segregationist residents in Birmingham waited at bus terminals to confront the Freedom Riders, who had been abandoned by fearful drivers escaping life-threatening attacks. Still, the violence against the rising liberation movement could not force back the relentless waves of defiance.

Clay began 1961 at a rapid pace through matchups against eight opponents on his ascent to become a top contender. On his January 17 birthday, the 19-year-old defeated Tony Esperti in a quick three-round technical knockout. He took down Jimmy Robinson next, after a flurry of punches within two minutes of Round One ended the no-contest match. His publicity fight-talk revved up again in February for his upcoming match against Donnie Fleeman, who proved unable to handle Clay's speed, prompting him to surrender after the sixth round. In April Clay predicted that, "Clark will fall in two," following through with a second-round KO of the seasoned brawler LaMar Clark, who had a 43-fight winning record.

In June, Clay went the 10-round distance to win against Duke Sobedong by unanimous decision in the fight capital of Las Vegas. After the phenomenal win, he boasted how pretty he still was, unmarked after facing such an ugly, tough opponent, which raised the fight-talk another level. In July, he went the distance once more against high-ranking veteran Alonzo Johnson for a win in hometown Louisville. In October, after outclassing Alex Miteff in a six-round TKO that again drew audience cheers in Louisville, he said, "I showed tonight I can fight as well as box." Clay continued to adapt his talent, adding a new dimension of inside blows thrown from solid footing off his toes. Speed and accuracy while holding his head high in full view of the ring proved to set Clay apart. The momentum of upcoming events kept pace with his growing confidence with sights set on the heavyweight crown. His final contest of the year in November against Willi Besmanoff proved he was unstoppable in the ring during a third consecutive appearance in Louisville. Clay dropped his opponent to the canvas, delivering on his prediction "Besmanoff must fall in seven!" Remaining undefeated through eight fights sparked bold talk about his readiness to face champions Floyd Patterson and top contender Sonny Liston. Clay hyped his performances to the press stating, "I showed I have stamina, atomic energy and determination to go with my unequalled skill . . . I have the fastest fists in history." At this point, counting two victories the previous year, he had defeated 10 consecutive opponents on his fight card.

In a letter to Sister James Ellen early in his career, the rising star impressed his hometown friend with his command of the brilliant limelight:

> Dear Sister:
>
> I was very glad to hear from you. Tell every body that I said hello, and one day this week I will try to come and see you all, and I will try to bring one of the newspaper men with me and we can take a nice picture together for the paper. I think this will be very nice. Well I am sitting here at the table answering a lot of fan letters, hope to see you soon,
>
> Truly Yours,
> Cassius Clay
> 1961

As Clay rose to the occasion with each prizefight, the Sisters of Charity of Nazareth continued to write congratulatory letters that encouraged him to fulfill an overriding benevolent and devout mission:

Dear Cassius:

Congratulations again! Another big step toward your goal. We do not have the proper TV equipment for channel 32 so I did not see the televised bout, but from accounts of those who did view it you were in good form and gave a superb performance. We at Nazareth College who knew you in your amateur days are proud of you and want you to know that we follow you with our prayers and good wishes in the hope that you may continue to be an ambassador of good will to all and that you may further peace among men and the spread of the Kingdom of God in the hearts of men. In the words of Holy Writ "What doth it profit a man to gain the whole world and suffer the loss of [his own] soul?"

   Again, congratulations and all good wishes for good health, happiness and unending success!

Yours in Christ,
Sister James Ellen, SCN
Librarian
October 11, 1961

During time away from the ring in 1962, Clay attended an event in Detroit to hear Nation of Islam (NOI) leader Elijah Muhammad deliver a spiritual message that spread religious faith in Allah and espoused national-ist tenets. Twenty-year-old Clay was impressed by the Messenger, who inspired a proud race consciousness and self-respect to advance radical change toward self-determination within the African American com-munity. Since embarking on his demanding career, Clay had never lost touch with community developments, generously giving time and money to uplift lives, address the injustice of quality-of-life disparities, and keep the fight for equality in clear sight as it gained momentum. Clay met NOI minister Malcolm X, beginning a close friendship based on a shared faith in divine redemption promised by the Prophet Elijah Muhammad. Malcolm was a prominent spokesman for the Nation, who stayed on the boxing scene with Clay, influencing the spiritual growth of an aspiring world heavyweight champion. Leading up to the 1964 title fight against Charles "Sonny" Liston, they were united in a spiritual brotherhood committed to tenets that galvanized a nationalist movement for African American solidar-ity. Clay would become a champion of the people, with a vision of great-ness that encouraged African American independence and self-reliance in the fight for freedom. He demonstrated great fortitude in the battle against racial oppression, knowing that the commitment to the cause and his faith in God must be unwavering.

The usual fight-talk promoted Clay's 11th career match against young southpaw Sonny Banks on February 10, 1962. During his Madison Square Garden debut in New York City, a weakness in his defensive style was exposed early in the match. For the first time, a solid left hook to the jaw in Round One stunned and embarrassed the undefeated Clay. Dundee never forgot the unconscious freefall of his fighter, who hit the canvas, then stood right back up to finish the fight. He shouted, "Hold your right hand up to protect your jaw. All this kid's got is a left hook." Clay demonstrated his grit and astonishing fortitude throughout the challenge, defeating Banks for a comeback victory. Referee Ruby Goldstein observed an overpowering passionate drive to win, which abruptly stopped Banks in four. He said, "I've refereed the best. . . . and this kid Clay could one day be up there with them. . . . The kid's got heart to go with his ability." Clay would later remark, "Now everybody's waking up to the fact that I really am The Greatest." Defending against left hooks thrown in a classic southpaw stance would require more sparring practice by Clay to elude future downfalls.

The brutality of boxing was put in perspective when Banks died from ring injuries after a fight three years later. Clay stated, "Sonny Banks was a fine fighter and a good human being. We earned each other's respect in the hardest arena of them all, the boxing ring. My deepest sympathy goes to his family. This is a hard, hard sport, but we choose to do it knowing the risks. I pray for Sonny's soul and that he rests in peace." Clay was in his second year of professional boxing when two-time welterweight champion Benny "Kid" Paret proved that the brutal sport needed better oversight safeguards in the ring. In April 1962, Paret died at age 25 from injuries suffered during his 50th fight, a savage match against Emile Griffith that was stopped too late. A committee was formed to address the clarion call to ban boxing, following Paret's death from massive blows that continued after he was knocked unconscious leaning against the ropes. Clay was invited to testify in front of a New York State legislative committee that was investigating adherence to rules governing safety standards in the sport. He explained that boxing had changed since the days of Joe Louis, Sugar Ray Robinson, and Jack Dempsey. Already the number two contender for the heavyweight crown, in typical self-assured style, Clay told the committee that he expected to be the world champion in a year. The hearings revealed the sport had been negligent and had exploited its fighters by failing to provide them with proper health care. Clay was not indifferent to the serious injury he could inflict or suffer in the ring. He once said, "My strategy was to be as scientific as I could when I fought. I didn't want to be seriously hurt, and I didn't want to do that to anybody else either. My plan was to dance, stay out of my opponent's reach, and use my wits as much as my fists. I tried to get into the mind of my opponent and psych him out. I studied my opponents to learn their strengths and weaknesses."

Against another left hook master in February, Clay ended the hopes of his opponent Don Warner by the fourth round. He feinted punches, jabbed, and moved away instantly to avoid Warner's famously lethal knockout punch. The performance assured his corner that he could defeat reigning world heavyweight champion Floyd Patterson. Clay would fight four more times in the year after Floyd Patterson lost his crown to the menacing Sonny Liston during one of the fastest title fights in boxing history. During the Warner match, fight referee Cy Gottfried noticed the extraordinary skills of the young contender for the crown. He said, "This kid is something very special and will make the boxing world buzz. What's more, he knows it!" Clay seconded with fight-talk insults stating, "Now I want Fraud Patterson and the very ugly Liston. . . ."

By April, with a dozen wins under his belt, the fight world was put on notice about the new rising star. He stopped George Logan in his third fight of the year, adding another victory to the record books. Many took notice of his talents, including retired heavyweight champion Jack Dempsey, who predicted that he would win the title. Former champion Joe Louis said, "I know what it takes to win the world heavyweight championship, and I think Clay has got it." Clay next amazed with triple jabs that took down Billy Daniels in New York City. As flurries of flicking jabs were followed by right hands, Clay easily shifted gears, dancing in and out of counterpunch range. Alejandro Lavorante was next to fall under multiple punches in Round Five. After more than 200 fights, Clay's former coach Archie Moore stepped in the ring in November to face the famed boxing prodigy. Putting front-page sports reporters on notice, Clay boasted that the fight would be over in four rounds. Moore, who had started fighting before Clay was born, now discovered that he could not hold on through the savage pace. The fight was in front of a record-breaking sellout crowd in Los Angeles and shown on closed-circuit television in 53 major cities. Referee Tommy Hart ended the barrage of punches from Clay that first overpowered then outmaneuvered his seasoned opponent's tight defensive stance. Moore wryly explained the loss to his undefeated opponent when he said, "He's brainier than I thought and boxed a perfect fight." He was stopped in four just as predicted, prompting Liston to underrate Clay stating, "He won't last long with me. He's just a runner and I'd quickly catch up with him." Liston's fight-talk continued with remarks that were shockingly to the point. He concluded, "If he stands and fights, I'll kill him. If he runs, I'll catch him and kill him."

While Clay closed in on Liston's throne, he was well aware of desegregation setbacks in the civil rights movement, as reports of escalating violence unsettled mainstream America. Police brutality during peaceful protests crushed hopes for progressive reforms. In 1962, segregationists rioted when James Meredith became the first African American student to enroll at the University of Mississippi on September 30. President John F. Kennedy responded by ordering hundreds of national guardsmen, federal marshals, and US troops to protect Meredith while attending Ole Miss, where the brave student would go on to earn a political science degree.

In 1963, just after his 21st birthday, Clay started off a remarkable new year with a three-round victory against Charlie Powell on January 24. Powell admitted Clay was impossible to beat, telling the press. "He throws punches so easily that you don't realize how much they hurt you until it's too late." Although Clay was staggered in Round Two of the fight by a superbly multitalented athlete, he later dominated Powell for the win. Even at a young age, the rising champion demonstrated the seriousness of his humanitarian commitment. Clay donated a percentage of the fight revenues from his bout with Powell to help the families of dozens of men killed in the 1962 Robena Mine methane gas explosion.

Dundee motivated Clay to pick up the pace and score more points against his next opponent, Doug Jones. He told him the dream of a red-tomato Cadillac victory prize was not going to happen. Clay fought harder, proving he could land powerful punches to the body for the win. He boasted, "Hello tomato red . . . Goodbye Mr. Jones!" The rising champion fine-tuned his jab to win by unanimous decision in 10, missing the predicted fourth-round KO at a sold-out Madison Square Garden. His corner team believed that his physical maturity would be optimal for a fight with Liston by the following year, but ringside experts said that the title was way out of his league. Dundee defended Clay's unorthodox style, describing him as "a marksman" with a precise jab used to cut and stun his opponents.

Attention shifted outside the ring when the Louisville *Courier-Journal* published an interview about Clay being a member of the Nation of Islam that threatened to throw his career in jeopardy. Although news about his affiliation upset the boxing world, the trouble was contained after he went the tough 10-round distance to clinch the win against Jones. As the breaking news subsided about Clay's membership with the Nation, Reverend King made headlines when arrested on April 12 during civil rights protests in Alabama. He wrote *Letter from Birmingham Jail* in which he delivered his commanding civil disobedience message about a "moral responsibility to disobey unjust laws" keeping sights focused on the struggle. His words, "Justice too long delayed is justice denied," added a sense of urgency to the spirit of the civil rights movement. New seasons of defiance already underway took a turn for the worse following devastating storms of violence. Horrific confrontations across the South prompted President Kennedy to call racial inequality a "moral issue" as he advanced legislation that summer to defend citizens from violent racial discrimination.

Clay was photographed with Mississippi civil rights activist Fannie Lou Hamer at a time when the ultimate sacrifice was made by freedom fighters who lost their lives in the line of fire. She had been brutalized on June 9, while imprisoned for involvement with a voter registration drive gaining precious ground across the South. Law officials pardoned for racist abuses knew that it was commonplace for unsolved murders of African Americans to be disregarded in the most segregated state in the country. Jim Crow laws were ruthlessly defended against desegregationists crossing resistance lines to defy history. Progress moved in slow rhythm in the racist heartlands of the Deep South, where bloody bayous overflowed with the deadly fallout. People fled to northern safe havens from this place, endemic with oppressive injustice by white supremacists. A desperate struggle for freedom had challenged the fragile faith in redemption over many generations. The departing travelers left behind longed for places where the beauty of magnolias flowered with fragrant richness in a forbidden promised land of dreams. Ancient hollers echoed from haunting slave plantations urged an escape from the tragic conditions of subjugated life. Those who stayed suffered extreme hardships where poverty enshrouded the survivors of a cruel season that left despair in its wake.

Tragedy struck a day after President John F. Kennedy introduced terms for civil rights legislation on June 11 to protect advancements toward ending rampant racial violence. Vengeful backlash in Jackson, Mississippi, claimed the life of NAACP field secretary Medgar Evers, shot by a sniper in the driveway of his home. It would not be until some 30 years later that the accused killer was sentenced to life in prison after authorities finally responded to years of legal pressure to bring the murderer to justice. Enraged conspirators continued efforts to derail the civil rights movement, which was gaining political power in racist territories across the nation.

After defeating Doug Jones, Clay would have to win a match against British champion Henry Cooper before securing a contract to fight Sonny Liston. Media attention peaked, as 21-year-old Clay grew even larger on Liston's radar at 6'3" and weighing more than 200 pounds. Liston remarked, "If they put Clay in the ring with me I'll be locked up for murder." Clay responded with fighting words, "Now for that big bum Liston and the world title." Before the overseas fight with Cooper at Wembley Stadium on June 18, Clay appeared on a June cover of *Sports Illustrated* for the first time with headlines announcing, "Cassius Clay Invades Britain." The magazine remained loyal to the "King of Heavyweights" with press coverage that would last more than a half-century. He had taken the world stage by storm, after his team took carefully measured risks to place him at the summit of professional heavyweight prizefighting.

Clay adapted his showmanship style to a London audience while on training runs alongside a horse-drawn carriage through Hyde Park. Intense fight-talk probably even frayed royal nerves at Buckingham Palace, rallying British critics against his boastful incursions. Clay predicted Cooper would fall like the landmark bridge in the nursery rhyme "London Bridge is falling down." Cooper retaliated, "People tell me to hang one on him and button his lip and I am looking forward to doing just that." Clay dismissed the berating comments, saying, "I'm not even worried about this big bum." He predicted, "It ain't no jive, Henry Cooper will fall in five!"

In front of 35,000 fans at Wembley Stadium, European champion Henry Cooper believed he could ruin Clay's chances despite the 4–1 betting odds of defeat. On the day of the match, the left-handed champion with an orthodox stance sized up the unique talents of his young opponent, known to have novice inside-fighting skills that could present an opportunity for an upset. Clay promenaded into the ring wearing a royal red robe with *Cassius Clay The Greatest* embroidery to accentuate his rhinestone-jeweled gold crown. From the start, he absorbed furious blows and outpaced Cooper with speed, spry footwork, and precision jabs thrown in flurries that connected as vicious blows to the head. He complained to referee Tommy Little that Cooper unfairly continued to rough him up after the bell sounded at the end of the round. Despite Dundee's shout-outs to "jab and move!" he instead danced and teased until returning to the corner with a bloody nose after Round One.

He opened cuts around Cooper's eye with blinding jabs in Rounds Two and Three but succumbed to the reflexes of a seasoned British champion, who stunned with a left hook to the jaw in the fourth. Clay dropped backward to the canvas as his arm tangled in the middle rope easing the unconscious freefall landing. When Clay hit the floor, the celebrity-studded crowd cheered for their hero. Within seconds their hopes were dashed when Clay sprang to his feet on shaky legs just seconds before the bell ended the round. Dundee shifted into damage control, thinking quickly to help his dazed fighter defy gravity. He used controversial time management skills between rounds that were referred to as "sleight of hand" by *Sports Illustrated* writers. When he pulled on an open tear in Clay's glove for officials to notice the damage, Dundee called the ruse "gamesmanship." He explained, "people said I cut the glove on purpose, but I actually didn't." Extra time caused by the damaged glove gained Clay vital seconds for recovery, while his team resorted to smelling salts to fully revive him for the start of the next round. Arthur Daley of the *New York Times* described Clay as being on "dream street" before demonstrating great heart by continuing to fight in Round Five. Cooper commented that Clay still had brutal lessons to learn in the ring from seasoned professionals. The three-time British Lonsdale Belt champion had knocked Clay down with his legendary left hook to the jaw that threatened to end a stellar trajectory. He observed, "Clay was out on his feet when he scrambled up . . . he didn't know what day it was. He should have been looking to stay down for at least eight seconds." Then the momentum shifted, as Clay miraculously came out for the next round with lightning-fast moves, pressuring Cooper to fall under the powerful force mounting from each blow. The crowd yelled to stop the fight when heavy bleeding from a cut over his left eye blinded Cooper in Round Five. He protested about the referee's end-all decision, saying it was just a matter of time before he would catch Clay again with his left for the win.

Clay told reporters his downfall from the left hook was caused by the distracting sight of Elizabeth Taylor sitting ringside with Richard Burton. Despite his 19-0 record and 14 KOs/TKOs, the second knockdown of his career added doubts about his ability to defeat Liston. He confessed that Cooper "hit me harder than I've ever been hit." The defeated Cooper would later say, Clay was "the fastest moving heavyweight of all time . . . the exception to the rule." Boxing commentator Larry Merchant later observed, "Ali rode the crest of a new wave of athletes—competitors who were both big and fast . . . combination of size and speed that had never been seen in a fighter before, along with incredible will and courage. He also brought a new style to boxing. . . . He changed what happened in the ring, and elevated it to a level that was previously unknown."

After the victory over Cooper, Clay returned home to ongoing conflicts in the civil rights struggle. On August 28, 200,000 people joined the March on Washington for Jobs and Equality, demonstrating to end disparities in economic opportunity. Reverend King delivered his "I Have a Dream" speech that day on the steps of the Lincoln Memorial after gospel singer Mahalia Jackson urged, "Tell them about the dream, Martin." Hundreds of thousands across the nation heard King share a vision of imminent freedom and equality for all. He spoke about his four young children, saying he hoped that they "will one day live in a nation where they will not be judged by the color of their skin, but by the content of their character." The world would learn his great vision, "I have a dream that one day even the state of Mississippi, a desert state, sweltering with the heat of injustice and oppression, will be transformed into an oasis of freedom and justice."

Instead, there was a violent turning point with deadly repercussions. Weeks later, the world mourned the news of bomb blasts that reached deep in sacred territory of the Southern Christian Leadership Conference in Birmingham, Alabama. On that besieged sacred Sunday, September 15, 1963, the racists' attack killed four little girls caught in a firestorm of violence at the 16th Street Baptist Church, marking a crucial new chapter for the movement. Under Director J. Edgar Hoover, the FBI withheld key evidence in the investigation, wasting precious time in the search for justice. It would take decades before three of the four accused killers were convicted and sentenced to life in prison. National outrage at the loss of young lives added more pressure on Capitol Hill to pass and enforce civil rights legislation drafted by President John F. Kennedy and Attorney General Robert F. Kennedy. The tragedy would be remembered 50 years later, when America's first African American president, Barack Obama, honored the innocent young victims by posthumously awarding the Congressional Gold Medal to Addie Mae Collins, Cynthia Wesley, Carole Robertson, and Denise McNair.

Tragic acts of violence continued to strike at the heart of America. The final episode in a devastating year occurred one bloody November day, when fatal gunfire in Texas ended the life of President John F. Kennedy. A powerful message of hate was sent through a suspected intricate network of perpetrators. A frightened nation fell prey to the horrific pattern of conspired retaliation, which extended its bloodthirsty path to the White House.

Clay stayed on track throughout those tragic days, until the prime time championship fight against the formidable Sonny Liston was secured. The match would set the record straight and usher in a new year of high expectations for the promising top contender. Clay addressed sportswriters who doubted the caliber of his ring skills by predicting Liston would fall in eight and explaining that his winning fight against Cooper was just a warmup before taking down seemingly invincible Liston.

3

CROWNING GLORY

A Freedom Fighter Enters the Humanitarian Arena

Ali vs. Liston II Victory Celebration.
World History Archive / Amaly Photograph

The time had come for Clay to face seemingly indomitable reigning champion Charles "Sonny" Liston at the Miami Convention Center. Armed with adrenaline-fueled might, Clay searched high and low for Liston with plans to psych him out before the fight. He analyzed the champion's taped fights, conferred with his team specialists, and publicly disputed his underdog odds. Clay even angered Liston at one point by showing up at his Las Vegas home before retreating to demanding training days. One of his tactics was to try threatening Liston's territory with a publicity scheme that involved wearing a blue denim jacket emblazoned with the words *Bear Hunting*, referring to Liston's style of mauling opponents. Liston responded by saying, "He should be locked up for impersonating a fighter."

On February 25, 1964, Clay was slated to fight Liston shortly after celebrating his 22nd birthday. Sports analysts expected Liston to cut off the ring with lateral moves, then return to his straight-line brawler style to catch the kid on the ropes. The tactical showdown would require Liston to contend with Clay's lightning-fast reflexes, then try to demolish the psychological edge reinforced by his masterful corner team. Dundee explained, "I didn't have to tell Cassius much. I just kept reminding him, 'You're quicker, you're smarter, you're not gonna take his shots. Don't trade with him, don't try to fight in close . . . in, and out . . . nail him!'" The champion, known for the ferocity of his jabs delivered with massive 15-inch fists, said, "The only way that Cassius can hurt me is not to show up for the fight." Clay pushed the boundaries of heavyweight bravado, forcing cracks in Liston's armor with demeaning psychological warfare when he said, "You big ugly bear . . . the traps are out for you." Dundee knew what fighters endure to reach the top: "The punches, the blood, the hurt, the pain. When all the training and promotion is done, it comes down to what a guy does in the ring." Clay not only had Dundee for psychological support; he also had Malcolm X, who reinforced a vision of greatness that strengthened the undefeated top title contender's belief that he could win. He helped tune out negative opinions intruding on the prized moment by telling Clay, "Do you think Allah has brought about all this intending for you to leave the ring as anything but the champion?"

The underdog was a quick scientific fighter who hoped to rely on defensive moves around the entire ring to skillfully position the ferocious brawler Liston outside his comfort zone. Over the last three years, Liston had fought for only brief minutes of early rounds, showcasing his mean attitude and knockout power. Nothing could dial down the intimidation factor for those who were brave enough to face Liston and the blows he delivered with his powerful, massive shoulders. Clay would try to counteract the strength of Liston's lethal left jab with exceptional speed and agility. Dundee told him, "When you get in the ring with this guy, stand tall so he sees you're as big as he is." Great champions like Rocky Marciano knew that Liston was a bully whose power would weaken when his sense of invincibility was shattered by each blow.

On Howard Cosell's radio show Clay told listeners, "I'm always nervous. I can't tell a lie, to hear the roar of the crowd, to feel the pressure

. . . but once I throw the first punch, I'll be all right." Clay's promotional antics and high-volume fight-talk were a publicist's dream come true. His handsome all-American boy-next-door appeal along with his virtuoso boxing skills and entertaining showmanship made him famous in households across America. Dundee recalled Liston telling Clay, "You can't punch hard enough to break an egg." Clay immediately sounded back, "Oh boy! You just stand there, and pretend you're an egg."

In August 1963, Clay released the comedy album *I Am the Greatest!*, a soon to be famous poetic rap on vinyl about coming to terms with his own greatness. The album was recorded by CBS Columbia Records for release six months before the championship fight against Liston. Brash assertions featured in sound bites from the album hit the airwaves, earning it a nomination for best comedy performance in 1964. Album liner notes written by Pulitzer Prize–winning poet Marianne Craig Moore admiringly described the grace of a champion. The rising star on the prefight publicity circuit introduced fight-talk that claimed he was too pretty to be denied the heavyweight crown. The boastful self-promotion advertised that he was the main attraction of the times ready for his close-up. His brash bravado would be used a half-century later by Apple, Inc. to feature the iPhone selfie. He announced from the beginning, "I am the greatest. I said that even before I knew I was. I figured that if I said it enough, I would convince the world that I was really the greatest."

Liston, the man on the throne, dominated heavyweight boxing with a menacing reputation. He had knocked out Patterson in Round One for the title win. Though Clay hurled insults at Liston—telling reporters he was "too ugly to be the world champ! The world champ should be pretty like me!"—behind the scenes, Clay admitted that he feared the ex-convict with the reputation as a Mob enforcer. The seasoned fighter, thought to be at least 10 years older than Clay, had fists that landed with bone-crushing power. The professional fight world perceived the Liston vs. Clay fight as a mismatch of epic proportions.

During his time in the Missouri State Penitentiary for armed robbery, the latest in a rap sheet of crimes, Liston had developed a strong bond with Reverend Alois Stevens, who influenced him to start boxing. In the prison gym, he perfected skills as a slugger building on his talent for inside fighting techniques to rule the center of the ring. Liston found his ticket to success with an organized crime syndicate that owned heavyweight prizefighting. He would rise to the top with a style that earned him a reputation as the most dangerous fighter of the times for his weight class. Following his 1953 professional debut, he had amassed 35 wins and 1 defeat by the time he faced Clay in 1964. The phenomenal winning streak conveyed an awesome dominance that scared away most top contenders from challenging him in the ring. Threatening stares told a dark story of surviving hard times, magnifying his tough image. The blues melody "Night Train" was often heard in the background during his training hours in the gym. On the run from a brutal father, he had escaped childhood abuse by thriving on mean streets in ways that guaranteed prison time.

Liston's manager, Joseph "Pep" Barone, was a reputed front man for the Lucchese Family under Mob bosses Frankie Carbo and Frank "Blinky" Palermo. Liston tried to dim the spotlight on his criminal past by showing a compassionate side, visiting the sick at hospitals and children at orphanages and elevating his image in political circles with President Lyndon B. Johnson. The boxing world Clay discovered was dominated by organized crime elements that set limits for various sanctioning bodies, front managers, boxing trainers, referees, fight judges, and even journalists. The world of prizefighting is notorious for attracting gangsters in pinstriped suits, oddsmakers, gamblers, celebrities, and fans seated ringside in the haze of thick billowing cigar smoke. Winning fight odds were not always based on honest rankings or merit. Instead, they were manipulated by predetermined fixed arrangements that exploited fighters ruthlessly to ensure profitable returns on bets. The team seriously considered keeping Clay out of closed-circuit media, the most lucrative Mob-owned enterprise. However, the presence of the LSG began shifting the scales in favor of better deals in the best interest of their fighter. The downfall of Frankie Carbo resulting from congressional investigations allowed his legal team to redefine the business terms of Clay's career, benefiting from the changed management hierarchy of the sport. Clay would impact boxing history as he set the record straight: "The biggest thing in the world is the heavyweight champion. And I'm not going to be just an ordinary heavyweight champion. I'm going to be the greatest of all time!"

Dundee told sports journalists that Clay had a style that Liston had never faced before in the ring: an unorthodox technique with hands held low, before launching quick cutting jabs from unpredictable directions that posed a threat to Liston. With an extraordinary sense of anticipation, he evaded punches with sharp reflexes, shifting the pace to send his opponent's fists sailing into thin air after missing the mark. Clay said, "I'll hit Liston with so many punches from so many angles he'll think he's surrounded." His incessant fight-talk before matches showcased his other talent for high drama. At the prefight weigh-in, the press reported that Clay was overcome by fear, constantly aggravating Liston with his nervous outbursts while emotionally carried away with showmanship antics that cost the team thousands in fines for disruptive behavior. Fast-jabbing Clay was handsome, sharp-tongued, and appeared to be a nervous wreck in the face of seemingly impossible odds. Dundee moderated the situation saying, "I've been telling everyone that this kid is a great fighter. The talk's only an act." Despite the promotional antics, the Miami Beach Convention Hall was far from sold out for the fight. However closed-circuit ticket sales soared. Event promoter warnings asserted ultimatums for Malcolm X to stay away that were ignored when he arrived in ringside seat number 7. Liston had taken a stand against segregated seating at theaters, saying, "I feel that the color of my people's money is the same as anyone else's. They should get the same seats. If not, I don't want those places to have the fight."

Liston, the no-contest 7–1 betting favorite according to Las Vegas oddsmakers, had proven he ruled the heavyweight throne by mercilessly amassing a stellar record before fight night. Clay had a response to Liston's menacing glare directed at the "naive kid" taking on the fiercest king of heavyweights. He taunted the "big ugly bear" with his mantra, "Float like a butterfly; sting like a bee; rumble, young man, rumble." The boastful provocation thrilled Liston, who flexed his muscles with anticipation of an easy payday. Sportswriters expressed the consensus view of seasoned fight officials, believing that no one in the division of licensed heavyweights could withstand the impact of Liston's powerful fists. Like everyone else who thought the fresh young contender was out of his element, famed comedian Jackie Gleason predicted that Clay would survive in the ring with Liston about 18 seconds, including three seconds the "Blabber Mouth will bring into the ring with him."

From the opening bell, Liston struggled to keep pace with Clay's overwhelming speed, as the young contender circled at a safe distance beyond the range of a potential knockout blow. The crowd was astounded, just as Liston was angered by the skilled precision of stinging left jabs from Clay that connected multiple times. Powerful blows to the body hurt Clay, who survived them with reassured confidence that he was tough enough to withstand the punches on his dancing feet. The disappointed Liston failed to find the mark for his lethal left hook during the chase in Round One.

The fight continued, showcasing Clay's superb scientific formula of flicking jabs, uppercuts, combination flurries, and graceful defensive moves in and out of range that outclassed the champion. Liston responded with an onslaught of massive punches. In Round Two, Clay was forced against the ropes on unsteady feet, when caught by the champion's legendary left hooks, as he moved in to cut off the ring. The massive blows put him in trouble, but Clay shook his head, emphatically denying that he was in serious pain. During Round Three, a welt under Liston's right eye and cut under his left glistened in the brilliant lights, showing off the effects of mounting punishment that weakened his defenses through the round. The adrenaline rush kept the champion fighting, but he overcommitted more punches to thin air. He braced for a barrage of punches from the skillful contender at this stage of the fight. The momentum shifted in Clay's favor causing physical damage that Liston had never experienced in the prize-fighting ring. The reigning champion was staggered when pressured against the ropes, salvaging just enough strength to land a few punches before the bell. Liston's corner team went to work treating eye cuts and tending to his left shoulder that had been injured earlier in the gym.

Clay lost focus near the end of Round Four, blinking his eyes to clear his sight, and Liston took advantage of the moment. Referee Barney Felix heard shouts from Clay's corner before Round Five. Clay yelled, "I can't see, Angelo. My eyes are burning!" Dundee recalled, "I put my pinkie in his eyes and then mine. It burned like hell . . . I tried to clean his eyes out, first with sponges and then towel. . . . But that didn't help." The corner team believed that a caustic solution used by Liston's cut man Joe Pollino somehow spread to Clay's eyes, blinding him well into the next round. During the commotion, Clay stood up from his stool, demanding that someone cut off his gloves and saying, "I want the world to know there's dirty work afoot here!" Just seconds before a disqualifying technical knockout decision, Dundee took charge, telling him, "Forget the bullshit. . . .This is for the big one son, the world championship. Now get the hell out there . . . AND RUN!!!" At the bell, Round Five began with a mad chase. Doctor Ferdie Pacheco said Liston came out at the start of the round "like a little kid looks at a new bike on Christmas." Midway through the round Clay's eyes cleared, causing another change in momentum that meant trouble for Liston's last-chance hopes. In Round Six, the crowd roared as Clay regained control, hitting Liston at will with signature jabs, dizzying combinations, and hooks that went unanswered, all the while dancing to the height of crowning glory. He threw punches that Bundini said, "could hit you before God gets the news." Clay shouted from his corner at reporters who had advised him to update his will, "I'm gonna upset the world!"

Liston spit out his mouth guard, signaling surrender before the bell for Round Seven. The ringside crowd heard announcer Howard Cosell say, "Wait a minute! Wait a minute! Sonny Liston is not coming out! Sonny Liston is not coming out! He's out! The winner and new heavyweight champion of the world is Cassius Clay." It was the biggest 20-minute upset in sports history. The distance had proved too far, the pace too fast, and the rising champion's determination unbeatable. Clay jumped for joy during his moment of victory that marked a new era of powerful fast heavyweight fighters. From his mighty throne, he shouted, "I must be the greatest . . . I talk to God every day . . . I shook up the world . . . I'm the king of the world!"

Hometown friends cheered for the newly crowned world heavyweight champion. Sister James Ellen wrote her congratulations in a letter the next day with an invitation to visit:

Dear Cassius,

Congratulations to the greatest!
    We knew that you would win even though the predictions of many favored your opponent.
    You have an amazing record. I know your past level headedness, good judgment, and loyalty to truth and honor will prompt you to keep your good record in all of its aspects. Prayers and continued good wishes for my favorite boxer.
    When you return to Louisville, you must include a visit to the college which helped you on your way to greatness.

Sincerely yours,
Sister James Ellen
Librarian
February 26, 1964

When Sister James Ellen wrote her letter, the day after his title win against Sonny Liston, Clay announced his conversion to Islam in front of an astounded crowd of reporters. In March, Elijah Muhammad publicly welcomed the new champion to the Nation of Islam by bestowing upon him the Muslim name Muhammad Ali. The announcement put the world on notice that the champion should never again be called by his former name. He said, "Cassius Clay is a slave name. I didn't choose it and I don't want it. I am Muhammad Ali, a free name—it means beloved of God, and I insist people use it when people speak to me." He showed deep conviction in defense of his devout Islamic faith against widespread public criticism. Although the reigning heavyweight champion of the world could not fight off the frenzy of aspersions that followed, he struck back stating to his critics, "I know where I'm going and I know the truth, and I don't have to be what you want me to be. I'm free to be what I want." He confronted extreme demands from reactionary members of the boxing world, while charting a unique course from his corner of the ring in the fight for equal rights and religious freedom. Ali chose to join the Nation of Islam realizing it would be one of several ways to participate in the civil rights movement during the 1960s.

The champion's fall from grace in the eyes of many Americans occurred when he boldly expressed pride in a faith associated with a reviled separatist group that alienated and offended parts of America. The announcement would define him as one of the most famous symbols of defiance in the country. The gathering storm of controversy closed in on the new champion, who now defended his title from the east corner of the ring bowing toward Mecca, like no other before him in the sport. He was the first Muslim in the world to hold the title, rallying millions of fans united by a strong alliance of faith.

Ali's announced membership with the NOI prompted his downfall in the eyes of mainstream America and raised awareness about converging movements for equality, justice, and peace. It was a dangerous time to take a progressive stand for revolutionary change in the country. News about his conversion spread like devastating wildfire through enclaves of ringside newscasters, who echoed the resentment expressed by certain venue pro-moters, boxing contenders, and fight fans who wanted to see him lose the title. Despite the hostility, his cosmic talent continued to advance his career. At age 22, the champion wore the crown proudly, having competed against the foremost heavyweights to build a perfect record of 20 consecutive pro-fessional wins by then. His toughest critics included prominent American publications that, like the news media, refused to acknowledge his new name. Howard Cosell was among the few boxing commentators to defy the angry cadre as they attempted to cast a shadow over the bright shooting star. James Baldwin captured in words the reaction to Ali's outright defi-ance of the status quo: "Any upheaval in the universe is terrifying because it so profoundly attacks one's sense of one's own reality. . . . The black man has functioned in the white man's world as a fixed star, as an immov-able pillar: and as he moves out of his place, heaven and earth are shaken to their foundation."

Ali found spiritual enrichment at this point on his journey in pursuit of a higher life purpose. The name given to him by Elijah Muhammad signified a sacred anointing and great esteem that imparted pride in the remarkable prizefighter. The Messenger seemed to deflect from the percep-tion that Ali was a rare black diamond on his crown of daring apostles. As

Muhammad Ali Praying to Allah in the Ring.
Photograph by Neil Leifer / Getty Images

the Nation of Islam welcomed the champion to the ministry, it also fervidly disapproved of public showmanship and the sport of boxing. Despite the contradictions, the name *Muhammad* meaning "worthy of all praises" and *Ali* meaning "most high," confirmed a valued alliance among the devoted. A sharp rise in membership and greater awareness in millenarian beliefs throughout the country followed his conversion. African Americans outside the Nation sensed the threat of government reprisals against the sect with nationalistic ideals inspiring resolute solidarity.

Herbert Muhammad, son of Elijah Muhammad, replaced the LSG when their contract with Ali expired. The champion's fight career was turned over to the enterprising Nation, which continued to protect him from organized crime exploitation at the contract table. The wealthy business empire controlled by Elijah Muhammad was built on the promise of

affluent independence free from the unjust power structure in racially stratified America. Lasting amicable ties with the LSG would prove strong when
Ali drove 300 miles from Chicago to Louisville to visit Bill Faversham, who
was recovering from a heart attack. The LSG transitioned the fighter to
his new management team but continued to protect his financial interests.

Just a few days after the world learned about the new champion's
religious conversion, Malcolm X split from the Nation of Islam, surren-
dering to ruthless political pressure. He had discovered that beneath the
veil of religious teachings, there was truth to the rumors of disreputable
behavior by Elijah Muhammad. Malcolm made public statements that
damaged the supremely revered image of the powerful Messenger. After
traveling to West Africa and the Middle East, where he was enlightened
by a traditional Islam practiced by people from diverse cultures, he was
inspired by a shared communion of faith in Allah through the spiritual
path to Sunni Islam. He returned with a philosophy that denounced racism, while promoting broader unity to advance the cause for equal rights.
A letter he wrote to Alex Haley, the ghostwriter of his autobiography,
described the holy journey that gave rise to blessings of a spiritual epiph-
any: "on this pilgrimage, what I have seen, and experienced, has forced
me to rearrange much of my thought-patterns previously held, and to toss
aside some of my previous conclusions. . . . Despite my firm convictions
. . . I have always kept an open mind, which is necessary to the flexibility
that must go hand in hand with every form of intelligent search for truth."
Diverging perspectives added to tensions between Elijah Muhammad and
Malcolm when he publicly shared his worldview: "as a result of my pilgrimage to the Holy City of Mecca, I no longer subscribe to the sweeping
indictments of one race."

The discord between the Messenger and Malcolm reached a critical threshold. Public statements Malcolm made offended the heart of a
nation in mourning, after the assassination of President John F. Kennedy
on November 22, 1963. Comments that were widely accepted to mean
the assassination was a consequence of appalling violence, unleashed with
impunity against African Americans, that returned home to its powerful
source of origin. The next month, Elijah Muhammad suspended Minister
Malcolm from Harlem Temple No. 7. After the controversy first erupted,
a thoughtful friend made Malcolm an offer that briefly dimmed the glaring,
contemptuous spotlight on his life. Ali, then a top contender known as Cassius Clay, extended an invitation to Miami while training for the first title
fight against Sonny Liston. Malcolm reminisced about the visit: "But always
I must be grateful to him . . . he . . . invited me, Betty and the children to

Malcolm X and Muhammad Ali in New York City, 1964.
Everett Collection / Amaly Photograph

come there as his guests." While Clay was preparing to face Liston, Malcolm had confidence in the rising superstar, who became committed to a deeper life purpose guided by faith in Allah.

As for Liston, he continued to insist his skills were superior. After all, he had only lost one match in 10 years before Ali won the title: "I still say the kid can't fight. I'll shut him up in the return when I'm fully fit." British heavyweight champion Henry Cooper was not surprised about the aging champion's downfall when he explained, "He thought that Ali was just a brash kid, a loudmouth. He said, 'I could beat him with one hand' . . . Ali had a lot more than Liston ever thought he'd have . . . when you're past that peak, when you're stale or over the top . . . you keep saying, 'I'll do it the next round.' And the next round never seems to come." Rocky Marciano assessed Ali's stellar ring talents, "There is nothing around to touch him. He's so good he can make your fight his fight. He may be the fastest ever. He's so alert [that] you can't get a good shot at his chin and he is always moving away when he does get hit. You can't pin him against the ropes."

Reverend King sent Ali a congratulatory telegram after his championship victory. Senator Edward Kennedy was later given a pair of boxing gloves as a gesture of support and admiration for the Kennedy brothers' stand for African American civil rights. President John F. Kennedy had paved the way for President Lyndon B. Johnson to enact the Civil Rights Act of 1964. After Johnson signed the Act on July 2, the surge of racial violence seemed to subside for a few weeks. Then in August, the discovery of victims in an insidious hate crime raised fears to an intolerable level. The FBI found the buried bodies of three missing Congress of Racial Equality activists, who had been shot at close range by Mississippi Klansmen. The world watched as the fight for equality and justice raged on across the nation. Reverend King would later express faith that racism would be conquered one day: "How long will prejudice blind the visions of men. . . . How long? Not long because no lie can live forever."

In the summer of 1964, after the ultimate crowning achievement in boxing, the world heavyweight champion traveled to African countries on a visit that was praised as a return to the Fatherland. His visit to Ghana was organized by Pan-Africanist president Kwame Nkrumah, a hero of Ali's who served as his guide through the country. In Kumasi he received a hero's welcome from thousands of young metropolitan admirers. The champion made an appearance draped in traditional Kente cloth, once adorned by kings, as he rallied cheers from the crowd before an exhibition match with local boxing talent Jojo Miles. People greeted him with ritual welcome ceremonies that acknowledged his esteemed status as a great world champion fighter for the people. He connected personally with many fans and stayed highly visible by attending a stadium soccer match. There were many international publicity press sessions, personal interviews, university lectures, and social gatherings with government officials during the several weeks of his visit. He captivated the entire country, which graced him with plots of land to build a permanent residence in Ghana.

Then he traveled to Egypt for a two-week visit, where he was welcomed by President Gamal Nasser. In Cairo, Nasser embraced Ali and presented him with gifts and a key to the city, recognizing him as an honorary citizen. Airport security included military guards that were pushed to the limit when Ali arrived to meet an uncontrollably jubilant crowd before a press conference. The experience was in extreme contrast to his arrival at American airports, where he had largely been ignored since his announced membership with the reviled Nation of Islam. He joined other worshippers in prayer at Egyptian mosques and went sightseeing at the famous historic monuments. He explored the pyramids of Giza before leaving for Lagos, Nigeria.

Ali mingled with fans at the airports, randomly teaching star-quality boxing skills as he playfully sparred among the fascinated crowd. The heavyweight champion with unshakeable confidence remained outspoken against racism, war, and religious intolerance around the world. He was viewed in Ghana, Egypt, Nigeria, and Senegal as an empowering icon of courage for Africans and African Americans at the height of the civil rights movement, influencing the course of history. Consistent with his fearsome reputation in the ring, his involvement with the struggle for equal rights and justice remained relentless throughout his lifetime. His strength of character projected a bold self-pride that uplifted African Americans and impressed upon the world perspectives intended to evoke a spirit of humanity. As a renowned activist and humanitarian, the cross-cultural experiences he gained when traveling the world presented opportunities to inspire hope and spread his ideal vision of freedom, justice, and peace across geographic and racial boundaries.

Ali was photographed many times engaged in generous acts of kindness around the world. His community outreach united people and encouraged them to work together toward a better tomorrow. He had a huge impact on disadvantaged people of all religions, cultures, and national origins. Donations of his time and proceeds from large fight revenues to fund education programs and scholarships continued well beyond his rise to fame in the 1960s. Some of his visits to help those in need with generous gifts, expressions of love, and lasting impressions broadened his humanitarian reach across the globe and remain unpublicized to this day. It is estimated that 22 million people worldwide were impacted by Ali's hunger relief initiatives over the years of fighting in the humanitarian arena. His appearances outside the ring at fundraisers amassed millions for various causes and charities. The champion also donated a portion of ticket sales from main event fights and exhibition bouts to hospitals and other humanitarian endeavors throughout his career. Ali said he did not speak about all of his charitable giving, since true generosity involves expecting nothing in return.

Before defending his title against Cleveland Williams in the mid-1960s, he toured college campuses in the South, taking time between bouts to meet with faculty and students. He spread an empowering message that encouraged academic excellence and uplifted students with the promise that they would all play important roles in serving humanity to build a brighter tomorrow. At intimate gatherings and speeches to large audiences, where he signed thousands of autographs, Ali left lasting impressions that inspired pride, hope, and the pursuit of dreams. During his prizefighting career, he made unforgettable impressions at historically African American colleges. Across the nation he emphasized the importance of education, advocated an end to bullying, and encouraged the youth to discover a greater purpose in life.

On January 2, 1965, Reverend King assembled support from churches to organize campaigns for African American voter registration in Atlanta, Georgia. Marches to assert constitutional voting rights met with violent opposition from Selma to Montgomery, Alabama. The demonstrators that bravely continued to advance the cause fell victim to brutal segregationist law enforcers. Protection was provided after national broadcast news showed images of the Bloody Sunday violence against peaceful marchers trying to cross the Edmund Pettus Bridge.

Early in 1965, revolutionary changes underway continued to incite brutal reactions from rural towns to major cities around the country. The Nation of Islam attracted headline attention when an explosive breakpoint was caused by the shifting balance of power between Elijah Muhammad and Malcolm. Violence ensued, as the Nation's leadership reacted to the increasing support for the new orthodox Muslim Mosque, Inc, where Malcolm promoted an imposing alternative worldview: "I believe in human beings, and that all human beings should be respected as such, regardless of their color." Professor Manning Marable cited politics as the final strike against Malcolm when tempers flared with the competing interests between mosques. Malcolm stated, "It is a time for martyrs now, and if I am to be one, it will be for the cause of brotherhood. That's the only thing that can save this country." Malcolm's written plea for peaceful unity in a published letter to the Messenger was answered by a savage storm of lethal gunfire, which some believed came from forces that had infiltrated Black Nationalist territory to silence zealous revolutionary voices. Malcolm's eulogy was delivered by friend and celebrated actor Ossie Davis, whose words honored the courage of an "unconquered" soul, on the day that Harlem gathered "to bid farewell to one of its brightest hopes." He enlightened those who were doubtful of Malcolm's importance in the African American community: "Many will ask what Harlem finds to honor in this stormy, controversial, and bold young captain. . . . And we will answer and say to them . . . in honoring him, we honor the best in ourselves." The insight Malcolm shared was a profound spiritual awakening that would continue to threaten the unity of the Nation long after his death. Malcolm promoted the civil rights struggle as part of an international humanitarian fight for justice and freedom. The movement for social change he envisioned would inspire a broad-based unity, spanning geopolitical distances across diverse ideological, cultural, and racial lines. The influence of his legacy expanded the framework of equality and justice for African Americans to an international human rights platform with his Organization of Afro-American Unity (OAAU).

Years later, Ali would express regret for turning away from Malcolm after Elijah Muhammad forbid any association with the outcast minister. In the book, *Soul of a Butterfly: Reflections on Life's Journey*, written with daughter Hana Ali, he confessed, "Turning my back on Malcolm was one of the mistakes that I regret most in my life. I wish I'd been able to tell Malcolm I was sorry, that he was right about so many things. But he was killed before I got the chance. He was a visionary—ahead of us all." In time, Ali would eventually break free on a spiritual path influenced by Malcolm's legacy, at a sudden turning point in the history of the Nation. The death of Elijah Muhammad on February 25, 1975, would end his four-decade reign and signal a new beginning for the Nation's evolving temples, which opened their doors to spread orthodox Islamic teachings with worshipers of all races. The chosen successor and son of the Messenger, Imam Wallace D. Muhammad, was known for traditional Islamic scholarship. Ali would become one of the founding members of the orthodox Sunni mosque that rejected the Messenger's separation of the races doctrine. Harlem Mosque No. 7 was named El-Hajj Malik El-Shabazz to honor Malcolm and his embrace of ancient teachings from the holy Qur'an. Ali bared feelings about his evolving faith when he expressed gratitude to the Nation of Islam that gave him a cause greater than himself to fight for in life.

On May 18, Sister James Ellen wrote two letters before the rematch against Sonny Liston, one written to Ali's mother Odessa that expressed concern about his membership with the Nation of Islam: "It is most unfortunate that he was caught up in the Muslim group. I think he can still be salvaged when he finishes up this rather complex Liston affair. . . . I want Cassius to know that all of the Sisters here at the college remember him and regard him highly." Her second letter to Ali acknowledged his compassion and importance during revolutionary times in the struggle for human rights and peace: "Your contribution has made inroads in the here-and-now problems of race, creed and color."

An ominous atmosphere muted the usual flamboyant fight-talk before the Ali vs. Liston rematch in 1965. On May 25, police security at the fight held in Lewistown, Maine, was arranged to protect the event from threats of retaliation against Elijah Muhammad's followers. Members of the Nation of Islam were positioned around the ring on protective watch over Ali, who was booed as he entered the ring an underdog. More controversy surrounded the fight when the champion dropped Liston with a blinding right less than two minutes into the first round, sending the audience into an uproar. Liston, who was favored by oddsmakers in the rematch, lacked the physical stamina or the tactical arsenal to weather the impending storm. The press called the blow that ended it the "Phantom Punch," but Ali called it the "Anchor Punch." Ali made contact in the blink of an eye, ruining Sonny Liston's career just moments after the fight began. The champion had the final say, concluding, the punch was "a perfect right-hand to the jaw. He's not going to get up after that. . . . Don't feel bad, Sonny was closer and he didn't see it either."

One ringside observer, former world heavyweight champion James "The Cinderella Man" Braddock, thought that Liston had been hurt earlier by a massive punch that started to capsize the ship, setting the stage for the knockout blow to finish him off. Another former champion, Rocky Marciano, studied the videotaped fight and noticed that Ali snapped the punch, adding velocity just before impact. Jersey Joe Walcott defended the outcome of the fight explaining, "It didn't make any difference if I counted or not . . . Liston was in a dream world. . . ."

On August 6, President Johnson signed the Voting Rights Act of 1965. It outlawed racial discrimination in the voter registration process and empowered African American voters to elect advocates for equitable rights. Groundbreaking legislative victories began to narrow the great divide by outlawing segregationist practices that prevented full citizenship. However, the deeper problem of economic inequality persisted, giving only the privileged few rights to the American Dream. Marginalized communities were denied entry to golden avenues of success, and lives were placed in the cruel stranglehold of ruthless politics. The persistent common denominator of poverty, from marginalized northern inner cities to subjugated southern rural communities, existed worlds apart from America's celebrated majesty. Just days after the Act was passed, a new wave of violence erupted on the West Coast. Six days of rioting began on August 11 in Watts, a marginalized neighborhood of Los Angeles, following the arrest of a young African American motorist by a white California highway patrolman. Thousands of California's National Guardsmen assembled to restore order after allegations of racist police brutality against the motorist incited outrage in the community. Reverend King assessed the mounting despair from intolerable economic and racial inequality persisting in America. He anticipated more violent clashes coast to coast, where residents of oppressed inner cities continued to tread water in the wake of powerful riptides of injustice.

In the prizefighting arena, Floyd Patterson had been America's celebrated champion, becoming the youngest heavyweight champion at age 21. He fought Sonny Liston in 1962 and 1963, losing both the title and rematch fights to the proven invincible power slugger. President Kennedy and Eleanor Roosevelt had been fans in Patterson's corner, cheering on the young fighter who symbolized America's defense against the corrupt criminal elements that managed Liston. Facing Ali on November 22 would allow Patterson the chance to represent America and win back the crown from the despised Nation of Islam. Mainstream America sided with Patterson, who was appalled by Ali's membership in a Black Nationalist organization. In the October 1965 issue of *Sports Illustrated*, Patterson commented, "I have nothing but contempt for the Black Muslims and that for which they stand." Patterson provoked Ali by calling the champion "Cassius Clay." But Ali demonstrated the importance of his name and proved he was worthy of his honored place on the throne by dominating Patterson mercilessly. Ali declared, "No contest, get me a contender. . . ." He demanded a show of respect for his crowning achievement: "Floyd would be smart to come out and make a national apology." He was determined that his proper name would be announced on the world stage. The press criticized Ali for cruelty in the ring, which prolonged Patterson's agony until a 12th-round TKO. Dundee said, "a lot of people forget that, when the bell rings, Ali is a fighter, a tough guy." Patterson would eventually praise the gifted champion: "I never fought anyone who moved as well as he did."

A year after winning the heavyweight crown, Ali told *Sports Illustrated* writer Gil Rogin that he felt he was born for a greater purpose, for accomplishments beyond the arena of championship boxing. Ali would discover his calling at the forefront of a rising national antiwar protest movement with an unwavering commitment that would astound the world. The influence of his growing legacy expanded the framework of equality and justice for African Americans to an international human rights platform. He fearlessly responded to the claims from his detractors, "They're all afraid of me because I speak the truth that can set men free."

4

COURAGE UNDER FIRE

The People's Champion vs. the US Government

*In the late 1960s, Muhammad Ali
lectured at Cal State University.
California State University, Los Angeles. John F. Kennedy
Memorial Library, Special Collections & Archives*

Muhammad Ali continued his altruistic fight for justice, making his presence known on several fiercely combative fronts. He explained his position, "I have nothing to lose by standing up for my beliefs. So I'll go to jail, so what? We've been in jail for 400 years." He defended the heavyweight crown through 1966, when an Army draft notice arrived, beginning the fight of his life against the US government. In February, the US Army broadly reclassified draft standards, making the 24-year-old Ali eligible for military service during the escalating war in Vietnam. Rumors surfaced that he was targeted by the government for his outspoken membership in the radical Nation of Islam. He responded with characteristic defiance to the devastating blow. American attitudes toward Ali became even more critical after his antiwar statements hit media airwaves. His abrupt press statement ruined plans to fight in a number of venues throughout the country when political pressure turned state boxing commissions against the outspoken champion. A point of no return was reached the moment he conveyed his intention to refuse the draft.

Confidence that Ali would prevail was expressed in a letter from Sister James Ellen:

Dear Cassius,

It was good to hear your melodious voice the other day on the telephone but I was sorry you could not make it to see me in person. I would very much enjoy an old time chat with you.

I just want you to know that I am for you and I believe that you believe in good things. We all make a few mistakes in a life-time. The only people who make no mistakes are the people who do nothing. You have reason to be depressed over the bad press you have received recently—but I do not pick and drop friends by the papers—and I grow stronger in my desire to stand by my friends when many others are turning against them. . . .

I judge from some of your statements in the paper that you find a balance and a stabilizing power in some of the confusion in which we find ourselves at times—when you turn to God in prayer. This confirms my belief that you are intelligent and have ability to make good judgments in choices and decisions. Our God is the God who saves. . . .

Sister James Ellen Huff
March 22, 1966

The April 11, 1966, issue of *Sports Illustrated* featured the headline "Cassius Clay: The Man, the Muslim, the Mystery." The published interview brought his religious beliefs to the forefront of his draft refusal as his statements made headlines across America. Filing as a conscientious objector proved a costly choice, forcing him to defend his title outside the country for disappointing prize winnings at welcoming arenas in Canada, England, and Germany. The next contender was five-time Canadian champion George Chuvalo, who in 85 fights had never been knocked down. Chuvalo commented on the champion's speed and spirit, saying, "damn fast. . . . He's a man of integrity, a man of good heart." The fight at Maple Leaf Gardens in Toronto went the 15-round distance on March 29. Ali revealed his battered hands to the press when he mentioned George's head was the hardest thing he ever punched. Two months later, a May rematch with Henry Cooper brought Ali back to England, where his popularity drew thousands of starstruck fans to his side as he strolled through familiar London Town. Rocky Marciano and Richard Burton were seated with 46,000 others to watch Ali's superb performance, in which he showed off the Ali Shuffle before defeating Cooper in Round Six on cuts. He next faced Brian London in August, outclassing him in a third-round knockout. His last fight on the European tour in September brought him to Frankfurt, Germany. After overcoming tough challenges from the southpaw's right jabs, he defeated Karl Mildenberger in a 12-round TKO.

Ali returned home after conquering Europe, facing Cleveland "Big Cat" Williams two months later. The Big Cat was a powerful two-handed fighter, who had won 65 of his 71 fights, many by impressive knockouts. An audience of about 35,000 filled the Houston Astrodome in November 1966, breaking the record for attendance at an indoor event. The Big Cat was mesmerized by Ali's speed, punching precision, agile footwork, and bravado. Experts, including his critics, believed it was Ali's most brilliant performance. Howard Cosell said, "The greatest Ali ever was as a fighter was in Houston against Cleveland Williams. That night, he was the most devastating fighter who ever lived." Ali continued to defend his title by extending his record to 27 wins, but not everyone was proud of him. Harsh criticism from former champion Gene Tunney, known as The Fighting Marine, appeared in a telegram: "You have disgraced your title and the American flag and the principles for which it stands. Apologize for your unpatriotic remarks or you'll be barred from the ring."

On February 6, 1967, Ali entered the ring with Ernie Terrell, who refused to respect his name and continued to call him "Cassius Clay." Ali controlled the pace throughout the torturous 15-round fight and won by unanimous decision. At the sound of the final bell, the answer to Ali's question—"What's my name?"—remained unanswered by Terrell. *Sports Illustrated* writer Tex Maule wrote that the fight was a "wonderful demonstration of boxing skill and a barbarous display of cruelty." Ali responded, "using my slave name. . . . That made it a personal thing. . . ." At the same time that some mainstream sportswriters refused to acknowledge the name Muhammad Ali, they showed respect for Rocco Francis Marche-giano, when he changed his name to Rocky Marciano and Walker Smith Jr., who had chosen the name Sugar Ray Robinson. Animosity toward Ali outside the ring continued to be pervasive, especially in political circles that interrupted his career plans. Back on January 20, at the urg-ing of the US Justice Department, the Kentucky Draft Board delivered a powerful blow and rejected his conscientious objector filing. In private moments with his idol Sugar Ray, the pressure devastated the 25-year-old champion, bringing him to tears. On March 22, two months after the Draft Board decision, Ali fought top contender Zora Folley at Madi-son Square Garden in New York City, where the audience witnessed a mutual respect between the fighters and great achievements in scientific boxing. Folley fell to defeat in a seventh-round KO admitting, "There is no one around today who can beat him. I know, I've fought them all." He also offered cautionary words of advice for Ali's next opponent: "He's smart. The trickiest fighter I've seen. . . . He could write the book of boxing, and anyone that fights him should be made to read it first." Ali was undefeated in the first seven years of his professional career after 29 matches.

The perfect storm in modern American history had arrived for a country devastated by the explosive confluence of escalating racial hostil-ity, political assassinations, and prolonged war. The nation continued to be afflicted with violent outrage over federal desegregation laws that failed to discipline racist practices in the Delta of a brutal southern stronghold. Ali was transformed into a hero to many in the eyes of a world veering toward perilous revolutionary change on the human rights front. In time, he received praise from many pulpits. During a speech heard at his Ebene-zer Baptist Church, Reverend King expressed his admiration for Ali's courageous defiance in refusing the Army induction order days earlier. "As Muhammad Ali puts it, we are all—black and brown and poor—victims of the same system of oppression."

The mutual esteem King and Ali shared was witnessed on rare public occasions when these allied spirits from vastly different arenas united in the fight for freedom and justice. Persistent old-world attitudes brought Ali back to Louisville with Reverend King to support fair housing demonstra-tors. Peaceful protests in March 1967 had turned violent over the next month, when the police resorted to extreme measures that would disband the rally. Ali joined Reverend King to support the ongoing hometown protests. The Fair Housing Campaign that continued in mid-April pre-sented another opportunity for Ali to make statements to the press about his stand against the war. He would later say, "Why should they ask me to put on a uniform and go ten thousand miles from home and drop bombs and bullets on brown people in Vietnam while so-called Negro people in Louisville are treated like dogs and denied simple human rights? No, I'm not going. . . ." Ali spoke publicly about the mistreatment of people in his hometown community when police brutality against demonstrators erupted in the streets. The desegregation protests were also a moment that appeared to express a departure from the separatist ideology espoused by the Nation of Islam that stood in opposition to the integrationist civil rights movement. He announced, "In your struggle for freedom, justice and equality, I am with you." Reverend King publicly expressed support for Ali's decision to refuse the draft. He addressed parishioners from his pulpit saying. "No matter what you think of Mr. Muhammad Ali's religion, you certainly have to admire his courage."

Ali stood beside Reverend King as a friend in the cause for civil rights in Louisville. A history of burning crosses cast a searing heat across the landscape, symbolizing the fierce resistance to integration pressure in the South. President Johnson would sign the Fair Housing Act of 1968 on April 11, a full year after the open housing marches first brought attention to the civil rights movement in Kentucky. The National Baptist Convention, the largest African American denomination in America by the late 1960s, joined the ranks of advocates who urged support for the fallen champion. Ali announced to the world, "I am proud of the title 'World Heavyweight Champion' which I won in the ring in Miami on February 25, 1964. The holder of it should at all times have the courage of his convictions, not only in the ring but throughout all phases of his life. It is in light of my own personal convictions that I take my stand in rejecting the call to be inducted into the armed services. I do so with full realization of its implications and possible consequences. I have searched my conscience and find I cannot be true to my belief in my religion by accepting such a call. My decision is a private and individual one. In taking it, I am dependent solely upon Allah as the final judge of these actions brought about by my own conscience."

High-profile African American athletes rallied around the champion in a show of support for his decision to become a conscientious objector. The Cleveland Summit held on June 4, 1967, was organized by Jim Brown, former star running back for the NFL Cleveland Browns. He called on several of the most influential athletes of the times to meet with Ali. Bill Russell, Willie Davis, Bobby Mitchell, and Lew Alcindor (later known as Kareem Abdul-Jabbar) were among the other stellar athletes who spoke to Ali. They left the meeting convinced that Ali was sincere about his religious beliefs. NBA All-Star Bill Russell said, "He has an absolute and sincere faith." The athletes held a news conference the next day to express their undivided support. Ali's actions inspired other athletes to step out of their traditional roles and speak out against injustice. The public display of respect from admired sports legends was intended to bridge the gap between Americans with different political views and ease resentful feelings across the country. Many viewed Ali as the target of government reprisals for outspokenness about his progressive beliefs and convictions.

The date was set for Ali to report to Houston, Texas, for induction into the Army on April 28, 1967. The final bell sounded as the champion faced trial after refusing to step forward as instructed three times at the Army induction ceremony. A federal grand jury in Houston ultimately responded to Ali's public statement, "I ain't got no quarrel with them Vietcong" by charging him with the crime of draft evasion on June 20. The maximum sentence was handed down: five years in prison and a $10,000 fine. His legal team arranged to keep him free on bail during the drawn-out appeals process. As public criticism spiraled out of control, he was called a disgrace to the sport and stripped of the title by the New York State Athletic Commission (NYSAC) and World Boxing Association. The NYSAC immediately suspended his boxing license before other states followed suit. Ali faced a cruel exile from the sport when every state refused to clear him to fight. Under FBI director J. Edgar Hoover, ongoing surveillance was ramped up and infiltrated every aspect of his life.

Arguing that Ali had made several claims that appeared racially and politically motivated, the government created doubt in the sincerity of his conscientious objector case. Ali was clear in his decision about the draft, explaining he was meant to fight in a war to lift and elevate people. In later writings he would tell the world, "The price I paid was nothing compared to what I gained. I lost the championship title. I lost three and a half prime fighting years. I lost financial security and public acclaim. . . . A title that no man or government could ever take away: I was the People's Champion . . . even the Nation of Islam tried to persuade me to accept the induction order . . . I didn't believe that was God's plan for me."

A letter from Sister James Ellen expressed understanding about his introduction to the ministry of the Nation of Islam and included a prayer for the embattled freedom fighter:

Dear Cassius,

The announcement of your ministerial office is not a complete surprise as I recognized in your "very" young days your religious quality.

   The enclosed prayer of St. Francis is the only copy I have at hand . . . but I think it expresses what, or at least something of what you idealize. Ponder it carefully and let me know if I am right. Draw close to God. God is Love and Life eternal. This life and love is my prayer for you, for me and for the world so much in need of Love.

Sister James Ellen Huff
August 25, 1966

Sportscaster Howard Cosell, who was also an attorney, spoke out publicly and provided legal commentary to expose the mishandling of Ali's case. He observed, "There'd been no grand jury empanelment, no arraignment. Due process of law hadn't even begun, yet they took away his livelihood because he failed the test of political and social conformity." While his conviction was on appeal, millions of supporters charged the air with rallying cries that echoed around the world. When he asked, "Who's the heavyweight champion of the world?" they answered, "YOU ARE!" British philosopher Bertrand Russell told Ali, "They will try to break you because you are a symbol of a force they are unable to destroy, namely, the aroused consciousness of a whole people determined no longer to be butchered and debased with fear and oppression. . . ."

   While banned from the ring, Ali remained in broad public view, lecturing at universities and reminding everyone he was the heavyweight champion of the world. All the while, he vehemently spoke out against the war, spread sacred teachings of Islam, and joined sportscasters in boxing commentary, providing favorable ratings for television networks. He continued to focus on uplifting the community stating, "My new job is freedom, justice and equality for black folks, to bring them the knowledge of their true selves." Changing perspectives on race and class in America rallied grassroots action to end unjust politics. An evolving awareness about systemic discrimination and the denial of economic justice transcended boundaries and led to unified action. A proud race consciousness conveyed by the Black Power movement was captured in the song by James Brown expressing Black pride out loud, shattering demeaning stereotypes when it rose high on the charts with frequent radio airplay.

Admiration for the heroic People's Champion was growing around the world, as he risked everything rather than fight in an unjust war. His impact broadened during his years of exile from the ring, as antiwar sentiment was nearing extremes. Many who believed that soldiers defending America are honorable for their loyalty, bravery, and sacrifice in the commitment to defend America were impassioned with new demands for ending a misguided war. Although Ali still had his share of critics, adulation by millions for his humanity resonated widely. The world watched as he confronted setbacks in the fight for equality and the prizefighting ring. Ali continued to be visible in troubled places around the nation, remaining outspoken about racial inequality after inner city uprisings. In 1967, he was photographed in Watts by friend Howard Bingham, two years after racial unrest escalated into mass rioting against police brutality in 1965.

Behind the high-profile attention in 1967, Ali privately impressed Chicago gang members enough to end plans for a showdown riot against police officers on the West Side. When the gangs assembled at the Senate Theatre, he warned them about the dire repercussions for the ghetto community and their families. He persuaded them to abandon the violent rebellion idea in front of a lone hidden reporter who witnessed the gifted peacekeeper in action.

The Vietnam War was escalating in 1967, when Reverend King gave a speech at Riverside Church in New York City called "Beyond Vietnam: A Time to Break Silence" that denounced the unjust war. Against the background of escalating military action in Southeast Asia, he stated that America was engaged in "one of history's most cruel and senseless wars." An historic alliance with President Johnson came to an end when he publicly criticized the US government as "the greatest purveyor of violence in the world." Reverend King spoke out about the "cruel irony" of African Americans dying on the battlefield for a country that denied them full citizenship. The antiwar comments cost him not just the White House but support from old allies unwilling to accept the unfavorable truths about covert foreign policy decisions during the war.

Secret plans by the Joint Chiefs and President Johnson to accelerate the war offensive brought more soldiers into the line of fire, breaking promises to bring the war to an end. Reporter Walter Cronkite went to the battlefield of Saigon in February 1968, broadcasting war scenes back home to prime-time news. President Johnson's disapproval rating skyrocketed even higher that year, as personal commentaries by Cronkite and other reporters in combat zones expressed the disillusionment descending over the country. Admiration for the heroic People's Champion was growing around the world, as he risked everything rather than fight in the war. His impact touched millions during his years of exile from the ring, as antiwar sentiment continued to intensify. Although Ali still had his share of critics, adulation by millions for his humanity resonated, and he emerged as the most famous symbol of defiance in the world.

On February 27, 1968, Cronkite reported a turning point in consensus opinion about the war. He ended the nightly news with a statement to America: "We've been too often disappointed by the optimism of the American leaders. . . . Both in Vietnam and Washington, to have faith any longer in the silver linings they find in the darkest clouds. For it seems now more certain than ever, that the bloody experience of Vietnam is to end in a stalemate." President Johnson watched the broadcast, telling his press secretary, "If I've lost Cronkite, I've lost Middle America." Reverend King and Ali made extreme sacrifices that brought worldwide attention to the unjust Vietnam War, which would finally end in 1975 when Saigon was overrun by the North Vietnamese army.

Reverend King raised the intensity of protests against injustice, by preaching the Word of biblical prophecy to inspire advances in the civil rights movement. On April 3, 1968, he delivered a speech in Memphis, Tennessee:

> I just want to do God's will.
> And He's allowed me to go up to the mountain.
> And I've looked over.
> And I've seen the Promised Land.
> I may not get there with you.
> But I want you to know tonight, that we, as a people will
> get to the promised land!

As the country was desperately adrift at a harrowing crossroads, Reverend King's unrelenting conviction rallied the movement and brought his followers out of an abyss of hopelessness. Revelations spoken in gospel cadence sounded the way toward justice prevailing over a savage culture of subjugation. Knowing his life was endangered, he continued to chart a course toward peace. From the mountaintop, he invited humanity to a place of spiritual refuge away from demoralizing oppression. With the Promised Land in sight, he withstood threats to his calling as his spirit blazed with arresting faith. His vision of the mountaintop resonated with daring assurance precious hours before news of his assassination caused shockwaves around the world. Reverend King was assassinated on April 4,

1968, exactly one year after his controversial antiwar speech in New York City. Senator Robert F. Kennedy was the first to release the tragic news to the nation. A quote from his favorite poet Aeschylus expressed the depth of an everlasting sorrow in the wake of the tragedy: "Even in our sleep pain which cannot forget, falls drop by drop upon the heart, until, in our own despair, against our will, comes wisdom through the awful grace of God."

With news of Reverend King's death, riots erupted in more than 100 inner cities where uncontainable outrage filled the streets. A season of torrential bloodshed would end with another violent storm when the assassination of Senator Robert F. Kennedy occurred two months later on June 6, 1968. America suffered through tragic times of deep loss, searching for a powerful voice of reason that would end the rampant violence.

By 1969, Ali was discussing his possible return to the ring with Howard Cosell. This departure from the Messenger's instructions caused the Nation of Islam to turn its back on their most famous member. In April, his one-year suspension from the NOI was publicized in *Muhammad Speaks*, which headlined the response "We Tell the World We're Not With Muhammad Ali." Ali remained devoutly committed to his religious beliefs, asserting that his faith in God made him a Muslim, not membership with the Nation: "My prayers, my sacrifices, my life and my death are all for Allah." The world began to realize that Ali had been following his conscience when he made profound life-changing decisions.

Ali remained publicly outspoken about social injustice, while his draft evasion case continued its course through appeal after appeal. He was free to travel the university lecture circuit and became a prominent symbol at peace rallies as the antiwar movement gained momentum among a rebellious youth culture. By the 1970s, students at over 100 American universities were protesting the invasive war maneuvers devised by the Pentagon. On May 4, 1970, students at Kent State University were killed by deadly crossfire from National Guardsmen that rained blood over home territory, unleashing a thunderous outcry of criticism.

Legal pressure intensified for a comeback by the People's Champion to his rightful place in the ring. Although Ali was still in legal trouble, supporters Atlanta mayor Maynard Jackson and Georgia state senator Leroy Johnson had mounted support through powerful constituents to host the champion's return. The NAACP filed suit against the New York State Athletic Commission that had first suspended his license to fight. In 1970, *Esquire* magazine featured a statement signed by a long list of celebrities that said, "We Believe That Muhammad Ali, the heavyweight champion of the world, should be allowed to defend his title." Segregationist Georgia governor Lester Maddox called on the Justice Department to weigh in against plans for the champion's first match since defeating Zora Folley in 1967. At the urging of prominent African Americans with political clout, Atlanta would become the first city to welcome him back for a fight against Jerry Quarry, on October 26, 1970, at City Auditorium.

After such a long absence, his competitive winning spirit would be tested on fight night. Ali was returning past his prime to an era of new heavyweight fighters. He would absorb more punishment to win rounds, dancing away from counterpunches less often on agile feet. Governor Maddox proclaimed a day of mourning when Ali stepped into the ring to participate in a sporting event that attracted millions of viewers worldwide. The international media spotlight captured cheers from celebrities, politicians, and ardent fans, and 5,100 ringside who filled seats to capacity. Despite death threats against him, the first-round bell sounded in the electrified arena. The promotional fight-talk was subdued, with Ali getting right down to business against a tough cunning fighter. Ali found his bearings after Round One with stinging jabs, combinations, and seasoned ring science. The younger Quarry was thrown off by an unorthodox style that forced the fight Ali's way. Referee Tony Perez officiated until Quarry's corner stopped the fight in the third round on cuts, advancing Ali's career record to 30-0. After the fight, Coretta Scott King presented him with the Martin Luther King Jr. Memorial Award that she said honored "a champion of justice, peace and human dignity." Civil rights leader Ralph Abernathy then described the returning champion's powerful impact as the "March on Washington all in two fists." After hard-fought rounds against injustice, the breathtaking comeback of the People's Champion inspired African American pride throughout the country. A bold renaissance spirit moved millions to celebrate the return of a remarkable champion to the golden age of boxing.

Ali's comeback coincided with bitter dissent toward a Nixon White House that was responsible for continuing a deceptive war policy, which now faced overwhelming public pressure to reduce troops on the front lines. Powerhouses in publishing increased government criticism, as Ali gained support among the growing number of antiwar subscribers. The *New York Times, Life, Sports Illustrated, Ebony, Time, Newsweek,* and *Esquire* were among the many publications that featured Ali through the years of government trials. His supporters around the world protested the decision by the New York State Athletic Commission and World Boxing Association that unjustly denied his right to the heavyweight title.

The lawsuit by the NAACP against the New York State Athletic Commission that had stripped Ali of his title and license to box was successful. Ali won back his right to be licensed in the state when the judge determined that he was entitled regardless of his draft evasion conviction. Craig Whitney of the *New York Times* covered the story in an article entitled "3-Year Ban Declared Unfair." Madison Square Garden once again turned on the spotlight for Ali as the 28-year-old champion faced the powerful Oscar Natalio "Ringo" Bonavena, who had knocked down reigning world heavyweight champion "Smokin'" Joe Frazier. Ali missed his prediction after shouting to the press, "He'll be mine in nine!" The grueling fight went the 15-round distance, with Ali timing his flicking jabs during the dance around his opponent for a strong finish. After Bonavena was sent to the canvas three times in the 15th round, he experienced the first TKO defeat of his career. During the fight, Dundee noticed that Ali's reflexes, agility, and speed had changed through the lost prime fighting years. Ali shouted his ultimatum to the press, "I want Joe Frazier."

In the eyes of the world, Ali had emerged as the People's Champion when the fight establishment first banned the undefeated world champion from boxing in April 1967. When he finally returned to the ring, he was a mature fighter who had to adapt his style to compete with a new generation of fast young heavyweights. He viewed the return matches against Quarry and Bonavena as preludes to recapturing the heavyweight title. In spite of cautious team guidance, Ali had a sense of urgency to win back the crown from reigning champion Joe Frazier. Although he had lost some of the speed that characterized the early golden years, Ali felt ready for what would be the epic "Fight of the Century." He set the stage for the championship match by stating, "Nobody has to tell me that this is a serious business. I'm not fighting one man. I'm fighting a lot of men, showing a lot of 'em, here is one man they couldn't defeat, couldn't conquer. My mission is to bring freedom to 30 million black people."

5

RETURN FROM EXILE

A Humanitarian Champion Prevails

The Fight of the Century at Madison Square Garden, 1971.
Bettmann / Getty

People around the world admired Ali for his proven self-sacrifice to uphold his principles. Bernie Yuman from Ali's management team described what millions had witnessed about the champion's character. "Most people would give up their heart and their soul to become the heavyweight champion of the world; he gave up the heavyweight championship of the world to keep his heart and his soul."

After years in exile from the ring, Ali returned to prizefighting a different fighter. He no longer danced through three-minute rounds slipping away from counterpunches within milliseconds of impact. At times, the magic of stinging jabs hurled with lightning speed still amazed, allowing him to continue gaining the competitive edge through the heat of battle. More often, he absorbed blows with resilient fortitude against the toughest heavyweight opponents he had ever confronted in the ring. He adapted his style to compensate for the physical changes he experienced as a mature fighter, with softer reflexes and legs that no longer glided him effortlessly out of range to outdistance his opponents. Yet in the gym, as he sparred with Luis Rodriguez, the fastest welterweight in the world, Ali proved he still had the skills reminiscent of his early golden years to elevate the pace in the fight. When Ali returned to the ring, he realized, "Everything changes. Governments change, kings fall, people change. I've changed."

American attitudes were changing when Ali denounced the escalating Vietnam War. There was a growing movement among those outraged by the foreign policy decisions that resulted in rising casualties throughout the long, drawn-out war, seeming to have no end in sight. On the comeback trail at the height of the antiwar movement, the renowned champion prizefighter received a hero's welcome. A *Sports Illustrated* article by Mark Kram on October 26, 1970, entitled, "He Moves Like Silk, Hits Like a Ton," revealed Ali's impressions about his return to the ring. He was quoted as saying, "I never thought I'd be back again, here again. Back in my old life again. All those years." After defeating two top contenders, only Smokin' Joe Frazier stood in the way of Ali regaining the crown that had been taken from him in 1967.

Ali had become internationally renowned during his fight for social justice, religious freedom, and racial equality in the 1960s. The world watched his return to championship boxing with high hopes that he would regain his rightful place as the crowned champion. His impact outside the ring would continue to be as great as his career achievements in the fierce heavyweight boxing arena. He identified with the liberation struggles of people from different cultures, appearing on a televised show discussing the Irish freedom movement. At home, he recited a human rights poem he wrote to express the truth that racial injustice was ever-present in America. His lyrical protest inspired by the 1971 Attica prison riot brought to light suspicious motives involving the shocking executions of African American inmates attempting to surrender to the guards after a rebellion. As national public opinion increasingly turned against the Vietnam War, the famous fighter was seen in a more favorable light as a revered champion. His support of the people's struggle for justice transcended sports, transforming him into a cultural icon for African American pride and independence.

He was adrenaline ready in anticipation of the fight against the reigning champion of the world. However, his team felt more time was needed to fine-tune a scientific approach designed to defeat reigning champion Joe Frazier. As he prepared for the fight, the outcome of his legal appeal to overturn his draft evasion conviction could threaten his freedom at any moment, so Ali chose an early opportunity to fight Frazier at Madison Square Garden on March 8, 1971. Ali defined the character of the Fight of the Century with symbolic references to the People's Champion taking on the adversarial political establishment represented by Frazier. Against a backdrop of oppressive politics, he set the stage for the title bout and defined the stakes for those involved: "They identify with my struggle. Same one they're fighting every day in the streets. If I win, they win. I lose, they lose. Anybody black who thinks Frazier can whup me is an Uncle Tom. . . ." The fight-talk continued, with Ali telling the media he was the one who represented the struggles in the African American community. The heavy blows continued, as he insulted Frazier's intelligence with comments to the press about him being too ugly and dumb to be the world heavyweight champion.

"The Art of Ali," an article written by Martin Kane for the May 5, 1969, issue of *Sports Illustrated*, described Ali as a classic boxer fast on his feet, who threw punches with a lightning flick of his wrist. Ali's style transition was described by one sportswriter as going from "superman to extraordinary" after years banned from the ring. Ali knew that Frazier would be willing to endure an entire weapons arsenal for the one chance to position his devastating left hook. Though the times were changing, the Ali mystique of invincibility still attracted unprecedented public attention. The New York venue drew thousands of people, who cheered his name during walks in Central Park before the championship fight at Madison Square Garden. The fight, which was advertised by a massive multimedia campaign, would be broadcast in 50 countries, to an estimated 300 million viewers with ringside commentary in 12 languages. The estimated $2.5 million purse to each fighter set a record for a one-night main event.

Like their contrasting ring styles, the fighters came from vastly different backgrounds. At a young age, Joe Frazier left behind rural poverty in Beaufort, South Carolina for New York City before finding success in Philadelphia. He trained by running up all 72 steps to the building entrance of the Philadelphia Museum of Art for endurance, a training run later portrayed by Sylvester Stallone in a scene from the critically acclaimed movie *Rocky*. In 1965, wealthy financiers formed Cloverlay, Inc. to support the 1964 gold medal Olympian's professional boxing career. The reigning world champion ranked high among the best inside fighters in boxing history, with a solid gold left hook. His crouching bob-and-weave style had a powerful forward motion that inspired trainer Yancey "Yank" Durham to nickname him "Smokin' Joe." He was compared to Rocky Marciano when his punches brought contenders to their knees in the ring. Cornerman Eddie Futch had discouraged Frazier from entering a WBA tournament organized to fill the vacated seat left by Ali in protest over the decision to strip him of the title. He would ultimately capture the world heavyweight crown when he defeated titleholder Jimmy Ellis in 1970. The Fight of the Century brought together two undefeated champions who had a brief friendship during Ali's exile until they met in the ring for the first time. The 27-year-old Frazier stood 5'11" and had won 26 career fights with 20 KOs/TKOs. The 29-year-old Ali stood 6'3" and had a 31-0 career record with 22 KOs/TKOs.

Ali had always been a perceptive fighter with keen hunting instincts, known for his psychological jabs that infuriated opponents and led to their downfall in the ring. Dundee assessed his impact: "He destroyed a generation of fighters by boxing with his hands down." Martin Kane described Ali's boxing style and slugger fighting technique that characterized Frazier in another *Sports Illustrated* article entitled "The Slugger and the Boxer." The fight crowd knew Ali would make it a physical as well as mental exchange of blows to lure opponents into his fight plan. He boasted, "There's not a man alive who can whip me, I'm too fast. I'm too smart. I'm too pretty." There were many people uninterested in the sport who paid top dollar for ringside seats at Madison Square Garden to see Ali recapture the title. His boxing style would astound them with unrivaled legendary hand speed that delivered fluid punches that cut down his opponents. Ringside viewers consisted of the most famous celebrities in Hollywood, the glitterati crowd, worldwide media, and enthusiastic fight fans including astronaut Alan Shepard, the commander of the Freedom 7 spacecraft.

Millions around the world were cheering for Ali from the start of the promotion buildup for the championship match. The moment had finally arrived after years of defending his religious freedom. Heavyweight champion Joe Frazier had used his clout at the White House to ask President Nixon to reinstate Ali's boxing license. Then feelings of betrayal ruined a friendship, when fight-talk in the demeaning style of a Gorgeous George wrestling venue became more than Frazier could tolerate. To no avail, boxing promoter Butch Lewis told Frazier, "He's not disrespecting you. This is Ali! This is what will make the payday. This is not personal." Many were surprised to learn, after the showmanship antics out of the spotlight,

Ali "was just a nice, quiet, calm person." As a proud champion ranked high on his throne, Frazier would not stand for the ridicule, especially from the man he stood by during rough times in exile. By the sound of the opening bell, their friendship was over.

Fight-talk from Ali was amplified to extremes by directing negative media attention toward Frazier, who he referred to as an Uncle Tom fighting for the establishment. Frazier had earnestly told the press, "If there is anything I can do to help black people, or help anybody, I'll do what I can." Ali's brand of gamesmanship infuriated Frazier, who was still favored by oddsmakers unconvinced of an Ali comeback win.

Ali's theatrics continued into fight night, as fans in an arena filled to capacity watched the drama unfold before the bell. Frazier entered the ring wearing a robe embroidered with the names of his five children. They had experienced unanticipated and unintended fallout when bullied at school by kids who sided with Ali, the more popular contender. Ali wore a red satin robe and white shoes accented by red tassels that swayed around his ankles. He warmed up in the ring dancing, throwing punches, and waving at the crowd, then intruded on the champion's corner. As he tapped on Frazier's head to test the tough target, it seemed he was insulting the champion by mockingly searching for signs of intelligent life. The provocation had the expected effect, as they stood in the center of the ring with Referee Arthur Mercante and angry Frazier sneered at Ali, "I'm gonna kill you!" The fierce rivalry between the two great champions, which began with this fight, would last for decades after the final bell.

Standing in Frazier's corner, trainer Eddie Futch anticipated that Ali would use the ropes to conserve energy, then move in clinching to pace the fight. He would continue the psychological warfare to inflame Frazier's temper, force his defenses down, and shake his confidence. From the start, Frazier showed that he could absorb heavy punches as he searched hard for the chance to land his famous left hook. More than 20,000 people watched in the arena as Ali circled Frazier, who moved in tight to turn the fight in his favor. As the ringside crowd stood up screaming for Ali, he responded by leading the heated fight action with damaging hurled fists, feinted punches, and stinging jabs. Frazier bobbed and weaved, trying to dodge the blows and demeaning fight-talk in the ring.

In Round One, Frazier stayed true to his unrelenting slugger style, landing a signature left hook that Ali brushed off like a passing breeze as he circled the ring. The referee warned the fighters to stop talking and the momentum changed, with the two fighters standing toe-to-toe exchanging punches. Suddenly retreating to the ropes, Ali took brutal punches from the headhunting reigning champion in the second round. The next two rounds winded Ali as he shouted at Frazier, who set a furious pace. Before forced to the ropes to evade Frazier's missiles, Ali landed rights with combinations and stinging jabs before he tangled up Frazier in powerful clinches. Ali shook his head at intervals to assure viewers that he was not hurt, evoking laughter and applause from the crowd. Dundee was not amused at this point in the match, which had a faster exchange between the fighters without the expected KO upset. During Rounds Six and Seven Ali mostly avoided the ropes by moving on his toes, adding uppercuts to combinations while shifting momentum to his corner. Before the start of Round Eight, the crowd chanted "Ali! Ali! Ali!" Psychological plays were exchanged by each fighter in that round, when Ali dropped his fists, daring the champion to hit the mark. Frazier pulled Ali off the ropes closer to him, giving Ali an opening to land a one-two combination and inspiring the crowd to chant his name—"Joe! Joe! Joe!"—when the round was over. During Round Nine Ali dazzled, danced on his toes, and dominated the fight, throwing sharp reflexive punches that outclassed Frazier. The referee split the fighters locked in a clinch that counted two points against Ali. Arthur Mercante observed, "Most guys are just in there fighting, but Ali had a sense of everything that was happening, almost as though he was sitting at ringside analyzing the fight while he fought it." Ali fell back to the ropes in Round 10, when he withstood a ferocious thunder of left hooks to the body from an exhausted Frazier. Ali yelled to his team, "He's out!" Ali finished the precious remaining seconds of the round with left-right combinations and multiple jabs scoring desperately needed points.

During the fight, Ali held the advancing Frazier back with one arm. Dundee warned Ali to stop clowning around, telling him not to underestimate the tough world heavyweight champion. A devastating turning point came in Round 11. Frazier appeared to brush off his exhaustion when he landed a massive left hook to Ali's jaw, staggering him in a daze. Bundini sprayed water at Ali to accelerate his recovery on his way back to the corner after the bell. Ali survived, drifting back to his team to recharge the pace. Ali reached the corner where Dundee reiterated the winning strategy by yelling in his ear "get back on your toes . . . get off the ropes . . . use your jab." The damage became obvious in Round 12 when Ali struggled to protect his face, which ballooned to extreme proportions from his injured jaw. Round 13, between low-impact coasting, Ali then went to the ropes as Bundini desperately shouted, "You got God in your corner, Champ!" Frazier was showing the heavy damage, as his eyes swelled after absorbing close to an hour of tremendous counterpunches. By the end of Round

14, damage to both fighters astounded Mercante, who commented, "I was surprised that it went 15. They threw some of the best punches I've ever seen."

Ali, sensing that precious seconds remained in the final championship round, searched for his last chance at a knockout. Instead, that opportunity opened for Frazier. When Ali set up for a right uppercut, he made room for Frazier's left hook, which instantly landed him on the canvas. Describing the moment that devastated worldwide hopes, Bundini said, "That punch blew out all the candles on the cake." He gave Ali a lifeline to help him to shore, throwing water so high into the ring on fallen Ali it reached the ringside seats. Facing a fine and suspension for the infraction, he defended his impulsive reaction, stating, "I was trying to revive my soldier." Although Ali miraculously stood up almost as quickly as he fell, the unanimous decision went to Frazier, making him the undisputed world heavyweight champion. Upsetting the expectations of millions for an Ali comeback win, Frazier maintained his claim to the throne at the summit of heavyweight prizefighting.

Former champion José Torres commented, "incredible left hook that Ali was hit with. That was Frazier's best punch, and Ali took it on the jaw. Nobody takes that kind of punch and stays up. . . . But then he gets up. . . ." Millions around the world who expressed heartfelt disappointment over the loss still believed Ali was the true heavyweight champion. The first loss of Ali's professional career brought Bundini to tears. Both fighters were taken to the hospital where doctors determined the physical toll of the battle. It was not until years later that Ali shared that he thought his jaw had been broken, along with his perfect fight record.

Ali faced a barrage of reporters the day after his devastating defeat by unanimous decision. He treated the situation matter-of-factly, concluding, "Just lost a fight, that's all . . . more important things to worry about in life . . . probably be a better man for it. . . . News don't last too long." A reporter interrupted the impressive nonchalance, searching for a visceral response from Ali by commenting, "Joe said he didn't think you wanted to fight him again." The insinuation provoked Ali to jab back instantly, saying, "Oh, how wrong he is."

Media throughout the world reported on Ali's massive fall to earth; still he assured fans that the defeat was no reason to leave the sport like a washed-up fighter. The Ali star seemed to shine even brighter in the cosmos when he demonstrated gracious sportsmanship: "I never thought of losing, but now that it's happened, the only thing is to do it right. That's my obligation to all the people who believe in me. We all have to take defeats in life." Frazier was left wondering what other worlds he had to conquer to win the universal appeal experienced by the People's Champion. Ali used fight-talk to set up a rematch and kept hope for second chances alive, telling Joe, "No man ever beat me twice."

Ali's impact outside the ring continued to grow impressively. In this decade he would be recognized as one of the most famous people in the world. The US Supreme Court convened in April 1971 for a decision in the draft evasion case. Government accusations had consistently expressed racially motivated, political reasons for Ali's stance against the war to disprove the sincerity of the Muslim beliefs he pointed to in his defense. However, a pivotal flaw threatened the government's premise. The Supreme Court justices raised a crucial question at the close of the trial to expose misleading arguments by the US solicitor general. In an attempt to sustain a guilty verdict, government counsel reversed its opinion and answered that Ali had been sincere about his religious beliefs. The inconsistency, which marked a denial of due process, enabled eight justices (with one abstention) to unanimously overturn the conviction without setting a precedent on June 28, 1971. The justices concluded, "For the record shows that the petitioner's beliefs are founded on tenets of the Muslim religion as he understands them."

The summer solstice marked a life-defining turning point in time for Ali. At the suggestion of Supreme Court law clerk Thomas G. Krattenmaker, Justice John Marshall Harlan II from Kentucky was persuaded to closely examine *The Message to the Black Man in America* by Elijah Muhammad and the *Autobiography of Malcolm X* to compose the legal opinion and to understand Ali's conscientious objector defense. Justice Harlan's opinion, which showed admiration for Ali's "integrity of character," concluded that the claims presented by the Justice Department misrepresented the truth. Despite the overturned conviction he was still resented by some, but he was admired by millions for bringing international attention to the antiwar movement, while keeping social problems in the forefront. Ali biographer Thomas Hauser observed, "At a time when America was being torn apart, when the government was lying to its people, he was speaking the truth as he saw it, if not as it really was."

Around the same time that Ali was vindicated, disturbing truths about an unpopular war surfaced when published excerpts from a document known as the Pentagon Papers appeared in the *Washington Post* and the *New York Times*. Dr. Daniel Ellsberg, a military analyst, leaked some of the top-secret study on the Vietnam War. The 44 volumes highlighted aspects of misguided policies followed by the Department of Defense during the war. The moral justification for the war fell short when the government's real purpose was revealed: to obstruct Communist regimes from expanding, rather than the liberation of South Vietnamese friends from a Viet Cong insurgency supported by the Communist North. The research revealed that President Lyndon B. Johnson broke campaign promises by escalating the war effort through covert military maneuvers that increased American and Vietnamese casualties to pressure Ho Chi Minh to the negotiating table. By 1965, analysts had reported that the fight was unwinnable, yet the Johnson Administration decided to expand the war offensive. Secretary of Defense Robert McNamara believed the Pentagon Papers would be a valuable historic record of wartime mistakes to educate future generations. In his published memoirs, McNamara revealed tragic truths: "We were wrong, terribly wrong. We owe it to future generations to explain why." A redemptive turning point was reached as President Nixon finally brought an end to the Vietnam War in 1973, after antiwar protesters became a powerful force during the moral crisis unfolding in America.

After his conviction was overturned, Ali's management arranged a fight schedule for an international comeback. Starting in the summer of 1971, Ali would prove his talents over his next 14 matches, taking on a manic competitive pace. By 1974, he would again be a top contender, in line for a championship fight against the newly crowned champion George Foreman. Successes and setbacks along the way challenged him like never before, as he rallied the support of millions during his ascent. It would take four years after his return to the ring in 1970 for Ali to reach the summit for the second time. Ali proved to the world that his principles were more important than wealth or his title. He shared his sage advice about his challenging return to the championship spotlight: "Success is not achieved by winning all the time. Real success comes when we rise after we fall. . . . Some mountains are higher than others, some roads steeper than the next. There are hardships and setbacks, but you cannot let them stop you. Even on the steepest road you must not turn back."

6

COMEBACK FORTITUDE

The People's Champion Goes the Distance

Ali on the Ascent.
Photograph by Ken Regan / Getty Images

In 1971, Ali began a long ascent to regain the coveted championship belt awarded to those reaching the zenith of heavyweight prizefighting. He described his prowess in the ring with comedic wit: "If you sign to fight me, you need speed and endurance but what you need most is to increase your insurance." A series of competitive challenges during 15 fights would add a stunning defeat and celebrated victories to his record by 1974. His physical skill and mental fortitude were both put to the test during this new era of great heavyweight champions. During his manic world tour between 1971 and 1974, Ali was all business as he faced opponents on several continents. Although he would never recover the prime boxing years he had lost while banned from the sport, Ali showed the world great performances reminiscent of his glorious reign as the undisputed young heavyweight king. Boxing fans had hoped to see his masterful fighting skills reach a personal best in the years after he defeated world champion Sonny Liston, but now he would have to go the brutal distance to win back his rightful place on the throne.

After his devastating loss to Frazier, the crucial Supreme Court decision to reverse his draft evasion conviction lifted his sights toward the crown and renewed his unrelenting drive to regain the title. Although many felt the comeback dream was too great a distance, even for the extraordinary 29-year-old, he would prove that the loss to Frazier was just a momentary setback. The next 10 consecutive victories brought him closer to another championship fight. Ali's resolve would be tested over and over again through fight after fight on his perilous ascent toward once again becoming the world heavyweight champion.

On July 26, 1971, he faced former sparring partner and childhood friend from hometown Louisville, Jimmy Ellis, at the Houston Astrodome. Angelo Dundee was in Ellis's corner with Ali's blessings for the first match since the Supreme Court win. The familiar fight-talk was amplified by media sound bites from Ali: "Ellis is ugly. He's so ugly he ought to donate his face to the National Wildlife Bureau." Ellis responded, "I don't care if I never win another fight as long as I live—if I win this one." At the bell, Ali danced in and out of reach, dropping his arms to entice his opponent to throw a knockout punch. Ellis endured a series of stinging jabs and uppercuts that forced him to the ropes, where Ali showed mercy for the disarmed fighter. In that moment Ali said he was thinking, "I was just waiting for the referee to stop it, not because Jimmy's my friend but because he's a man, like me." Referee Jay Edson stopped the fight for a 12th-round TKO win. Ali's demonstration of compassion, rare in a brutal pugilistic sport, caused many objections after the bell. The fight crowd was on notice that Ali would show heart in the ring. He was long past the anger displayed in his bloody battles with Patterson and Terrell, to whom he taught brutal lessons about respecting his name. Buster Mathis was next at the Houston Astrodome on November 17, as Ali once again displayed mercy by allowing his opponent to finish on his feet for the win by unanimous decision. For his final match of the year, he flew to Zürich on December 26 to face the German heavyweight champion Jürgen Blin for a KO win in the seventh round.

Ali began 1972 with a journey of a lifetime in prayer at the spiritual center of the Muslim world. His pilgrimage to the holy city of Mecca was a sacred experience that brought him to Mount Arafat where the Islamic Prophet Muhammad once stood. He shared his feelings about the Hajj with the press. "I felt exalted by the indescribable spiritual atmosphere there as over one and a half million pilgrims invoked God to forgive them for their sins and bestow on them His choicest blessings." A year later on January 27, the Paris Peace Accords were signed, answering heartfelt prayers for a cease-fire resolution and the withdrawal of American forces from Vietnam.

Ali's whirlwind 1972 fight season would include bouts against Mac Foster, George Chuvalo, Jerry Quarry, Alvin "Blue" Lewis, Floyd Patterson, and Bob Foster, attracting new fans to the ring that year in Tokyo, Vancouver, Las Vegas, Dublin, New York City, and Lake Tahoe. In April, Ali entered the ring wearing a striking Japanese robe to fight Mac Foster in Tokyo. The unanimous decision victory advanced Ali's ranking, though the match went 15 rounds rather than ending in the predicted fifth by a knockout. There were three rematches starting in May when he faced Canadian champion George Chuvalo, who had mastered a tough fighting style many compared to undefeated champion Rocky Marciano. Ali stayed on course, winning a unanimous 12-round decision in front of a cheering Vancouver crowd. The contender on track for the title publicly reminded crowned champion Frazier that he was fighting on precious borrowed time before The Greatest of All Time would win back the title. Ali faced Jerry Quarry next in another rematch broadcast from the fight capital of the world in Las Vegas. Ali forced his opponent to back down when cuts ended the match in a seventh-round TKO. Summer in Dublin brought thousands of fans to see his signature style as he moved on dancing feet, throwing flicking jabs until Alvin "Blue" Lewis fell victim to an 11th-round TKO on July 19.

In 1972, Ali purchased new training grounds that he named *Fighter's Heaven* in the Pennsylvania township of Deer Lake before his 40th career fight. The expansive rural grounds had log cabin residences, a prayer center, and a gym. Anyone was welcome to visit the champion while he fine-tuned skills in exhibition sparring rounds. Ali's father painted honored boxing names on boulders around the camp, including Sugar Ray Robinson, Joe Louis, Rocky Marciano, Floyd Patterson, and Jersey

Joe Walcott. Ali did roadwork on a grueling trail he called "Agony Hill" to build his endurance, vital for going the winning distance to the championship.

The next fight would reunite two great champions who were now on friendly terms. Floyd Patterson would mention old resentments saying, "I called him 'Cassius Clay,' but I didn't like it when he called me 'the rabbit' either," alluding to a timid nature. They came together, casting aside bitter times. Patterson admitted, "When we talked in private, I was surprised at how much I liked him. He was a nice guy. Believe it or not, he even seemed a little shy." Patterson had also supported Ali's right to freely fight in defense of his title in an *Esquire* magazine article he penned in 1966. He said that the heavyweight champion was treated too harshly for his religious affiliation and views on the Vietnam War.

The night of the fight on September 20, under the bright lights of Madison Square Garden, Patterson used the seasoned championship skills that had won him the title twice in his career. Patterson's quick rights controlled the pace, challenging Ali to break through his tough defensive style. Then Patterson succumbed to a cut eye in Round Six that swelled shut by the end of Round Seven. At age 37, Patterson ended two decades of record-setting professional prizefighting after the match was over.

Ali's final win of the year occurred on November 21 against Bob Foster in Lake Tahoe where a fierce fight schedule ended on another high note. Ali was cut over the left eye before he knocked Foster down multiple times in Rounds Five and Seven for an easy KO win in Round Eight. The first obvious cut Ali suffered in his professional career was put in perspective by Dundee, who said, "Now people know he's got blood. . . ." Ali asked referee Mills Lane to stop the fight saying, "I don't want to hit him anymore. There's no point."

On Valentine's Day, the heavily favored Ali faced Joe Bugner in a tough match at the Las Vegas Convention Center. Ali went the distance to win the unanimous 12-round decision. He was adorned in a white robe with sparkling rhinestones and colorful gemstones he received as a gift from friend Elvis Presley. The jewel-studded words across the back read the "People's Choice," expressing the world's love for Ali. Bugner described facing the most creative fighter of all time after he lost the fight. He told the press, "I tried to fight him instinctively because it's impossible to have a set plan against Ali."

Ali glittered under the bright lights, wearing the same robe, when he faced Ken Norton at the Sports Arena in San Diego, California, on

March 31. Since his downfall two years earlier against Frazier in the Fight of the Century, the 31-year-old Ali had been undefeated, winning 10 straight matches. Norton, who held an impressive 29–1 record, presented a major challenge to Ali's winning stride during his 43rd career fight. Ali experienced serious physical injury in the ring when his jaw was broken in Round Two. By Round Three blood spilled from his mouth, exposing the extent of the damage that Norton had inflicted. Demonstrating his legendary style and extreme raw courage, Ali refused to quit. He said, "I was thinking about those 19,000 people in the arena, and [ABC's] 'Wide World of Sports,' millions of people at home watching in 62 countries. So what I had to do was put up a good fight, go the distance and not get hit on the jaw again." His tearful corner braced for the worst as the courageous fighter struggled with debilitating pain to avoid an upset that would ruin his plans for the championship.

Ali fell to defeat in a 12-round split-decision that raised serious doubts about his ability to win back the title. *Sports Illustrated* included stories featuring him still sounding off with fight-talk through his broken jaw after the loss. Ali enlightened the press about the extent of his toughness through the ordeal: "Imagine you have your jaw broken and have to fight ten more rounds against Norton." After the match, Ali was piecing together his future, while surgeons pieced together his broken jaw for 90 minutes at the hospital. Ali's detractors celebrated the downfall in high style, feeling no pain. The stakes for a successful comeback were raised dangerously high during this most challenging stretch of his ascent. Howard Cosell expressed what many felt about Ali's defeat, that it signaled the end of the legend, when he stated, "Losing to Norton was the end of the road, at least as far as I could see." Ali's record slipped to 41-2 with 27 KOs/TKOs, and the press continued to speculate on whether the Norton fight was the finale of a brilliant career. Ali held onto his dream, but he would never wear that dazzling robe in the prizefighting ring again.

Ali confronted unflattering press coverage when he returned to Agony Hill, facing difficult miles ahead for his late summer rematch with Norton. Oddsmakers still favored Ali, despite the short timeline to get in shape for the fight. During media fight-talk, Ali expressed foreboding doom, saying that the chances were slim-to-none that his tough opponent would win at the Forum in Inglewood, California, on September 10. Norton's jab-resistant defensive stance made Ali adapt his style, as he faced Norton's strategically paced moves throughout the 12-round bout. Then Ali stormed center ring, standing toe-to toe with Norton, slugging him with swift combinations through the final minutes for a decisive win. Ali was forced into a desperate gamble, holding back his advancing opponent just enough to gain the edge. The crucial fight ended in a close split-decision that put Ali back on track to face reigning champion George Foreman. Ali told the press, "I know it was close, that's why I finished fast just to remove any doubts about the winner."

On October 20, after jetting to the Indonesian capital of Jakarta, Ali won his 45th fight against Dutch heavyweight champion Rudi Lubbers before a stadium crowd of 25,000. It was the first professional prizefight ever held in the country with the largest Muslim population in the world. It was one of many developing nations where the impact of Ali's activism would be felt. Fans surrounded his corner of the ring chanting his name. Ali's commitment to helping those in need anywhere in the world would lead him back to Jakarta many years later to deliver medical supplies and food during a visit to Harapan Kita Hospital for Children before he continued his travels to confront the dire circumstances of Moroccan street children. He also answered an urgent call for humanitarian help with American missionary Sister Sponsa Beltran in the Ivory Coast after discovering the plight of displaced Liberian refugees, many severely wounded and incapacitated fleeing embattled conflict zones.

With the championship match clearly in sight, Ali shared thoughts about his career that were surprising to some: "I'll get out of boxing once I've finished my business with Joe Frazier and taken my title from Foreman." He would continue to chart a course toward great achievements in the humanitarian arena by using his powerful platform to better the world. To further peace and brotherhood, Ali would create *Healing: A Journal of Tolerance and Understanding*, a book intended to inspire a spirit of unity through enhanced understanding, tolerance, and respect. He would receive high praise for his extraordinary fundraising and charitable giving efforts over the decades, which included raising money for local mosques around the world to help advocate for religious tolerance and spread his faith. The many accolades throughout his life included an award from the World Economic Forum's Council of 100 Leaders for promoting dialogue about Islam to promote religious understanding across faiths. Among the organizations on his long list of beneficiaries were the Cradle Adoption Agency, the Special Olympics, the Make-A-Wish Foundation, and the Muhammad Ali Parkinson Center at the Barrow Neurological Institute. His collaboration with actor Michael J. Fox also raised substantial funds for Parkinson's research.

Whether it was teaching tolerance and understanding, feeding the hungry, teaching the tenets of his Islamic religion, or reaching out to children in need, Muhammad Ali was devoted to making the world a better place for all people. He contributed unlimited time and raised generous sums of money for causes in the United States and throughout the world. During his travels, he brought attention to sick children and those with special needs, encouraged young students to stay in school, and even supported British boys clubs on overseas visits. The impact of his global mission strengthened communities by helping to break down barriers to greater opportunities, enabling the free pursuit of dreams of gold. To forge avenues for peace, he petitioned global leaders to join the humanitarian movement and helped establish the Children's Peace Foundation, which gives children a voice in promoting peace around the world.

In the early 1970s, Ali's lifetime of humanitarian endeavors was just beginning to unfold. He was only one fight away from facing the reigning champion to regain the world heavyweight title. Frazier was his next opponent, also vying for a chance to become the top contender in line for a championship fight, after losing the crown to George Foreman in January 1973. Frazier had been training hard in his North Philadelphia gym, inspired by a Fight of the Century poster of Ali knocked to the canvas by his signature left hook. Madison Square Garden sold out for the long-awaited Frazier-Ali rematch on January 28, 1974. The fight, billed as Super Fight II, brought two former heavyweight champions to the ring three years after their last match. The fight-talk jabs from Ali were toned down, as he focused on the serious business of determining who would be the next in line to reclaim the title. A genuinely bitter rivalry had been building for years since Ali's return from exile. Ali wanted to avenge the Fight of the Century defeat, and Frazier wanted to silence his critics who claimed that the crown belonged to Ali. Before the epic fight, a nationally televised brawl on *Wide World of Sports* captured an infuriated Frazier wrestling on the floor with his archrival. Ali had insulted Frazier's intelligence in retaliation for offensive comments Frazier made about his jaw injury during their championship match. Frazier stormed off and the New York State Athletic Commission fined both fighters for unprofessional behavior.

On fight night, Ali was the first to enter the ring, bouncing on his toes, moving in circles, and shadowboxing with swift combinations. Frazier stepped into the ring flexing his arms and homing in on his target in forward motion. Ali took the lead at the opening bell, dancing around the ring in constant motion and staying off the ropes. Frazier geared up his left hook, repeatedly flexing his shoulder muscles, bracing for the opportune moment to strike. Ali moved off the ropes while bearing down on his opponent in tight clinches, broken free by referee Tony Perez. Right from the start,

Ali landed combinations that demolished Frazier's defenses with several powerful lefts. He staggered Frazier early with a right hand in Round Two. Ali dominated round after round by throwing easy flurries, then tying up Frazier, cutting off his firing range to prevent inside blows. In Round Five, when Frazier came on strong and set the pace, Bundini shouted, "Float like a butterfly! . . . Keep dancing, champ!" Frazier taunted Ali while scoring repeatedly with lefts and rights during Rounds Six and Seven. Ali winked at ringside commentators after Frazier belted him, showing that his efforts had little impact. In Round Nine Frazier laughed at Ali, daring him to come closer. Ali accepted the invitation to go toe-to-toe, landing a flurry of seven punches, as his bloody nose exposed signs of damage from previous rounds. By Round 11, Frazier was well behind on points, narrowing down his options to a knockout win. Frazier swung wildly, hoping to strike gold as Ali threw flurry after dizzying flurry. Dundee shouted, "Stay there, Baby. Stay there! . . . Fifteen seconds left!" By Round 12, with one minute left, Ali was still on his toes never letting Frazier close the distance. He circled the ring, leading in and out of the Ali Shuffle with gliding foot speed. Frazier lost by unanimous decision at the final bell, ending his mission to destroy Ali's comeback. The media was informed of Ali's assessment of the win against Frazier: "I left him chasing my shadow." Throughout his long rise to the rank of top contender, Ali firmly believed that "The fight is won or lost far away from the witnesses—behind the lines, in the gym and out there on the road, long before I dance under those lights." Ali's championship match hopes were well in reach when he would next face undefeated reigning champion George Foreman.

7

ORACLES AND MAGIC IN KINSHASA

Muhammad Ali vs. George Foreman

Ali Overlooking the Congo River on the Esplanade in 1974.
Photograph by Neil Leifer / Getty Images

After the Frazier rematch, Ali would face George Foreman in a fight to recapture the throne seven years after he had been stripped of the title. He warned the reigning champion in lyrical fashion, "Float like a butterfly, sting like a bee, George can't hit what his eyes can't see, now you see me, now you don't, he thinks he will, but I know he won't." The world-renowned People's Champion entered the ring in Zaire against an undefeated Foreman for a highly publicized battle called the "Rumble in the Jungle." Once again, a moment of truth had arrived for Ali to prove he was the greatest prizefighter to ever wear the crown. Oddsmakers overwhelmingly favored Foreman, the young, seemingly invincible powerhouse slugger who emulated the formidable Sonny Liston.

The universe expanded exponentially at the highly publicized moment Ali stepped off the plane in Zaire (now known as the Democratic Republic of the Congo) to fight for the heavyweight crown. At the height of his fame in 1974, Ali brought worldwide attention to this African country, which he admired for achieving an independent Black Nationalist ideal. He said, "I've never felt so free in my life. Free from America where I'm not really free." He embraced Zairian people in the streets, who had been waiting for the chance of a lifetime to meet him. Basketball star Dikembe Mutombo, a native of Zaire and a humanitarian in his own right, said, "He changed my life. . . . He changed how the people of Zaire saw themselves, and in turn how the world saw them."

The $10 million spectacle in the capital city of Kinshasa was the product of united forces, including the innovative deal-making virtuoso Don King. After venturing into the prizefighting business, he managed to influence the president of an African nation to sponsor one of the most famous heavyweight championship fights in history. King gained the spotlight as a top producer who turned profitable returns from lucrative fight contracts into bountiful bankrolls. He was notorious however for exploiting talented fighters by way of rumored underworld connections. In a *Sports Illustrated* article, journalist Mark Kram described the boxing promoter in surreal terms, "a 50-carat setting of sparkling vulgarity and raw energy, a man who wants to swallow mountains, walk on oceans, and sleep on clouds." He parlayed with theatrical style, using Shakespearean quotes to thicken the plot and Socrates for wise philosophical discourse that seemed to give substance to the art of the deal. The fight, promoted by King with Pan-Africanist pride, was publicized as the homecoming for two awe-inspiring champions. He also organized a music festival with a soul and blues groove that showcased African American entertainers in the Fatherland. B. B. King, the Spinners, and James Brown led the lineup that also included Miriam Makeba and African jazz musician Hugh Masekela, both world renowned for their anti-apartheid music, which spread the news of rebellions happening across townships in their South African homeland.

Since 1965, President Mobutu Sese Seko had been behind the nation's Pan-African military dictatorship looking for a way to promote the country. Intent on publicizing a contrived image of his magnificence, Mobutu used money from a multibillion-dollar government fortune to bring the fight to Zaire. In stark contrast to the luxurious life of their despotic ruler, who gained personal affluence through rapacious corruption, the Zairian people suffered impoverished conditions. Ali was not blind to the country's hardships when he said, "I loved the people in Zaire so much, and they were great to me, too. . . . A country run by Blacks!" He announced the donation of a portion of his prize winnings for construction of a vital community hospital. The impact of his contribution endured on many levels long after the Rumble in the Jungle. The Oscar-winning documentary *When We Were Kings* captured Ali taking endurance runs through poor neighborhoods, where he was recognized with love for his heroism outside the ring. He symbolized the powerful spirit of solidarity in the global struggle for justice, equality, and freedom. The country was captivated by his quest to regain the crown and rallied behind him during his ascent to the heavyweight throne in Africa.

The fight took on a mystical dimension when oracles foretold that Zairean *féticheurs* practicing witchcraft would cast spells to magically disarm the powerful Foreman in the ring. Ali had his own take on the impossible odds, telling the press, "I've had appointments with danger, sneered at doom, chuckled in the face of catastrophe, stood fearless in the hour of horror. An occasion like this is fitted to me." His magnetism drew an estimated 60,000 entranced fans who chanted in Lingala, *Ali, bomaye. Ali, bomaye.* He clarified the emotional phrase, which meant *Ali, kill him!* by saying. "Of course, I did not want to kill him, but I did want to win." He announced his fight plan in simple terms: "I'm gonna dance!" With bets overwhelmingly against Ali, press stories about the ill-fated underdog communicated a sense of impending doom. The articles recalled publicity from his first title fight 10 years earlier at age 22 against the reputedly indestructible Sonny Liston. Howard Cosell expressed the doomsday sentiment when he said, "The time may have come to say goodbye to Muhammad Ali. Because honestly, I don't think he can beat George Foreman." Team Ali braced for the worst, fearing serious damage to Ali early in the fight. Although many around the world were concerned with the odds, they remained hopeful he would miraculously overtake the reigning champion. Ali tried to brighten the defeatist outlook with the confident refrain of words exchanged with his team: When he asked, "What am I going to do?" they replied, "You're going to dance!"

The battle to crown the rightful heavyweight king brought together two fighters with extremely contrasting styles. It was a match between high-velocity boxing skills and sheer knockout power. Foreman had dethroned the undisputed heavyweight champion "Smokin" Joe Frazier using powerful punches, earning him comparisons to Liston. He had demolished the steady advancing pace set by Frazier with such force that the overwhelmed champion was sent to the canvas several times during the two-round TKO. By 1974 the tough 25-year-old Foreman had an astounding record in the sport, having knocked out heavyweight opponents in no-contest fashion within two rounds during his last eight fights. Among those KO'd were Norton and Frazier, who had both marked Ali's record by adding two losses by decision. With a tough attitude and a record of 40 wins, no losses, and 36 KOs/TKOs, Foreman expected to be champion forever when he stepped in the ring to face Ali. He had been forced to go the distance only three times in his 40 professional career fights, proving he had a talent for demolishing opponents with his awesome power. The meanest heavy-weight around simply planned to take off his robe, quickly knock out Ali, and return to his dressing room before breaking a sweat.

Ali brought his scientific boxing skills to the dangerous challenge, pacing sharp precision jabs from unpredictable angles with fluid speed. Having amassed a record of 44 wins and 2 losses by age 32, Ali was a tough, cunning fighter with rare fortitude who would test Foreman's endurance, speed, and ring experience like never before. The history of deaths in the dangerous fight arena haunted Ali's corner. His team knew he would never quit in the quest for the coveted crown, even if he was in dire straits. Boxing aficionados reported that Ali would need a miracle to survive in the ring against Foreman. Sugar Ray Robinson and other great fighters knew that to be a world champion you must believe in yourself when no one else will. Dundee publicly stood behind his fighter, telling the press he believed Ali would win back the world championship title. The corner team still braced for the worst in case the fight world was right in its belief that he had no chance against Foreman's crushing right hand. Dundee conceived of only one winning strategy: Ali would have to dance and jab his way to victory. Assistant trainer Wali Muhammad expressed grave fears: "I thought George Foreman would break him in two. The plan was to dance for six or seven rounds, tire Foreman out and when he tired move in on him." Ali seemed to have conjured magical powers in preparation for the fight boasting, "I've wrestled with alligators, I've tussled with a whale; I done handcuffed lightning and put thunder in jail. You know I'm bad. I have murdered a rock; I injured a stone; and I hospitalized a brick. I'm so bad I made medicine sick." Ali confidently predicted Foreman would collapse after 10 rounds, telling the press, "when George gets tired, I'll still be dancing. I'll be picking my shots, beating him at will. If George Foreman don't get me in seven, I'm telling you now, his parachute won't open."

Foreman, who had been Liston's sparring partner, was intimidating in the gym leaving his powerful imprint on the heavy bag from the very first punch. Suddenly, the fight scheduled for September 24 had to be postponed for several weeks to allow Foreman to heal after his eye was cut in a sparring accident. Ali derided Foreman at every turn calling him "The Mummy." He said, "I've seen George Foreman shadowboxing and the shadow won." International Hall of Famer Cus D'Amato, who characterized Foreman as a bully, told Ali he should hurt him with the first punch of the fight for the early advantage, then use psychological warfare to wound his ego.

On October 30 at 4:00 a.m. Zaire time, millions around the world watched as a stadium filled with thousands of fans chanting for Ali to defeat Foreman. Drew Bundini Brown announced, "The King has come home to reclaim his crown." A four-story portrait of Mobutu placed high above the ringside crowd commanded the attention of a spellbound country. The sky-blue ring glowed under the bright lights like a patch of a dawning new day breaking through the dark brewing storm clouds over Kinshasa. Before the opening round, the fighters stood face-to-face in a huddle at center ring as they went through the formalities with referee Zack Clayton. Foreman's fierce staredown did not faze Ali, whose fight-talk bravado appeared to recite a declaration of war. The intimidating exchange, which reached a fever pitch during the face-to-face confrontation, drew attention from the press. Foreman said before, "He's playing with fire getting into the ring with me." Ali assured Foreman, "You're gonna meet the greatest fighter of all time!"

The extreme heat and humidity would weigh heavily on the action, slowing the fighters' movements on the softening canvas. The red and white ropes fastened around the ring had slackened from the dampness. Ali studied these conditions to develop a tactic that was kept secret from everyone to preserve the element of surprise. His strategy involved a risky defensive trap to weaken Foreman for a knockout victory. A winning outcome in the fight was paramount to defend his moral rightness and regain the crown unjustly taken from him during the conscientious objector trials. A glimmer of hope was inspired by the superman mentality he expressed to the world, "I'm so fast I can run through a hurricane and don't get wet." Still, the 3–1 betting odds against him predicted a sheer power over speed advantage described by Foreman's cornerman Dick Sadler, who said, "The best way to slow down a ring is with a hard left to the jaw, a right hand to the heart, and left hook to the kidney. Though I'm not saying that my fighter's a kidney puncher." Archie Moore, also in Foreman's camp, shared his wise experience, cautioning Ali was a smart skillful warrior prepared to use powerful elements of scientific boxing to take down Foreman.

Before the opening bell, Ali removed his ceremonial white robe with black trim matching his white satin trunks with black side stripe. George added vibrant color to the ring, wearing red velvet shorts with a white side stripe matching his long robe with *World Champion* lettering. At the beginning of Round One, Ali moved aggressively to the center of the ring surprising Foreman with two lightning jabs in combination with stunning straight right-hand leads before he danced out of reach. More fast flurries were thrown to confuse his opponent into lowering his guard, creating an opening for more right-hand leads that connected. Foreman was slow to respond, unfamiliar with maneuvering at the tremendous pace dictated by a circling contender bent on proving his superior speed. Ali used all the skills he had mastered in 46 prizefights with hundreds of rounds of professional competition under his belt. In his corner after the bell, he raised his fists in the air to conduct the crowd that erupted with the chant, *Ali, bomaye!* Foreman turned up the pressure to own Round Two by cutting off the ring, forcing Ali to the ropes to fend off wild massive punches. Dundee yelled, "Move, Ali! Move!" A change in strategy shocked everyone. Ali leaned way back on the slack ropes, resting like an easy target with raised arms shielding his face from the barrage of punches. At that moment, many braced for a brutal end to the fight as Foreman raised the pain threshold. Ali played mind games and found chances for rapid-fire counterpunches during the launch of his secret weapon called the "Rope-A-Dope." He insulted the champion who wasted energy with powerful punches that missed the mark in reckless fury. Like chastising a hopeless student, Ali told Foreman, "You are just an amateur, George. Show me something. Hit me hard." While watching the fight in Stade du 20 Mai, Norman Mailer thought the experience was an ordeal that was as "oppressive, as the closing of the door of one's tomb." Frantic shouts from his corner demanded that Ali get off the ropes, where he risked serious damage by the most powerful slugger of the era. Bundini flew into a panic, pleading, "Dance, champ; dance!"

The spectators fell silent in Round Three as Foreman landed explosive blows to Ali's ribs with emotional firepower that wasted precious energy. Ali responded nonchalantly: "Is that all that you got, George?" Foreman paused from target practice for a moment to decide on his next move just before the bell sounded to end the round. Foreman walked back to his corner, showing troubling signs of wearing down. Ali stared him down, as if to say he was just warming up in the fight for the greatest prize in the sport. In retrospect, Foreman would write about the verbal exchanges they had during the championship fight when Ali said, "I was world heavyweight champion when you were still a kid in school, so you ain't got nothing going for you here."

In Round Four, after Foreman landed a massive blow to the back of Ali's head, Ali then hurled lightning combinations that staggered Foreman after he gave the cunning contender an opening by dropping his arms near the end of the round. Ali would later reveal, "I started throwing punches at him in the fourth, George finally woke up and thought, 'Man, I'm in trouble.' He was shocked." By the fifth, visible signs of damage were apparent on Foreman's swollen face when Ali shouted to the press "What did I tell you?" The Rope-A-Dope was working, causing Foreman to lose his stamina over the next few rounds. Archie Moore shouted for Foreman to finish off Ali with powerful blows to the body. Ali leaned against the ropes, absorbing hits that none of Foreman's previous opponents had survived standing. Foreman's inability to floor Ali clouded his perception with self-doubt, shifting the momentum. Ali threw bursts of counterpunches, sensing that the end was near. While Foreman was tied in clinches, Ali told him, "Man, this is the wrong place to get tired. . . . You are in trouble."

By the sixth round, Foreman was showing extreme strain from repeatedly overextending punches with little impact. Ali shrewdly revved up the pace knowing, "George just didn't realize how hard I am to hit and how hard I can hit." He said, "There was George, trying to scare me with his serious look—he got that from his idol, Sonny Liston." Ali continued to slip away within inches of powerful blows launched by Foreman's fists that missed the mark by split seconds. Ali recalled, "I purposely left him some openings and he wouldn't take them . . . George was dead tired. . . ." Bundini stepped onto the edge of the corner ring shouting at Ali, seeming to encourage him to take advantage of Foreman's fading pace.

Ali refused to dance. Instead, he adapted his style to ring conditions by going back to the ropes to conserve energy, as Foreman raged forward with massive painful blows under the heart. Dr. Pacheco feared that after all the hurt Ali endured in the ring, physical damage would surface years later. Ali wrestled Foreman's head down, using all his weight to wear out the surge of adrenaline power. Moving from side-to-side on the ropes and bouncing away from blows while shielding himself with his forearms helped Ali survive. Media cameras captured the dangerous full-tilt action during the risky balancing act on the ropes. In an interview for *USA Today,* Dr. Pacheco recalled that Ali told him "This guy can't hit at all . . . I'm going to knock him out this round." Pacheco responded, "Well, hurry up.

The rain's coming." Ali expected to reach a turning point by the seventh round, when Foreman would tire enough to become an easy knockout target. In Foreman's corner, the big plan had always been to catch Ali before he could avoid the knockout striking distance.

The opportune moment after Ali executed his secret plan to outsmart Foreman into tactical mistakes had come into play. Foreman was losing sight of his bearings because of the mounting frustration. He underestimated the endurance needed to go the distance through the rounds to conquer Ali when he continued to slip behind round after round, unable to keep pace in the fight. Even with maximum effort, he lacked the speed to deliver the signature lethal punch while Ali leaned over the edge of the ring, braced against the slack ropes. Incessant taunting from within striking distance finished off Foreman's confidence in his ability to knock out Ali. Fight fans and Dundee knew that Foreman was strong enough to knock down an oak tree. The challenge he faced was Ali's overwhelming speed in the ring.

Foreman slowly left his corner for the start of Round Eight confronting a dramatic change of pace with the brewing storm in Kinshasa. Many of his wild punches cut through the air, while body blows that did hit the mark seemed to do no visible harm to his opponent, who was in tremendous physical condition. Ali was extremely vulnerable defensively leaning on the ropes when behind on points with the constant threat of a knockout blow from Foreman. He withstood intense pain, then increased the velocity of his punches while spryly dancing across the ring luring Foreman to his downfall. Ali had suddenly rushed off the ropes, delivering blows to the head that backed up Foreman, now drenched in heavy sweat from rounds of overheated exchanges. Ali then sprang into action with a combination that knocked Foreman to the canvas. The impact set off a shockwave in the stadium when the stunned, exhausted champion lost direction and fell. Foreman tried to recover from the thunder of blinding combinations angled over his shoulder and delivered with cunning marksmanship.

Ali's final right cross landed before the champion spiraled off his feet to the canvas in front of the electrified stadium as fans roared, *Ali, bomaye! Ali, bomaye!* In a stunning upset, Foreman failed to beat the count after finally rising back on his feet. He staggered out of the ring to his dressing room, obscured by the swarm of security that rushed into the ring to protect Ali from thousands of elated fans. Completely surrounded by guards, Ali was riding high on the glory of the miraculous victory that defied the odds.

Foreman was unprepared to go the distance against a top contender with unrivaled speed, power, endurance, and an arsenal of cunning tactics. He was devastated for a long time after losing the world title to an underestimated opponent. Replaying the course of events in his mind, Foreman realized, "after the fight I could think of all sorts of excuses. The ring ropes were loose. The referee counted too fast. The cut hurt my training. I was drugged . . . I wish I'd just said the best man won, but I'd never lost before, so I didn't know how to lose. He outfought me and outthought me." Foreman continued trying to set the record straight about the knockdown: "It's never been said that I have been knocked out." He admired Ali for not throwing another punch after landing the right to the jaw, which sent Foreman over the edge into semi-consciousness. Foreman knew that most fighters would have taken advantage of the vulnerable moment: "I was going down, stumbling, trying to hold myself, he saw me stumbling. . . . Ordinarily you finish the fighter off; I would have. He got ready to throw the right hand, and he didn't do it. That's what made him, in my mind, the greatest fighter I ever fought."

After Ali's tremendous victory, the first torrential downpour of Kinshasa's rainy season disrupted satellite communication with the rest of the world. Through the storm at daybreak, local news about Ali winning back the coveted crown was all that mattered for the two-time champion. The final trial on the road to redemption was his most satisfying, proving the strength of his resilient spirit. In an outpouring of love, the Zairean people lined flooded streets for over 40 miles to see the champion's motorcade, as it returned to the residential compound. Photographer Neil Leifer captured the reigning champion before the win in a serene place, when the dawning hues welcomed a momentous new day on the esplanade overlooking the Congo River. It was a moment of reflection that captured a great champion, with the courage to prevail in the face of extreme odds to rightfully recapture the coveted throne. His remarkable athletic fortitude astounded his critics, who believed he was a washed-up fighter with a hopelessly long way to go on the comeback trail. At times, it was unrivaled willpower that carried him through brutal rounds, mystifying those who anticipated his tragic downfall in a dramatic defeat. By adapting his innovative tactics to unusual ring conditions, he succeeded with intuitive skill and his psych-out approach to defeat the awesome Foreman for the ultimate victory. Ali would again defy the odds and explain his winning mindset: "Impossible is just a big word thrown around by small men who find it easier to live in the world they've been given than to explore the power they have to change it. Impossible is not a fact. It's an opinion.

Impossible is not a declaration. It's a dare. Impossible is potential. Impossible is temporary. Impossible is nothing."

Hours after his victory, Ali spent time performing magic tricks in tender moments with children whom he met while celebrating in the streets. His popularity soared when the storm relented, allowing global media networks to showcase his phenomenal ascent, sportsmanship, and multitude of accolades. By December, *Sports Illustrated* featured him on the cover as Sportsman of the Year, a decade after he first won the title against Sonny Liston. He was awarded the Hickok Belt, given to America's most outstanding professional athletes. *Ring* magazine selected him as Fighter of the Year, turning the page after refusing to give Ali the title during the exile years. On December 10, 1974, Ali reached a new level of national acceptance. The two-time world heavyweight champion was invited to the White House to meet Gerald Ford, who wanted to unify the country after the tragic events of the tumultuous last decade. In April 1975, just four months after Ali's visit, Saigon would fall despite the strict terms established by peace agreements.

Foreman admired Ali as more than a legendary boxing champion, calling him a great man who should be celebrated for his humanity and standing strong through challenging times. After the title loss in Zaire, Foreman fell into a deep depression. He said that he "believed the sky had fallen" until he found a spiritual calling that turned his life around with new purpose. Foreman gave credit to Ali for his own boxing career: "I'd become a boxer, because I wanted to be like Muhammad Ali."

A few months after the fight in Zaire, Elijah Muhammad passed away, bringing Nation of Islam members at mosques nationwide under the leadership of his son, Imam Wallace D. Muhammad. The temples, renamed the World Community of Al-Islam, practiced orthodox tenets of the holy Qur'an learned from the Imam's theological studies. Teachings about sacred Islamic beliefs enlightened many in the Nation through the conversion. Ali explained, "Wallace taught the true meaning of the Qur'an." The devoted rejected the separation of the races doctrine to follow the religious tenets of Sunni Islam, a faith shared by people of diverse races, cultures, and nationalities. Ali explained the evolution of the faith, a dramatic departure from early doctrines. Those years, he said, were "the time of our struggle in the dark and a time of confusion in us, and we don't want to be associated with that at all." Herbert Muhammad, another son of Elijah Muhammad, had a strong bond of brotherhood with Ali. He continued to manage the boxing career of the crowned champion.

The legendary Muhammad Ali, whose name became widely synonymous with the phrase "Greatest of All Time," was admired by millions around the world for more than his athletic achievements by the time he regained the title in Zaire. There were critics who still harbored resentment for past actions by the young rebel of the 1960s, who stood with the Nation of Islam and then refused to serve in the Vietnam War. But more importantly, the world champion had pursued a twofold ambition with unwavering conviction—winning the crown and advancing the fight for religious freedom, equality, and peace. His celebrated greatness in the ring would only be the prelude for his true purpose in life, turning his celebrity into a focus on humanitarian causes that would impact the world for future generations.

Ali continued to demonstrate the breadth of his humanity on the vast world stage by relentlessly raising his voice to represent those unjustly denied the chance to speak. In 1975, he spoke to graduates at Harvard University about the Civil Rights Movement, Black Nationalism, and the racial discrimination faced by African Americans. The student body admired him for his courageous stand to break down barriers to equality.

Ali would return home to defend his title four times that year. One of those fights was again orchestrated by Don King, who mesmerized the universe with an epic Ali-Frazier mega-millions rematch billed as the "Thrilla in Manila."

8

THRILLA IN MANILA

A Fight to the Brink

Ali Training on the Gym Speed Bag.
ZUMA Press / Alamy Photograph

After winning the crown for a second time, Ali remained undefeated for the next three title defenses in 1975 with two successive TKOs before his 50th fight, won by unanimous decision. Once more, worldwide attention was drawn to the ring for his 51st fight, an epic rematch that would test the extreme limits of human endurance. Smokin' Joe Frazier, powered by a relentless forward-moving bob-and-weave style, was fiercely determined to regain the title. Ali would confront his archrival for the third time in the Philippines, where the contest would be remembered as one of the most brutal in prizefighting history. The reigning champion warned his opponents, "If you even dream of beating me, you better wake up and apologize." The champions would withstand hundreds of damaging blows until one raised his fists high above the bloody ring to celebrate a miraculous victory. In an event promoted as the "Thrilla in Manila," the championship rounds would demand all the might of two great fighters battling to the brink for esteemed glory.

Ali defended his crown against opponents in and out of the United States before facing Frazier in Manila. In March, the first contender of the year was 6'5" Chuck Wepner, who braved the 15-round distance in front of an Ohio crowd of nearly 14,000 at the Richfield Coliseum. An official clean knockdown was ruled after Wepner, who may have stepped on Ali's foot in the ninth round, landed a right to the body that sent the off-balance champion crashing backwards on the canvas. Ali resumed the fight, using his superior boxing moves to win by TKO 15 seconds before the final bell. Wepner described how he was outclassed by the speed of Ali's blinding jabs: "He wouldn't hit you with just one punch; it was two and three in combination." The 33-year-old Ali had specific thoughts about his performance: "I'm gettin' old, but I remain 'The Greatest.'"

In May, Ali faced a tough fight against Ron Lyle under the bright Las Vegas spotlight. He used the Mirage tactic with raised fists pressed together to shield his face, deflecting tremendous punches with his forearms. He teased and taunted Lyle, who eventually managed to break through the peek-a-boo game with a surprise right uppercut that gave Ali a black eye. Still, it was just a matter of time until it was all over. The champion brought his signature style to the bout, finishing the fight with an 11th-round TKO. Ali waved in Referee Ferd Hernandez to stop the fight after a final flurry dazed Lyle into twilight consciousness. Ali told the press that he was not in the ring to cause unnecessary punishment: "It was obvious I had Ron beat and that's why I encouraged the ref to step in and stop it. . . . He gave me a hard time in there, but there was only ever gonna be one winner."

The next venue, the first title fight in the majority Muslim country of Malaysia, was a July rematch with European heavyweight champion Joe Bugner. The People's Champion attracted a crowd of 20,000 at the Kuala Lumpur airport before he defeated Bugner by unanimous decision in Merdeka Stadium. Ali had sailed sky high on public adoration since regaining the title, while Joe Frazier was seated ringside to size up his chance to dethrone the reigning champion. Once more, Ali would light the fuse of explosive fight publicity, telling the press in Manila, "Got some unfinished business with the gorilla, Joe Frazier. . . ." As the fight-talk toughened Frazier's will to win, many felt that Ali crossed a line with the shocking tone of his excessive insults. Determined to settle the score, Frazier was well prepared to go the distance with his rival at any cost to prove worthy of the championship belt. He trained hard to fulfill ambitious plans he had made from the start of his boxing career to knock Ali off the throne.

Principal dealmaker Don King orchestrated the multimillion-dollar Ali vs. Frazier III championship with the endorsement of Philippines dictator Ferdinand Marcos. As the fight for democracy advanced, the Marcos regime would be ousted years later after a history of human rights atrocities, widespread corruption, and theft of billions of dollars. The 15-round prizefight drew a record-breaking audience to the ring, where the two-time heavyweight champion would defend his place on top of the world. Many believed that Ali had reached the pinnacle of greatness and had no other mountains to conquer. Legendary battles fought both in and out of the ring defined him as a hero in the hearts of millions worldwide. Ali agreed to the final match with Frazier, a fight that would come to be considered the most violent of the Ali-Frazier trilogy. An indomitable reigning champion faced his toughest contender, who sought to mend his wounded pride with a second title victory.

The world discovered that Frazier despised Ali, who claimed all the glory as the true heavyweight king. He had proclaimed himself as the Greatest of All Time even after Frazier became the undisputed world champion by defeating him in the Fight of the Century. Frazier harbored deep resentment, feeling betrayed by a disrespectful friend he had helped through hard times in exile. The fight-talk insults would win Ali a psychological edge in the heartless world of professional prizefighting. He succeeded in outraging Frazier by ridiculing him with renewed intensity at every opportunity. Frazier suffered an incessant storm of taunts meant to destroy his image as a worthy contender for the title. Ali profiled Frazier as a traitor to the African American community who conformed to the demands of an oppressive power elite. The Uncle Tom label seemed fitting to those unaware of the great obstacles Frazier had overcome since his childhood struggles with poverty in rural Beaufort, South Carolina. He endured financial hardship living in the inner-city ghettos of New York and Philadelphia while pursuing ambitious dreams. As a young man in search of success, he was reassured along the way by the emotional support of his family. Joe's parents could not afford a formal education for their son, yet he said the encouragement they provided had helped to make his dreams come true. He turned professional under the management of a wealthy team of businessmen organized by his trainer Yancey "Yank" Durham under the name Cloverlay, Inc. Eddie Futch, who was promoted to trainer after Durham's death in 1973, said he was responsible for teaching Frazier his tactical bob-and-weave style. Frazier had many hard-won achievements before capturing the prized heavyweight crown, but he remained an unsung champion, veiled in the shadow of Ali's greatness. He would say, "Being a fighter made a good living for me, but that wasn't all. I loved fighting. . . . It gave me an opportunity to prove myself, to stand up and say, 'I'm the best; I matter; I am.'"

Eleven months since regaining the title, Ali would face Frazier in the toughest match of their legendary rivalry. Ali had to adapt his style to compensate for fading skills, which would be put to the test in every round of the competition. He knew that the fierce challenger could absorb extreme punishment and would fight with courageous determination each minute of every round. Frazier dreamed of the moment when his lethal left hook, powered by years of animosity, would knock Ali off the summit forever. He was prepared to fight to the finish. Ali was forced to fend off an aggressive slugger style with unrelenting drive that pressured his defenses. By the last seconds of this rematch, it would be obvious to many after the tremendous physical toll that both fighters realized they had reached a career finale.

In a *USA Today* article, Dr. Pacheco described the Ali technique of self-promotion: "Ali is a master put-on. He can make anyone feel stupid. He took on (Howard) Cosell and made him look ridiculous." Ali injured Frazier's sensitive ego with highly demeaning fight-talk depicting him as a gorilla, too ugly and ignorant to hold the title. His vilification of Frazier as a shameful sellout resulted in bitter fallout in the African American community. The charades continued as Ali mounted heavy insults jabbing at Frazier's character to upset his tough confident attitude.

Many thought the championship match generously offered Frazier a last chance to defeat Ali and settle the score. He had faded into the background, obscured by a cherished heroic champion who commanded the bright arena spotlight. Ali's nemesis hoped to destroy the idea that he was a washed-up fighter with nothing left to show after an impressive 10-year record. The former reigning champion committed his soul to the Manila match, prepared for anything to win the championship belt. Ali described the threat to his hard-won territory from the talented Frazier: "he had what I was vulnerable to—a good in-close left hook . . . Joe stayed on me, always on my chest; and from out of nowhere he'd throw the hook." Frazier was the roughest opponent Ali would ever face during a remarkable prizefighting career. The Ali mystique of invincibility was damaged during the Fight of the Century, sending the fallen champion back to Agony Hill endurance runs on a long ascent to reach the summit once again. Deep resentments brought complex feelings to the explosive fight, as Ali continued to rev up the publicity machine to destroy Frazier's winning spirit. A potent emotional mix of anger, fear, anxiety, and pride intensified the drive to prove who was the better man.

The former world heavyweight champion counterpunched Ali's flurry of insults, calling him by the offensive slave name "Clay." Raising his voice in response to the outrageous rants of psychological warfare that held worldwide attention, Frazier reassured everyone that he was in control of the situation: "He's still trying to make himself believe. But it is too late, way too late. I got the noose around that cat's neck." A negative opinion about Ali came from Mark Kram, a *Sports Illustrated* writer in Frazier's corner who tried to demystify the famous persona of the champion. "He has all the problems that human nature gives us. He's not a museum figure. He's the greatest fighter in history. Period. Why isn't that enough? Why does he need to be more?" Ali biographer Thomas Hauser answered, "Because he is." The champion responded to his detractors by admitting that the critics made him work harder. Ali continued to beat the war drum loudly, undeterred by the criticism that focused on his mean streak. To no avail, Eddie Futch tried to help Frazier ignore the incendiary fight-talk, aggressive gamesmanship, and media antics Ali used to psych out his competition. Dundee was pleased to discover that, "Muhammad's under Joe's skin . . . Joe actually hates him, which is good. It creates emotion."

Extreme animosity was an unexpected fallout from the fight that would haunt the two champions for decades. Ali defended his flamboyant fight promotion style: "Showmanship is a large part of both boxing and magic as well. I called my opponents names and boasted of my abilities and beauty, and often predicted the round of my victory to infuriate them so they would make mistakes." Frazier struggled verbally to fend off derogatory remarks in front of the world to prove he was a worthy contender. He explained, "I was no philosopher or poet . . . I was a fighter known in the trade as Smokin' Joe." Beginning with the Fight of the Century, when he faced extreme provocation from Ali for the first time, lingering resentment over the years would intensify his angry attitude: "Nineteen seventy-one was the year I made a New Year's resolution that I was going to dust that butterfly off. I was going to clip his wings." Four years later in Manila, he pledged to avenge the unforgivable betrayal, rephrasing the fight plan in tougher terms: "I want to hurt him. I don't want to knock him out. I want to take his heart out." The fight-talk reflected an aspect of the cruelty that characterized the brutal sport of boxing.

Ali, the most famous athlete in sports, attracted worldwide attention to the fight drama by targeting Frazier without mercy. An estimated $9 million purse was allocated for Ali while Frazier would receive about $5 million. Many felt that Ali was giving Frazier a last chance to revive his waning career by offering a rare opportunity for a huge payday. They would enter the spotlight of the fight ring together, electrifying audiences for the last time on October 1, 1975. From the demand for ringside seats to multimedia coverage, and closed-circuit network revenues, Ali had tremendous drawing power. An estimated 700 million people in 65 countries would watch the contest in Quezon City, including fans more interested in Ali than the sport of heavyweight prizefighting.

It was a hot tropical day with high humidity, as the temperature reached more than 100 degrees Fahrenheit. The venue in Araneta Coliseum was filled to capacity. Torrid heat hit the ring like another fierce contender, bearing down on the fighters surrounded by about 25,000 in attendance. There was an adrenaline rush of heavy punches at the first bell, setting a pace that miraculously would not slow down. Frazier, gearing for an upset victory, aimed repeated body blows to weaken Ali's legs and essentially tear down his primary defensive weapon. Ali worked hard to outscore his opponent, as he infuriated Frazier to the limit with distracting verbal taunts. Ali dominated the beginning rounds, opening with a fast break in hopes of an early knockout. Frazier stayed true to his unrelenting slugger style, landing a signature left hook that Ali brushed off like a refreshing breeze across the ring in Round One.

Ali stayed flat-footed in the center of the ring, exchanging punches with Frazier, who appeared to aim powerful hooks at an indestructible wall. Frazier pressed forward aggressively, forcing Ali against the ropes, where he hunted for the knockout finish with brutal left hooks. Ali unleashed the tremendous power of his right fist, raising the pain threshold to a point that rocked Frazier off balance several times. Bundini chastised, "He won't call you Clay no more." Frazier smiled, seeming to let

Ali know he was tough enough to endure the fastest jabs in heavyweight history for the next 14 rounds. He would elevate the threat level against Ali by shifting his momentum to fast and lethally furious. In the second round, the champion braced for an onslaught of punches, defensively positioned on the ropes, as Frazier sensed victory. Ali landed a series of rights with signature stinging jabs, then tangled Frazier in powerful clinches, weighing down on him to control the pace of the fight. Referee Carlos Padilla reprimanded Ali about the move, which could cost the champ penalty points.

In Round Three, Frazier gained the advantage withstanding brutal punishment. Ali was heard speaking nursery rhymes to infuriate Frazier: "Jack be nimble, Jack be quick. . . ." He was unconvinced his opponent would last through the tidal wave of blinding flurries that won him two championship titles. He brought the full arsenal of punches to find the winning combination to break down Frazier's inside fighting style. When the round was over, Ali blew kisses at the crowd that was astounded by the high caliber fight action. By Round Four, Ali showed signs of drifting off pace from the repeated blows against his body. Bundini pleaded, "Stay mean with him, champ!" Ali's precise, flicking jabs at Frazier's head could not cloud the determined contender's mind with doubts about winning. Although there was mounting damage from Ali's blinding flurries, the blows could not deter his powerful forward charge.

Before the start of the next round, Ali conducted the ringside audience as they cheered his name. The crowd roared in the fifth round when the champ, fighting on the defensive in his own corner, drove the team into a panic. He leaned against the ropes taking heavy rapid-fire punches to the body. Frazier maintained the furious pace that trapped him in the barrage of an explosive arsenal. The crowd chanted Frazier's name as he turned the fight his way with the seismic impact of his punches. Everyone heard Dundee shout, "Get out of the goddamn corner. Stop playing!" Frazier tasted victory, launching massive missiles that relentlessly attacked Ali's ribs, weakening his legs through the round.

Frazier reenergized in the sixth, aiming to kill Ali by belting him with wide powerful hooks that affected the ability to steady his legs. He rested his head on Ali's chest, able to feel a racing heartbeat at intervals of the battle. Easy victory bets favoring Ali were now cast in doubt. The corner teams worked quickly to cool down their fighters with towels soaked in ice water. Dundee, through with Ali's antics, told his champion, "We blew those rounds. You don't rest on the ropes against Joe Frazier. . . ." Ali danced in Round Seven, then retreated to the ropes again under pressure from bone-crushing punches that Frazier launched at an accelerating pace. The verbal jabs against Frazier continued to distract the focus. Ali said, "Old Joe Frazier, they told me you were washed up." Frazier responded, "They lied, pretty boy."

Ali regained the offensive, forcing Frazier to crouch and cover up against the velocity of his punches in Round 8. Joe rebounded with lethal blows forcing Ali to the ropes after multiple jabs by the champion failed to hit the mark. By the ninth round, Ali had to survive painful low body blows delivered by Frazier, who was trying to force down his defenses. Still, Ali recovered enough to outclass Frazier by dancing around him with reflexive well-timed jabs in his unique scientific boxing style.

Appearing exhausted in Round 10, Frazier still managed to whip left hooks that caused deeper damage to Ali's body as he again retreated to the ropes. Ali finished the precious final seconds of the round with combinations, scoring points that evened the fight. After the bell paused the murderous pace, Ali said back in his corner, "This is the closest that I've ever been to dying." Bundini pleaded, "Go down to the well once more!" The team rushed around their champion, keeping him hydrated and treating the wounds as he sat collapsed on the stool with his head down. Dundee realized that the fight was far from over at this point, when it had become an evenly matched battle of wills on the world stage.

Team Ali worked to revive their overexerted champion in the searing temperature for the start of Round 11. Between rounds ice water rained down on Ali from Bundini who helped fend off the oppressive heat as the champ sat slumped in the corner. Dr. Pacheco knew that Ali would endure unbearable punishment through Rounds 10 to 15. Under the merciless spotlights in the stifling Coliseum, the fighters were forced to the brink of survival. The ring doctor observed, "no man could take this punishment for long." Biographer Walter Dean Myers wrote, "Every fight hurts. Every fight damages the body. Some damage the soul." What Dr. Pacheco called the "Championship Causeway" happened during the last five rounds of the brutal contest, bringing a sense of urgency for it to end. Ali danced to control the pace while his fists searched for a knockout landing. The fight reached a life-or-death turning point. Each fighter was barely hanging on. There were visible injuries to Frazier's swollen eyes, and Ali's face was bruised after the painful exchanges in Round 11.

Bundini was brought to tears when Ali was taking a severe beating from Frazier's savage hooks that pinned him against the ropes. At this point, there were many who thought that Frazier would win back the title. Then suddenly the round belonged to Ali, who reached deep down into the well and lifted himself back up on his toes to launch blows with long-range precision. The impact put Frazier in trouble when his eyes nearly closed from extreme swelling that severely narrowed his field of vision. Ali opened a cut over Frazier's right eye, while his left was already visually impaired by an accident suffered while training in the gym years earlier. Frazier's mouth was bleeding as both fighters remained determined to conquer. They would be forever changed by the extreme brutality of the fight. During the next three rounds, Ali fought masterfully like a defending two-time world champion against Frazier. The rhythm of his bob-and-weave motion was disrupted by the crushing pace of Ali's combinations. The bell sounded for the 12th as Ali's corner once more chimed in, "Get off the ropes!"

In the 13th round, Frazier staggered backwards, struggling to advance through the assault in search of a knockout opening. He became an easy target for Ali, who fought to close out the match with both fists in play. But the bloodied Frazier would not fall to Ali's rising fury unleashed against his indomitable spirit. Frazier's mouthpiece was knocked out and landed in the ringside seats without stopping his advance. An iron will carried him through the final moments of the round, appearing to accept the risk of fatality in the battle. Coach Eddie Futch would have to decide the distance for his fighter, who had lost sight of Ali's powerful rights freely alternating with stinging left jabs.

After winning the round with the help of his team, the champion resumed the fight for survival. Round 14 would demand every ounce of strength and courage from both fighters just to remain standing through the mounting injuries. Dundee described this most challenging stage of the match with the fighters on the brink as the point when the men are separated from the boys. Dundee pulled Ali up to his feet before pushing him toward the center of the ring for the start of the round. Ali showed remarkable grit, delivering powerful punches that repeatedly blindsided Frazier, who was now in dangerous straits with both eyes nearly swollen shut, at the sound of the bell. The referee led Frazier back to his corner, where the fight doctor examined the extensive surface damage. On the verge of collapse in the opposite corner, Dundee ignored Ali's pleas to cut off his gloves, after giving more than seemed humanly possible throughout the fight. Although exhausted, the team knew he would never quit the brutal contest. Across the ring, Frazier pleaded with coach Futch to let him continue through the final 15th round. After telling the referee it's over, Futch embraced Frazier to console him while saying, "The fight's over, Joe. . . . The world will never forget what you did here today." Ali struggled to remain standing in his corner when he was declared the winner after Frazier's team retired from the match. He collapsed to the canvas from exhaustion with a swollen right eye, which was a superficial sign of much deeper battle wounds.

Ali confessed to the press, "only one fellow talked back to me that was Joe Frazier. I hit Joe Frazer with about 90 punches . . . hit him with everything. . . . " The warriors gave their all for the world championship fight. Ali said, "Joe Frazier is the greatest fighter in the world, next to me. He has my total respect. I apologize for some of the things I said before the fight, but it's my business to help the promotion. Anybody who bad-mouths Joe Frazier will have me to answer to." Joe would not accept the indirect apology from Ali spoken to the press, but publicly complimented Ali, praising him as a great champion. After the fight he said, "Man, I hit him with punches that'd bring down the walls of the city."

Dr. Pacheco assessed the damage to the aging champion, who now struggled to avoid serious health consequences after withstanding tremendous punches from Frazier. He knew Ali had reached the beginning of the end. The doctor noticed that Ali was already slowing down and there were noticeable changes to his speech pattern, which Pacheco attributed to brain injury. After Manila, many in Ali's corner believed that it was time for him to retire from the sport. He had reached a point in his career when serious health repercussions were inevitable if he continued the ascent. The warning signs were becoming pronounced at age 33, when he decided to cross a dangerous line in the sand by continuing to compete. Ali explained the hard-fought victory against Frazier: "That fight, I could feel something happening to me. Something different from what I'd felt in fights before. . . . It was like I took myself as far as I could go, and then God took me the rest of the way."

After Zaire and Manila, the world discovered that the sky was not the limit for Ali. Unconvinced it was time to hang up the gloves, he went on to fight 10 more telling bouts, while Frazier fought only twice more before retiring from the ring. Frazier first hung up his gloves in 1976, leaving behind the dream of becoming a two-time world heavyweight champion. An unsuccessful comeback fight in 1981 convinced him that it was time to walk away from the ring. Frazier left the prizefighting arena with a record of 37 fights, 32 wins with 27 victories inside the distance. The former champion was proud of his accomplishments, saying, "I never backed down and I've never backed off . . . I am privileged. I fought Ali three times." He devoted personal time to making an impact on the community, teaching young boxers the trade at his North Broad Street gym in Philadelphia. Athletic coaching, movie acting, and performing with his singing group, The Knockouts, kept Frazier in the spotlight. The former world heavyweight champion would be inducted into the International Boxing Hall of Fame along with Muhammad Ali, Sugar Ray Robinson, and Rocky Marciano and other great champions.

Ali knew that his fight-talk game seriously damaged egos, just as his cutting jabs destroyed the confidence of his opponents in the ring. Frazier was not ready to forgive him and could not let go of the deep resentment he felt toward the reigning champ. He finally seemed to accept Ali's apology in 1990 saying, "This has been going on too long. . . . We're two athletes of the world. . . . It's time to talk and get together. Life's too short." Despite the partial peace settlement between old rivals, several tries at full reconciliation were difficult as Ali continued to be celebrated around the world for being the consummate champion. Frazier held onto the animosity for decades, even after Ali wrote a poem called "The Silent Warrior" that acknowledged the importance they played in each other's lives as great champions of the sport. In a 2009 issue of *Sports Illustrated*, 34 years after the championship in Manila, Frazier claimed that he was no longer resentful of Ali and stayed true to the change of heart. He died at age 67 in 2011, only one month after being diagnosed with liver cancer. Ali honored him with a public statement: "The world has lost a great champion. I will always remember Joe with respect and admiration."

Ali continued to astound the world by remaining in the ring long after taking down many great champions. The epic fights fought past his prime against the seemingly invincible Foreman and the unrelenting Frazier were thought to be the victories that truly proved his athletic excellence.

Greatness on the humanitarian front continued when Ali was personally responsible for donating a portion of closed-circuit ticket sales to drought, poverty, and famine relief in the West African region of Sahel through the United Nations Children's Fund and Africare in 1975. At home, he reportedly donated $100,000 to the New York Hillside Aged Center for physically challenged senior citizens faced with financial limitations that would end funding for operating the programs. Once again, Ali demonstrated his compassion for the welfare of others. He remained a force for change, having a wide impact on humanitarian aid and diplomatic solutions for peace in far corners of the world.

Closer to home, major fallout rocked his corner when he ignored emotional pleas from the Fight Doctor to walk away from the sport. The aging fighter was warned about risks of further physical injury and the possibility of extreme irreversible damage to his health. The Greatest of All Time would continue struggling with diminishing returns on a punishing course to defend his title, fighting 10 more contenders in 120 rounds over the next six years with serious repercussions. The champion continued to draw millions of spectators to the fight arena, until a devastating defining moment stopped him inside the distance for the first time. Although he had dreams of gaining greater glory, he was outpaced by Father Time, heralding the final round for the legendary champion. Fight Doctor Ferdie Pacheco observed, "I knew the punishment he was taking was too much for any man, even him."

9

DANGEROUS CROSSROADS

Signs of Diminishing Returns

Ali at the Miami 5th Street Gym after Ali vs. Spinks I in 1978.
Photograph by Michael Gaffney © Michael Gaffney Photo

After the Frazier fight in Manila, Dr. Ferdie Pacheco, who had been Ali's fight doctor since 1962, said he discovered that the champion reached "the dangerous mental point where his heart and mind are no longer in it. It's just a payday. It's almost as if an actor had played his role too long. He's just mouthing the words." Ali admitted, "It's just a job. Grass grows, birds fly, waves pound the sand. I beat people up." Toward the end of his career, Ali still floated on air throwing his signature stinging jabs at the beginning of fights, but then the performance faded in late rounds when the dance was over, leaving him brutally outdistanced by the final bell. Champion Sugar Ray Robinson knew: "Rhythm is everything in boxing. Every move you make starts with your heart, and that's in rhythm or you're in trouble."

After the epic 1975 battle when the champion danced his way to victory against Joe Frazier in Manila, pleas for Ali to retire over health worries failed to stop the music, even when it seemed there were no other worlds to conquer. When Frazier retired in 1976 before a comeback match in 1981, Ali continued to fight many contenders, including Jean-Pierre Coopman, Jimmy Young, Richard Dunn, and a third matchup with former champion Ken Norton. After facing every top heavyweight on the scene throughout two decades of a golden age, he was moving into the last phase of his reign. An aging champion with fading skills would prove less often he could score in the final rounds to keep his crown. The once untouchable champion who danced under the bright lights to victory made many people wonder about the physical risks from repeated heavy blows at this dangerous crossroads in his career.

In 1976, aspiring to add more wins to his legendary record kept the 34-year-old Ali coming back into the ring, where he adapted his style to slowing reflexes. His desire to leave an unrivaled enduring impact on the sport was perhaps due to the sacrifice of his prime fighting years when he was unjustly banned from the ring. On February 20, Ali faced Jean-Pierre Coopman, who was knocked out in five when facing his idol. Then Ali went on to fight Jimmy Young, who tried to escape the line of fire by bending through the middle of the ropes to avoid stinging jabs during their April 30 bout. The third match that year, against Richard Dunn in May, would mark the last win by a technical knockout at this stage of Ali's career. In June, there was an odd match against martial-arts wrestler Antonio Inoki in Japan to prove who had the best fighting technique in the world. Ali suffered from serious leg injuries after the decided draw.

Ali trained hard, reaching top shape to fight tough contender Ken Norton for the third time in September. Referee Arthur Mercante noticed that Ali used every technique in his arsenal of scientific ring tactics to dominate Norton, including psychological warfare. Mercante said, "he was still the best boxer I've ever seen at coming up instinctively with what was necessary to win." Norton would agree: "He was the best fighter I ever fought, and I respect him. Very few men would give up the things he gave up for their beliefs, and I admire that. Hell, I even liked Ali. I liked him before we fought; I liked him after we fought; just not during." The fight went 15 grueling rounds to the final bell. Ali rallied enough in the last three rounds to earn the controversial unanimous decision win as the undisputed champion. Although Norton was unable to defeat Ali, he developed a deep appreciation for the endearing heart of the champion. He told a story about serious injuries from a car crash in 1986 that left him unconscious in the hospital with doubts about his future: ". . . I remember looking up and there was this crazy man standing by my bed. It was Ali, and he was doing magic tricks for me. He made a handkerchief disappear; he levitated. And I said to myself if he does one more awful trick, I'm gonna get well just so I can kill him." Norton revealed that Ali's visit helped him respond to treatment, which encouraged a brighter outlook for his recovery. He said, "So I don't want to be remembered as the man who broke Muhammad Ali's jaw. I just want to be remembered as a man who fought three close competitive fights with Ali and became his friend when the fighting was over."

After defeating Norton in his 55th fight, the winning streak was paused until plans for his next title defense eight months later against 22-year-old Alfredo Evangelista in May 1977. Ali's win against the young fighter from Uruguay, who had about two years in the professional ring, inspired Ali to tell the press, "You saw a miracle tonight. I'm 35 years old and I danced 15 rounds." Four months later, reality set in when he faced Earnie Shavers, one of the hardest punchers in heavyweight history. Shavers stepped into the ring with Ali armed with skills that had elevated his record at this point to 52 KOs/TKOs in 54 victories. At Madison Square Garden, Ali astounded with his fortitude under crushing blows, answering with precision jabs that rarely missed. Shavers launched powerful punches that pushed Ali to go the distance. A close call in the second round left Ali out on his feet drifting through the daze, managing to stay standing until the bell. By following the televised fight coverage, Ali's corner team learned that a knockout punch was the only way the challenger could win. During the hunt, Shavers waited patiently for an opportunity to deliver his devastating right and stop the mounting damage inflicted from Ali's flurries. By the last minutes of the fight, Shavers was dazed on his feet and falling behind on points, with only the ropes to depend on for support. Before the fight, Ali dubbed him "The Acorn" for his bald head, telling the press that "Acorns fall in September!" Instead, Shavers stayed on his feet fighting Ali, who occasionally defensively danced on his toes, while absorbing massive blows until winning the 15-round title defense by unanimous decision. Shavers praised Ali for the opportunity to improve his life with a big payday. He said, "I don't think there's a fighter in his right mind that wouldn't admire Ali."

After the win over Shavers, many observers realized that the sport was accelerating the aging process for Ali, each blow over the years making it harder for him to reach optimal physical condition. Symptoms began to surface that were likely from the physical damage the champion endured years before the fight with Shavers. Dr. Pacheco had noticed the wear and tear, including slurred speech and slowed reflexes, much earlier. Ali adapted to the physical changes he was experiencing by occasionally coasting through rounds, enduring massive hits, then turning the tables by setting the momentum of the fight. He demonstrated amazing fortitude when recovering from stunned senses after heavyweight punches pushed him to the edge of consciousness. Dr. Pacheco would quit Team Ali after a NYSAC medical report revealed evidence of kidney damage Ali had sustained from the fight against Shavers. He confronted Ali with details about the physical toll on his body, which exhibited the lingering aftershocks of concussive brain injury and other damage. At age 35, after 57 professional fights, Ali would never be granted a license for another venue in the state.

As with other champions who outstayed their welcome, Ali's performances in later years were scrutinized. Press coverage for the final rounds of his career included articles that questioned how much longer he would wear the crown. Dundee would realize, "I was young with him and now I feel old with him." The diminishing returns Dr. Pacheco warned the champ about became a hard-learned truth in the spotlight of the next arena. In training for upcoming fights, Ali continued to endure the high pain threshold he reached in Manila by keeping health considerations an afterthought. Madison Square Garden would no longer consent to showcase any more of his fights. Teddy Brenner, a main event organizer at the Garden told Ali, "You've proven everything that a great champion can possibly prove. You don't need this, Get out!" Ali still had dreams of fighting another day after the desperate win against Shavers.

Another contract guaranteed millions for the first opportunity of the new year in Las Vegas against skillful novice Leon Spinks, who was signed to fight the reigning two-time champion. Ali had defeated 10 challengers since regaining the title before selecting Spinks from a short list of potential opponents. Spinks was just learning to box when Ali won his first heavyweight title against the fiercest prizefighter in history, Charles "Sonny" Liston. By 1978, Spinks had turned age 25 with only seven professional fights. Since the start of his career in 1960, Ali had only two defeats on record by Frazier and Norton. The overconfident champion underestimated his tireless challenger, preparing only lightly before entering the ring.

The press placed easy bets on Ali, giving no chance for Spinks to win the title from his childhood hero. Ali anticipated that Spinks would tire when he was overpowered with a flurry of jabs. Instead, Spinks caught

Ali by surprise with a strong performance. Ali was hit in the jaw early in Round One, then Spinks trapped him against the ropes, surviving through clinches and landing consecutive rights that hurt the champion's early chances to dominate. As he stepped up the pace, the underdog roughed up Ali with pounding inside moves that left the reigning champion with a bruised face and cut lip. Dundee expressed the desperation point in the corner: "You've got to go out and win this round big, real big." Being forced toe-to-toe against Spinks weakened his chances of going the distance with a win. Spinks was staggered twice before exchanging thunderous left-right punches to the jaw that rocked Ali just before the bell. Sportswriters claimed Ali let down his guard while on the ropes trying to wear out his young opponent, wasting precious minutes referred to in *Sports Illustrated* as "reckless generosity." Ali landed several jabs in Round Seven, before being pressed to the corner by an onslaught of punches from Spinks.

Increasing pressure by Spinks in Rounds Eight and Nine continued to force the fight his way. In Round 10, Ali was at his best, firing shots at will that kept Spinks retreating to the ropes from fast accurate punches. The contender was pushed to 11 rounds for the very first time as the champ threw more flurries, but in Round 13 he fell off pace. Dr. Pacheco weighed in about Ali's performance in the 15th round: "He was fighting on memory; he was fighting on guts." It was over in a final flurry by Spinks, who had bounced back from blow after staggering blow even as the crowd cheered for Ali. The huge upset embarrassed Ali who rebounded psychologically, telling the press that he would be in shape to win the title for an unprecedented three times. Spinks said he idolized Ali, letting everyone know "I'm the latest, but Ali's still The Greatest." The fallen champion vowed to return championship-ready for the rematch against Spinks, vying for the third title win. He assured everyone that he was still the greatest when stating, "Leon Spinks borrowed my title; that's all."

Boxing was just the prelude for his enormous impact in the humanitarian arena as fans were increasingly impressed by Ali's achievements. The loss to Spinks did not interfere with his pursuit of human rights issues. That year, he addressed the United Nations Special Committee against Apartheid to boldly impart his message of peace with a powerful spirit of hope. He traveled to the struggling country Bangladesh as a hero who was granted honorary citizenship, before he returned home to support the "Longest Walk," a Native American protest march across the nation to fight government attempts to end treaty rights. He was invited to Russia by Leonid Brezhnev, where he prayed at a local mosque and spread his positive influence throughout the goodwill mission during the Cold War between the Soviet Union and the United States. In his lifetime, Ali fulfilled his goodwill missions to impact the well-being of others by joining forces with various organizations to confront extremely intolerable circumstances, delivering tons of food and medical supplies for disaster relief efforts in conflict zones. He focused attention on children in schools, hospitals, and orphanages around the world to spread joy and lift spirits in ways that inspired a vision of a brighter tomorrow.

Millions of people were impacted around the world by his rescue missions over the years of fighting for humanitarian causes. From his appearances at exhibition fights and outside the ring at celebrity fundraisers he amassed millions of dollars for various charities and deserving causes. He often donated a portion of main event fight ticket sales to hospitals and other compassionate endeavors. Despite using his fame to draw attention to certain causes, he remained private about some of his charity work, expecting nothing in return for the generous impact on many lives around the world.

He also took time away from the prizefighting ring to give advice to those incarcerated at the Rikers Island Correctional Center. Once again confronting injustice, he made high-profile appearances and made contributions to a defense fund in support of boxer Rubin "Hurricane" Carter, whose murder conviction was considered a human rights violation by Amnesty International. Ali was admired around the world for sacrificing prime prizefighting years in the ring for peace and demonstrating against pervasive discrimination in America.

Ali had a powerful reach and the world warmly embraced him in return. During a visit to Jamaica in the '70s that filled a stadium with thousands of fans, he received the key to the city of Kingston, which prompted a speech by Jamaican president Michael Manly praising his courage and mighty efforts to extend a helping hand to suffering people all over the world. Ali also received high-profile compliments as a global icon from Deng Xiaoping, paramount leader of the People's Republic of China, during his goodwill visit to the country. The invitation from the Chinese leader was designed to successfully lift the ban on boxing and revive the popularity of the sport. Ali joined prayer gatherings at the Great Mosque of Xi'an, met with students, and went to a local gym to teach expert workout routines. Crowds cheered the renowned heavyweight king, who embraced the people and dazzled aspiring champions with his Ali Shuffle bravado and artistry during his coaching sessions.

Ali trained intensely for the Spinks rematch at Fighter's Heaven in northern Pennsylvania near Reading's Highway 61. The sign "Welcome to Muhammad Ali Training Camp" marked the entrance to the log cabin campgrounds in Deer Lake. He welcomed the world to watch masterful sparring rounds before his attempt to become the first heavyweight boxer in history to capture the title three times. The camp buildings included a gym, residences, and a mosque built with wood from a deserted railroad bridge. Ali read the Qur'an in the morning before going out on the road for an hour-long endurance run. He finished the daily training routine at the gym, where visitors watched the talented world-class fighter condition his exceptional ring skills. After meeting hundreds of fans during the training days, he spent evenings with friends and family. Ali was determined to regain the crown after his defeat by the skillful Spinks, who had pressured Ali through the final rounds to throw off his jab. Team Ali planned a new strategy that involved staying in constant motion while throwing everything at his target to win back the crown. No time would be wasted on a defensive posture against the ropes, or expecting Spinks to cave in from exhaustion before Ali moved in for the knockout punch. The approach would conjure the style seen when Ali was in his prime, circling the ring on his toes and hurling precise stinging jabs, overhand rights, and uppercuts followed by left and right hooks in a stunning flurry of combinations. Throughout the challenge, he would keep Spinks off balance, stepping in and out of range as he put his jabs in play from every direction to outpace his opponent. Ali raptly focused his energy on the championship hour to come. He said, "I suffered and sacrificed more than I ever did."

Since defeating Ali, the young reigning champion had struggled with professional success and fame. His behavior in the limelight would jeopardize his crown. Spinks succumbed to a fast-paced social scene that demanded more attention outside the ring. His growing entourage brought distractions to his corner with serious consequences that involved his trainer George Benton, who suddenly quit during the rematch after coaching Spinks through the first title win. In the opposite corner, Ali prepared well to prove he was truly the Greatest of All Time.

On September 15, seven months after Ali's loss to Spinks, a planned rematch attracted over 60,000 spectators ringside at the New Orleans Superdome. An estimated 90 million people in 80 countries viewed the championship fight that could be record-breaking. Sportswriters focused on his enormous pride that weighed heavily on the chance of winning back the crown. As the odds-on favorite, he gave Spinks an expert 15-round boxing lesson in the center of the ring. He delivered on expectations, stunning the press with new tactics developed since the Vegas downfall. Ali circled him at a dizzying pace in the fifth, as Dundee shouted, "Where did he go, Leon? Where did he go?" After he had warned Ali early in the fight, Referee Lucien Joubert penalized him for clinching by giving the fifth round to Spinks. Through the next rounds, Ali amassed points from repeated combinations that assured his lead. He said, "Against Spinks the second time, my plan was simple. Jab, jab, and throw the right hand. If you got in close, tie him up. No rope-a-dope; fight the whole time in the center of the ring. And throw lots of punches at the end of each round. Closing a round right impresses the judges, and I wanted to give Spinks something to remember between rounds."

A third of the way through the match, Spinks lost step with Ali, who securely led the pace of the fight. Spinks struggled to keep balance under the weight of Ali's clinches, which slowed the momentum and pulled him down toward the light blue canvas. Spinks finally stopped smiling, as he searched for answers to the rhyme and reason of Ali's winning ring science. Ali held the advantage, controlling the fight by minimizing the chances Spinks had to land a knockout punch. Dundee interjected from the corner with a foregone farewell, simply saying, "Goodbye, Leon." Ali amazed fans when he danced through the fight on his way to the unprecedented heights of a third title victory. The cheers for Ali added weight to the impact of each punch absorbed by the outclassed Spinks. Ali would float and sting his way into the history books by the end of the 15th round, using reserve power to win by a unanimous decision. The fight was not picture perfect as observed by Dundee, who said, "It was beautifully sloppy. It was gorgeous sloppy. And it was the only damn way we were going to beat Spinks." Although Spinks had lost his crown in a desperate struggle, he was the first to congratulate his idol in the ring. Reflecting on his long career, Ali told the press, "my greatest fight was against Joe Frazier in Manila. But this was my most satisfying fight. It meant more to me." Many were unconvinced when he announced plans to retire: "I want to be the first black champion to go out on top."

His great compassion for children led Ali to visit the Newington Children's Hospital soon after he became the first man to win the world heavyweight title three times. On this occasion the press followed the champ as his affectionate bedside touch spread joy to each child located on all six floors of the hospital. His loving presence evoked a tearful emotional reaction from the deeply appreciative staff. Photographs that occasionally surfaced revealed the story of other hospital visits, human rights speeches at universities, and memorable images including a day spent compassionately holding hands with a St. Jude's childhood cancer patient.

Ali had been at a crossroads, fighting desperate rounds against a biological clock advancing him through health difficulties that affected a range of ring skills. The 37-year-old champion eased into retirement on June 15th the next year without defending his title. Ali had commanded the spotlight for almost 20 years, but knew that the time had come to leave the sport. Dundee would sum up his time with the champ at the very end: "We had traveled many roads together. . . .These were some of the best days of my life. . . ." Ali told the press, "I've been doing it for 25 years and you can only do so much wear to the body . . . I can see it. I can feel it." After 59 professional fights, Ali's only defeats had been against Ken Norton, Joe Frazier, and Leon Spinks. They were all ultimately defeated in rematches as the champion astounded his worst critics with his scientific boxing aptitude. The fight world knew that Ali had nothing more to prove. Still, the spotlight would lure him back into the ring a year later for a match with reigning champion Larry Holmes in Las Vegas. For Ali, his aspiration to leave an unbeatable chapter in sports history with a remarkable fourth title win was more powerful than the overwhelming odds against him.

After defeating Spinks, Ali's star still shined brightly worldwide. The courageous prizefighter reached a rare summit of achievement with three world heavyweight title victories by competing in the fight ring well past his prime. Even when forced against the ropes, he absorbed extreme punishment, willfully refusing to fall in defeat. The spotlight returned to his corner of the ring a year later as oddsmakers were not convinced he would be able to win the crown. Ali had reached another dangerous crossroads, envisioning the next unconquered summit he had to win to reign as heavyweight champion of the world for an astounding fourth time. Once again, Fight Doctor Ferdie Pacheco assessed Ali's attitude: "A champion doesn't think he can be beaten."

10

ASCENT TO GREATER GLORY

The Fourth Summit

Ali Shadowboxing in the Gym.
Trinity Mirror / Mirropix /
Alamy Photograph

By 1980, Ali had captured worldwide attention for nearly two decades of professional prizefighting. His plans to return to the competitive arena seeking a fourth title win astounded the boxing world. Many believed the highly respected prizefighter had nothing more to prove after decades in the boxing ring. He was the greatest heavyweight champion of his era, if not the greatest fighter of all time. Reigning world champion Larry Holmes, who was unfazed by the psychological warfare Ali used to break down opponents' confidence, would unleash the fury of his fists to defend his season on the coveted throne. The championship fight night would reveal that the toughest challenge Ali would face involved his winning spirit that compelled him to pursue daring dreams of greater glory.

In 1980, Ali reentered the ring, vying to be the first to reach the supreme pinnacle of achievement in heavyweight prizefighting with a fourth title. Famed dealmaker Don King worked his unique brand of business acumen to amass the megabucks behind the contract, which was rumored to be worth $8 million to Ali and $6 million to Holmes. Ali cast high hopes on the multimillion-dollar dream ticket to his 60th fight, which would once again draw worldwide attention. His winning spirit and his desire to be remembered as the greatest champion with an untouchable record in boxing overshadowed serious health considerations. After 35 fights, Holmes was in his prime as the undefeated reigning champion. Ali, the three-time world champion, dismissed worries from those who pleaded with him to give up the impossible dream by calling them overreactions.

Ali ignored the physical warning signs, projecting an invincible attitude despite fading ring skills that weighed on his high-stakes decision to return at age 38. Through the lens of greatness, he was convinced no one could stand in the way of his next chance for another title victory. True to form, he tried to deliver damaging psychological blows to his opponent, claiming Holmes was nothing compared to Liston, Foreman, or Frazier. The reigning champion sharpened focus on the cold facts by responding, "Ali's mind made a date now his body can't keep. . . . He was a great fighter but he stepped out of his time into my time . . . I know all there is to know about how he fights. Whatever he tries, I'll do what is needed to beat him. . . ."

Ali was risking serious injury in the ring. His slowing reflexes and speed had become more noticeable in recent years of going the distance with the hardest hitters in the sport. For nearly 20 years, Ali had defeated everyone he faced, and despite three losses to top-ranked heavyweights, he had evened the score by winning rematches to build an incomparable world-class record. Popular demand rallied 25,000 fans to ringside while others tuned in hoping to watch the underdog beat the heavy odds. Ali knew the feelings held by many admirers and the boxing world astonished by the comeback decision: "Mountains can't grow any higher." Those who shared faith in the dream would follow Ali's lead from tough training grounds at Fighter's Heaven to the eye of a brutal desert storm played out in Las Vegas.

Holmes had earned his place on the throne after an exceptional boxing education, including years of sparring in the ring with Ali at Fighter's Heaven. Ali faced complications with preparing to face Holmes when no state would license him to fight in the ring because of his medical history. Dr. Pacheco, who had walked away from Ali's corner in 1977 after medical tests had revealed serious kidney damage, observed that Ali "refuses to see himself as he now is, and can only see himself as he was. . . ." Ali was not ready to accept troubling physical limitations that would force him out of rhythm and out of time. Before the venue was set, the Nevada State Athletic Commission required a physical fitness exam to determine whether Ali was in sound enough health for a championship fight. Ali checked into the Mayo Clinic in Minnesota that summer, four years after the Fight Doctor complained that the champion was physically falling apart. The Mayo Clinic findings provided a positive assessment that was kept secret from the public. The test results cleared the decision to license him to fight in Las Vegas.

Looking to place the blame for endangering a legendary champion, many pointed to manager Herbert Muhammad, who did not publicly protest the return decision. Lonnie Ali explained her husband's trusted relationship with his manager, stating, "Herbert has been Muhammad's confidant, teacher, and friend. He's given him inspiration, guidance, and religious instruction. Now, what all that has been worth to Muhammad, only Muhammad can tell you." Ali trivialized the extreme risks for a fighter well past his prime in the championship ring with rough comparisons stating, "There was an old lady, 80 years old, finished the marathon in New York. That's 26 miles. I never ran 26 miles in my life, but an 80-year-old woman did it, and nobody made her stop." After going hundreds of rounds in the ring, he heard objections from Dundee, family, and friends who flatly told him he was too old for prizefighting. He informed the press about his firm decision, saying, "Angelo thinks I shouldn't be fightin'. . . . . But Angelo's not me. . . ." On more than one occasion, Dr. Pacheco had dared to tell the future Sports Personality of the Century that he should quit boxing forever. Ali revealed his thoughts stating, "I never let anyone talk me out of believing in myself." It would be a lonely, dangerous climb through rugged mountainous terrain to reach the envisioned pinnacle of glory. In the end, everyone knew the decision was up to Ali.

The outdoor venue placed Ali at the foothills of the Sierra Nevada Mountains to begin his dangerous record-breaking ascent. Sportswriters covering the Caesars Palace fight published several cover stories for *Sports Illustrated* about his incredible return to the ring that year. The presses kept rolling, delivering promotional sound bites that captured the dream of the heavyweight legend. On April 14, the article entitled "Look Who's Back! Muhammad Ali" raised the anticipation level. The next featured September 29 story had a caption on the cover to regally express the king's claim to the throne: "fourth time, Muhammad Ali Is the Heavyweight Champion of the World! Etc., etc. . . ." As he entered the ring, Ali impressed everyone with his youthful physique, magically conjuring illusions of a return to prime competitive years. At first glance, his physical image seemed to have won the race against time. *Sports Illustrated* writer Pat Putnam described the championship matchup as if it were a mirage in the desert, agreeing with experts unconvinced that Ali had a chance of surviving a single round in the ring against the physical prowess of the reigning champion.

Well before the opening bell on October 2, Ali took extreme measures to reach prime physical form, while struggling to quickly restore his championship speed, agility, and top physical conditioning after his absence. Dr. Charles Williams misdiagnosed an underactive thyroid and prescribed the drug Thyrolar, which Ali added to his daily regimen. The drug would act like a straitjacket after causing rapid weight loss, taking away vital muscle strength, and impairing his mobility in the ring. The medication ultimately immobilized him in the fight ring facing Holmes. Dr. Pacheco later explained, "Ali was a walking time bomb in the ring that night," drawn to the spotlight that trapped him against the ropes. Dr. Williams later concluded, "I may have placed him in jeopardy inadvertently."

Sportswriters took notice of the athletic physique Ali achieved for the fight, as if he had discovered a secret fountain of youth that restored him to prime fitness. His record of defying great odds in the ring continued to bring an element of surprise to the sport. He promoted the fight with his usual intensity, and his convincing winning mindset defied doubts about his ability to survive brutal championship rounds. Ali turned heads to his corner, until sportswriter Pat Putnam would report that Ali's physical appearance was just an illusion concealing the truth that he would never go the distance against Holmes. Ali ignored all the warning signs leading up to the fight. He was struggling at the one-mile mark on routine endurance runs just two days before the fight. It was later revealed that he suffered during training from restlessness, dehydration, and the inability to last the winning distance on Agony Hill at Fighter's Heaven. Reaching for perilous heights while using Thyrolar would have a dire impact on Ali through the fight.

Boxing experts believed that the fights after Manila in 1975 had caused irreparable damage to the greatest heavyweight fighter in history. Years later, the Mayo Clinic findings were released to Ali's biographer Thomas Hauser, who published the results. They had raised questions about Ali's neurological health, including coordination and speech pattern difficulties, impaired hand-eye coordination, and other mobility problems. Despite the findings, he was cleared for a license to fight in Nevada. Piecing together the serious signs of physical trouble would be a difficult lesson, as he pursued a stratospheric fourth title win.

On fight night Referee Richard Green brought the two fighters together at center ring. The sellout crowd, for an estimated record $6.2 million gate, started cheering at first glance of the legend on the dangerous ascent. Then at the opening bell, Ali moved to the perilous center of Holmes's universe, believing he could win. There would be a big reveal for the master of illusions who admitted later, "All I could think of after the first round was, 'Oh, God, I still have 14 rounds to go.' I had nothing. Nothing. I knew it was hopeless. I knew I couldn't win, and I knew I'd never quit." In addition to causing rapid weight loss and taking away vital muscle strength, the effects of the thyroid medication began to impair his mobility in the first three minutes of the fight. Sportswriter Pat Putnam would have a fitting title for his *Sports Illustrated* article, "Doom in the Desert," before the end of the opening round.

Ali slumped on his corner stool from exhaustion between rounds. The spell was broken, leaving fans wondering when and if a spark would reignite his stinging jabs. In Round Two it was clear that Ali was trapped on a precipice in the no-contest battle, clinging to hopes for a miracle without a way to escape the devastating fall. When he scored two rights after missing many soft punches, the crowd sprang to life cheering him on in the fight. Ali struggled to find his footing, prompting the corner team to take charge. Holmes continued to inflict bursts of pain on Ali that went unanswered.

More of the same action paced his fourth-round performance, which lacked Ali's characteristic agility, blinding speed, strength, and instinctive moves. The virtuoso talent that made Ali unique among heavyweights never materialized. At this stage of the fight, he showed visible signs of damage with a bruised left eye after a barrage of counterpunches pinned him on the ropes. As he leaned on them for support, the ropes held him up even through the agony of a powerful right hook that almost ended an era.

Obviously shaken by the blows, Ali amazed the fight crowd when pride kept him on his feet despite the tremendous pain.

In Round Five, Dundee warned Ali that he needed to find a way to answer the onslaught of blows from Holmes. He made attempts to find his bearings through heavy assaults in the fifth and sixth rounds, continually blinking his eyes trying to see past the daze from dizzying blows. Holmes knew something was wrong. He seemed to pace the fight with caution, while knowing he still had something to prove to silence his critics that favored The Greatest. Ali held his fists high to protect his face from further damage, opening his midsection to brutal flurries assaulting the body. When Holmes stepped back at intervals of his offensive, Ali sought refuge on the ropes unwilling to fall. He was injured with an obvious cut under the eye and bloody nose. Holmes looked to the referee, wanting him to intervene, and many in the crowd agreed that it was time to stop the fight. Ali was overwhelmed in the middle of the nightmare, prompting Howard Cosell to comment on what many felt: "It is sad to see this." Being given a license to fight cleared the way for Ali to show the world the repercussions of injuries compounded over years of brutal prizefighting. After staggering out of the worst moments of his career, he said, "In my youth, I set out to prove to myself and to the world that I could achieve anything I put my mind to. This was something that I had to do again and again."

In the seventh, Ali sparked the ignition by dancing, throwing jabs, arousing hope in the hearts of fans, who had been waiting for him to break into action. Suddenly the momentum faded like a brief flashback to prime competitive years. He repeatedly missed the mark, then nearly collapsed, motionless from exhaustion. After this round, he would be caught in a desperate psychological struggle to survive the massive beating while refusing to surrender the fight. Many knew Ali was a clever fighter who would not let himself get hurt. In the eighth, he shockingly stopped fighting and turned his back on Holmes to shield himself from further injury when his legs were shot. Dundee warned him that he or the referee would end the fight. Ali would never surrender, even at the point of no return in his motionless, stalled performance. Ali survived on his feet through extreme punishment until the ninth round. At that moment, Dundee realized that for the first time Ali could not go the 15-round distance. He barely made it back to his corner where Dundee told him, "This is your last round. One more round and then I'm going to stop it. . . ." Referee Richard Green went to the corner to find out whether Ali should continue. Still, Ali refused to cave in despite the ripping pain caused by round after round of brutal punishment. In Round 10, Ali was hit with devastating multiple combinations. Soon to be age 31, Holmes was in top physical condition, unchallenged by the slow pace of the fight. Concern was heightened when Ali was unable to defend himself from some 50 powerful punches within three minutes after the start of the 10th round.

The round ended no differently than the others, with Ali staggering back to his corner slouched on his stool in bad shape. He had withstood several hundred blows throughout the match. Referee Green rushed to Ali's corner for a closer look at his condition, then Dundee signaled the surrender. Bundini, who was in tears, could not accept that the championship dream was over, and pleaded for just one more round. Dundee shouted, "I'm the boss here. It's over!"

Dundee later commented, "When the tenth just brought him more hurt, then that was it." Responding to claims that he simply followed orders from Herbert Muhammad he explained, "They're saying that Herbert Muhammad as manager stopped the fight from the ringside but I didn't have to wait for word from Herbert. He gives me *carte blanche* when I'm in there." After 35 minutes in the ring, Ali's 60th fight was stopped inside the distance for the first time in his career.

The fight world knew that Holmes had tolerated numerous comparisons to Ali. Some felt he proceeded cautiously, but not compassionately through each round of the championship prizefight. Holmes made his feelings known, saying, "I love the man. . . . But when the bell rung, I didn't know his name." Holmes cried after the fight, speaking to the press about the legendary fighter who was an inspiration both in the glory of victory and in defeat. He said, "Boxing owes Ali everything . . . I love the man and I truly respect him." It was evident that Ali was in no shape to shadowbox through light training rounds when he stepped into the ring to win the title again. Ali shared his feelings after the damage was done, "I didn't like the idea of stopping the fight at that moment they did. I didn't know who stopped it. Now I realize what happened and what would have happened to me, I'm glad they did stop it. . . . Psychologically, I am all right. You have to be a champion in losing as well as winning."

After the fight Ali blamed the loss on side effects from the thyroid medication stating, "I spent three days at the Mayo Clinic . . . I passed every test. . . . " Dr. Pacheco responded, saying that granting Ali a license to fight was "scandalous," and that, "Just because a man can pass a physical doesn't mean he should be fighting in a prize ring." Although the drug did cause his fatigue, many were aware that his clean bill of health had ignored possible signs of brain injury, most evident in his speech difficulties. Instances of incoherent communication had become more pronounced after Manila, when he ignored signs of fading skills, which forced him to endure more punishment as he went the distance more often in his later fights. Ali only revealed the trauma he suffered in the ring years later: "You dream you've boxed six or seven fast rounds, and then you get tired, exhausted. You have nothing left. It's all gone. You have to quit." Blindsided by brutal reality after an extreme leap of faith, Ali contemplated retirement from the sport in his last chapter of a golden era.

The noticeable damage to Ali was an under-eye cut, superficial bruises, and bloody nose, but he suffered deeper permanent harm. Ali checked into the UCLA Medical Center a few days later, after close friend Howard Bingham noticed he was in very bad shape from the 10-round beating. In addition to assessing his superficial injuries, Dr. Dennis W. Cope and others became concerned about a possible deeper nervous system disorder and found a normally functioning thyroid. Even after the humiliation, confusion, and fear he experienced in his fight against Holmes, Ali would control the terms for how the last rounds of his legendary career would be fought. Despite the ensuing pushback from fight officials, Ali stayed true to his shocking words when he said, "I shall return." The glorious season of this golden age in heavyweight prizefighting would end soon after Ali made that promise to the world. He ignored the warnings and explained: "All my life I achieved the impossible by defying the odds, so after I lost to Larry Holmes in October 1980, I gave it one more shot."

Just about a month away from his 40th birthday, Ali continued to hold onto the dream of winning another championship title. He set the press straight about the challenges of aging in the competitive boxing arena: "Before the fight I remember telling the critics that I thought forty was a fun age, life was just beginning." It became clear that he wanted to go out with a win. Somehow, more medical tests settled concerns over his health, allowing clearance for his 61st fight against 27-year-old journeyman Trevor Berbick. In December 1981, fourteen months after recovering from his defeat by Holmes, Ali was forced to take the drama to the Bahamas, because no state boxing commission would license him for another fight. Ali persisted in finding the right venue, 50 miles off the coast of Florida, to finish his prizefighting career. The last stand in the city of Nassau was viewed as an unnecessary diversion for a legendary heavyweight king in search of a rare, graceful exit from boxing. In the scenic, serene island location, appearances were deceiving. Everything essential for a professional prizefight was treated like a disorganized afterthought. The timekeeping bell that sounds at three-minute intervals for each round of the fight was nowhere to be found. In a last-minute haphazard rush for a solution, someone discovered an available cowbell that was brought in as a substitute. After the last 10 rounds against Holmes, many people agreed with Dr. Pacheco, who realized that "Time makes more converts than reason." It was Father Time who would sound the final bell of Ali's career.

December 11, 1981, would usher in a difficult moment of truth for the exceptional champion. By the time Ali faced Berbick, he had recovered from the debilitating effects of Thyrolar, appearing to be in fine physical shape. Still, Berbick was viewed as a last stand to prove his fortitude and once again conquer the odds. As the fight began, Ali matched pace with Berbick, then his hopes of beating the odds faded with his performance in the last three rounds. He was slow to take advantage of openings to outscore his opponent. Boxing analysts commented on his lost timing by describing how he telegraphed his punches to measure the distance for blows that had little impact. There was an occasional counterpunch over the jab in Round Three, but still Ali staggered back to the corner at the end of the round.

A brief turning point in Round Four made spectator concerns seem short-lived. Dundee shouted to Ali, "This is number 5! We are halfway home!" Ali was against the ropes in Round Six when Berbick turned to the referee, attempting to stop the fight. At this point, live broadcast commentators said Ali should not have been permitted in the competitive fight ring. Referee Zack Clayton broke up the clinches that ensued after Berbick roughed up Ali. By Round Seven, Ali began to dance through the last rounds of the battle in legendary boxing style reminiscent of championship years in his prime. As Berbick misfired, Ali amazed commentators by demonstrating the seasoned experience that made him a three-time world champion. In Round 10, Ali held on through the barrage of punches as Berbick rallied into action for points he needed to win by the final bell. For the last time, Dundee cut off Ali's gloves as the ringside crowd closely surrounded the sentimental favorite during the score count. Berbick was heard shouting, "I love you. . . . Thank you! You made me!" Commentators acknowledged that, "In everyone's heart, Ali still remains 'The Greatest'." Dundee expressed his deep feelings: "Great men and great monuments don't relinquish their hold on anyone. And Muhammad Ali was both. Especially to me."

Photographers who had followed Ali's career for more than two decades captured dramatic images of his last fight, lost by unanimous decision. Acknowledging the close decision, Ali told the press, "Father Time caught up with me. I'm finished. I've got to face the facts." Ali admitted, "I thought I should go out boxing with the win. And if I couldn't go out with a win, at least I wanted to be throwing punches at the end." Emphatic statements by the press said it was certainly time for Ali to retire after the 10-round performance.

After more than two decades in the professional fight ring, the most celebrated partnership in boxing history ended on an island paradise. Since first meeting the ambitious teenage amateur boxer more than two decades earlier, Dundee had remained in Ali's corner during most of his prizefights, until the very end of a record-breaking ascent. The legendary cornerman coached Ali through major professional transformations, sharing the pain of heart-rending losses and the triumph of unforgettable victories while they traveled together around the world. Many agreed with Dundee when he assessed that the Holmes fight was the worst defeat of Ali's career. He reflected on a friendship, which began when young Cassius Clay dominated opponents with lightning speed in the ring: "His life was a happening era. He changed the whole concept of boxing, including the public relations part. He educated me. . . .There will never be anyone like him." Dundee passionately stated, "Muhammad had it all: natural talent, unbelievable speed and reflexes for a big man, skills, smarts, courage, you name it, he had it." Ali left a legacy of athletic excellence, with trademark poetic flourishes, humorous antics, and rousing repartee that endeared him to an international audience. Over the course of 56 wins, 5 losses, and 32 KOs/TKOs between 1960 and 1981, he became a uniquely iconic three-time heavyweight champion. Competitive championship wins against the fearsome Liston in 1964 at age 22, the powerful Foreman in 1974 at age 32, and the talented Spinks in 1978 at age 36 left an unforgettable impact, not just on the best heavyweights of his era, but on the world stage. Ali announced, "In the history of the world and from the beginning of time, there's never been another fighter like me."

As Ali faced growing health concerns in retirement, many believed he had fought for too long, pushing himself to dangerous limits that Dr. Pacheco believed harmed him forever. Back in 1977, before Ali fought Alfredo Evangelista, the doctor had warned that the champion was seen in an artificially rosy light, when he lost his passionate winning drive for the sport through advancing rounds. From medical tests, he knew that Ali was irreparably damaged when his condition was later assessed saying, "concussive blows to the brain. . . . It all progresses in a fighter's life. The legs go; his reflexes aren't what they used to be; he cuts more easily; the injuries accelerate. And the older you get, the less your recuperative powers are. Ali at age twenty-three could have absorbed Frazier in Manila and shaken it off, but at age thirty-three was another story." During a brutal fight against

Shavers in New York, for the last time from the corner, Dr. Pacheco had watched Ali survive while out on his feet after a seismic punch almost ended the fight.

The Fight Doctor weighed in to settle the speculation from uninformed doubters about Ali's condition: "people still wonder whether Ali's brain damage is due to boxing?" Biographer Thomas Hauser observed that Ali "deceived himself, massively" when he failed to reach championship form for the fight against Holmes.

The Nevada Athletic Commission had ordered testing at the Mayo Clinic in Rochester, Minnesota, three months before agreeing to license the 38-year-old Ali for the fight against Holmes. It was later revealed that the doctors observed unusual speech patterns, impaired finger to nose coordination, and difficulty hopping on one foot. Studies on neurodegenerative brain disease in professional boxers had been published decades earlier, confirming evidence that irreversible brain damage is an undeniable risk of the sport. Ali returned from retirement when almost age 39 having problems with slowed reflexes, fatigue, and slurred speech. His CAT scan results were dismissed as a benign condition with a congenital basis, while the other symptoms were treated as a temporary condition attributed to fatigue. Dr. Donald Romeo, who represented the Nevada State Athletic Commission that licensed Ali for the fight against Holmes, offered his perspective from the brutal mecca of boxing in Las Vegas. He stated that a fighter "takes some blows to the region of the kidneys and there's blood in the urine— big deal. . . ." Sportswriter Hugh McIlvanney commented on the health assessment which sounded indifferent to the possibility that Ali could risk permanent damage to the kidneys. He concluded that Dr. Romeo "seems to have learned his bedside manner from James Cagney."

Dr. Pacheco intervened years earlier with concerns that laid out the telling warning signs of brain injury. He offered his view on why Ali had failed to go the distance in the ring for the first time in his career against Holmes. The brutal blows Ali had sustained caused deeper injuries that forced his body's organs to work much harder to withstand debilitating physical damage. The doctor understood that the impact of Ali's trauma would advance in complexity. By 1984, concerns over slowed reflexes attributed to going the brutal distance too many times had progressed to arm tremors and more serious mobility problems.

One of the greatest eras in boxing ended when Ali hung up his gloves for good. Hundreds of feature stories immortalized the legendary champion. All forms of media kept international attention on the People's Champion, who followed his heart on a humanitarian quest over the years to help others in need around the world. Dr. Pacheco knew that Ali would continue to impress the world as he pursued his dreams and said, "I've never seen him fail, never seen him quit. He's a winner, always a winner." Millions admired Ali when he stated that the prizefighting ring was just an introduction to the world before his crucial mission to win human rights, freedom, equality, and peace for all.

When still dreaming of a fourth title win against Larry Holmes in 1980, Ali was recruited by President Jimmy Carter for a diplomatic mission in African countries to persuade a boycott of the Moscow Olympics. The effort was intended to protest human rights violations involving the Soviet invasion of Afghanistan. Although it was considered a failure, across Tanzania, Kenya, Nigeria, Liberia, and Senegal, he was still viewed as an exemplary hero for human rights who was gifted in diplomacy.

The Arab world embraced Ali as a great humanitarian hero, sports champion, and powerful member of a communion of faith in Islam. As an ambassador for peace, he remained at the center of negotiations to release hostages held in Lebanon by heroically offering himself in exchange for the prisoners. Although this extreme self-sacrificing effort was unsuccessful, he felt it was worthwhile to play this role in the crisis for a favorable influence on the captors. As the UN Messenger of Peace, he was well aware of the hardships endured by people throughout the world. He inspired dreams of success and the will to overcome disadvantages among students enrolled at Karte Sei High School for Girls in Kabul, Afghanistan, even as his personal battle with Parkinson's adversely affected his health. In 1987, a goodwill visit to Pakistan brought him in touch with mosques, schools, hospitals, orphanages, and government dignitaries to promote global humanitarianism. In 1988 he continued his lifelong missions to relieve suffering in the world, raising awareness about the plight of famine victims in Africa. When he visited the Sudan, he intended to shift the world's attention to the crisis, in an ongoing fight to eradicate poverty and help disadvantaged people, demonstrating his untiring commitment and fortitude.

In the 1980s, he also visited several cities in India and spent time with Prime Minister Indira Gandhi as millions of fans watched him in an exhibition match with a local boxing champion. He made a donation to Mother Teresa's Missionaries of Charity in Calcutta (Kolkata). Ali continued his global journey of love with increasing intensity for the rest of his life. In 1994, the horrific genocide in Rwanda prompted calls for extensive humanitarian aid and the mighty force of global political intervention. Ali used his celebrity to campaign for the US government and world organizations to aid Rwandan refugees displaced by the violence.

Ali remained involved with the well-being of children through The Rainbow Connection, an organization that makes wishes come true for Michigan children with life-threatening health conditions. The organization was incorporated in 1985, when he helped fulfill wishes and promote various support services for "wish families" in need of assistance. Ali also founded WORLD, the World Organization for Rights, Liberty, and Dignity, to alleviate poverty, aid victims in crisis zones, and advance equal rights around the world. In 1986, Ali received the Ellis Island Medal of Honor in recognition of his mission to increase knowledge, courage, compassion, and selfless generosity through his commitment to promoting idealistic principles that better humanity. It was his unwavering mission of caring for the less fortunate that demonstrated his unrivaled courage, boundless compassion, and great inspirational message.

Ali finally retired from the prizefighting ring after epic battles against the best heavyweights in the sport brought him unprecedented fame. Over decades, the magnitude of his success would extend across many continents as he led a golden age in professional boxing. During his ascent, participation in the civil rights movement and Black Nationalist fight for self-determination brought the struggle for social and political equality to the world stage. The next phase of his mission in the humanitarian arena would prove to be the most rewarding rounds of his life. With universal impact, he rallied cheers as the greatest sportsman of the 20th century, who inspired bold initiatives for peace. Ali often stated that the prizefighting ring was just a prelude for "The Real Fight Ring" to win human rights, freedom, and equality for marginalized people. At an unrelenting pace, now he pursued dreams of greater glory by confronting injustice with a relentlessly compassionate heart.

Ali found spiritual comfort from his religious faith, at a difficult turning point in the journey, when mysterious and troubling developments surrounding his health presented upsetting new challenges. Dr. Pacheco assessed the physical repercussions Ali faced: "Even Muhammad Ali is human and subject to the laws of nature."

11

LONG ROAD HOME

An Uncharted Course

Muhammad Ali Lights the Way at the 1996 Olympics in Atlanta.
Reuters / Alamy Photograph

When Ali retired from the prizefighting ring, his fame spanned across the world's continents, reaching billions of people. During his ascent to become the greatest champion of the 20th century, concurrent advances in the civil rights movement and Black Nationalism had rallied progressive action for social, economic, and political equality. Ali stated that the prizefighting ring was just a prelude to the big fight for human rights, justice, equality, and freedom.

For years after leaving the fight ring to travel the world for humanitarian causes, continuing to spread his message of faith in Islam, Ali searched for medical solutions to his advancing health problems. The champion who had stunned opponents with precision jabs as he gracefully circled the ring in fluid motion confronted endless rounds of debilitating physical symptoms, including fatigue, slurred speech, and unstable balance.

Remaining true to his legendary style, Ali would not let his health concerns interfere with his commitment to fighting injustice suffered by oppressed people around the world. The most enriching and fulfilling endeavors involved helping others in need anywhere: "It is after I retired from boxing that my true work began. . . . Now I dream about doing something to stop all the hating in the world. I dream about feeding people who are hungry. I dream about children learning how to read and write. . . ." As his health continued to decline, the People's Champion navigated uncharted territory in a fight with uncertain odds. Ali shared his view about the journey: "I have learned to live my life one step, one breath, and one moment at a time, but it was a long road."

The slurred speech that prompted ardent pleas by the Fight Doctor for Ali to stop fighting after the Thrilla in Manila was a mild prelude to far more serious repercussions of his decision to continue defending his reign. The countdown to the final bell involved 10 more fights after Manila, which amounted to hundreds of brutal fight rounds over his professional career. The dream of a fourth championship title win against Larry Holmes in 1980 had ended with him standing motionless in the ring absorbing a punishing barrage of punches.

Luis Sarria, longtime masseuse in Ali's corner, knew the fight scene was a cruel business even for a renowned champion: "Few cared for him as a human being." Sarria would come to regret not expressing his feelings in moments when he placed healing hands on the champ to ease the painful aftermath of brutal fights: "To tell a boxer to stop fighting is an insult. I did not have the strength to tell him, but I wish to God I had." John Schulian, a reporter for the *Chicago Sun-Times*, underscored the brutality in the Holmes fight. He said that it was supported by "people who didn't care one bit about the things he stood for his entire life. . . . You didn't have to be a rocket scientist to know at that point that Ali was facing brain damage."

Manager Herbert Muhammad said that his influence over Ali was not strong enough to alter his determined course toward greater glory. Before Ali's last fight, Dr. Harry Demopoulos at New York University consulted with 30 doctors, including specialists at the Mayo Clinic, before assessing that Ali appeared to have no serious damage to any vital organs after more than 20 years in the prizefighting ring. In a *Sports Illustrated* article entitled "Not with a Bang But with a Whisper," William Nack reported the statement by Dr. Demopoulos: "There's absolutely no evidence that Muhammad has sustained any injury to any vital organ—brain, liver, kidneys, heart, lungs—nervous system, or muscle or bone systems. His blood tests indicate he has the vessels of a young man." The findings cleared the way for the last fight of his career against Trevor Berbick. Just three years later in 1984 at age 42, Ali would be diagnosed with Parkinson's syndrome, a disorder characterized by gradual deterioration of certain nerve centers in the brain that control movement.

Perhaps Ali's dreams of greatness, which set his sights on ever higher mountains to climb, had been inspired by the idolized artistry of middleweight champion Sugar Ray Robinson. Between 1940 and 1965, Sugar Ray battled through 201 fights with just 19 losses, and he was considered the best pound-for-pound boxer in history. His innovative ring style led to a phenomenal record of achievements, celebrated until the end of his life at age 67 suffering from Alzheimer's. Marciano had been undefeated through 49 fights when he retired after just eight years in the sport, simply walking away at age 32 to spend more time with his family. Ali's career had spanned 21 years, with the aging process accelerating through the decades in the spotlight of the brutal fight ring.

In the aftermath of three world championship victories, Ali confronted the possibility of a progressive neurological disease that would cause him to lose control over his mobility and speech. Lifelong friend Howard Bingham remembered when Ali checked into the UCLA medical center in bad shape days after his brutal defeat at the hands of Larry Holmes. It is impossible to measure the destructive impact of each hit to the head in the championship ring or during sparring practice, where extreme physical tolerance is repeatedly put to the brutal test. Ali would endure the compounding damage of successive concussions from massive blows, when he was unable to dance out of range through the distance of later competitive matches.

In 1987, Ali's physician, Dr. Dennis Cope, stated that his condition was partly "caused by injuries to the brain from fighting" in the boxing ring. The Parkinson's syndrome diagnosis would not prevent Ali from pursuing the greater purpose he envisioned for his life after prizefighting. He established a partnership with the Parkinson's community through the Muhammad Ali Parkinson Center at Barrow Neurological Institute in Phoenix, Arizona. The Institute shares recent advances in medicines and surgical treatments for the fight against Parkinson's with patients and their families. He also was deeply involved with professional boxing regulation reform, including efforts to improve health care oversight and end the exploitation of athletes pushed to life-threatening extremes purely for profits in the sport.

In 1928, Dr. Harrison Martland began to study the long-term damage from boxing. He coined the term punch-drunk (or dementia pugilistica) to describe cognitive dysfunctions involving memory loss, disorientation, slurred speech, and dementia. Martland's study concluded that the declining trend continued for at least two years after leaving the sport. Decades later, research revealed that a degenerative brain disease called chronic traumatic encephalopathy (CTE) was associated with repetitive trauma to the brain. There is agreement that multiple jolts to the brain or even just one blow can cause progressive damage. During their careers, boxers endure more than a thousand blows to the head over the course of competitive matches and sparring practice through the years.

In 2002, three-quarters of a century after Martland's study, researchers began to investigate a pattern of CTE among National Football League athletes. After the sudden death of Super Bowl champion Mike Webster, who had died of a heart attack, traumatic physical brain injuries were discovered from the autopsy. Dr. Cyril Wecht of the Allegheny County Coroner's office, the presiding coroner in the Webster case, released the findings in a paper coauthored with other experts including his colleague Dr. Bennet Omalu, the neuropathologist who discovered the abnormal patterns in Webster's deep brain tissue. "Chronic Traumatic Encephalopathy in a National Football League Player" was published in the journal *Neurosurgery*. Symptoms of CTE can manifest as dementia, declining cognition, memory loss, balance and speech problems, or Parkinsonism with tremors and lack of coordination. The findings sent the NFL into damage control as they initially tried to discredit claims that a potentially life-threatening condition can develop among players after multiple concussions on the field.

Dr. Wecht said during our conversation about the current research on contact sports: "Nobody to my knowledge says that CTE produces Parkinson's disease. It produces a lot of problems that certainly, in some aspects mimic Parkinson's, but there's no direct relationship between these two. It is a neurodegenerative disease that is not at all rare. . . . The etiology is still unknown . . . Parkinson's does not lead to CTE nor does CTE lead to Parkinson's disease." In Ali's case, Dr. Wecht suggested that "he may have had two separate disease processes. . . . Indeed, most victims of chronic traumatic brain injury suffer what looks more like Alzheimer's disease rather than Parkinson's." Dr. Wecht explained the challenges of diagnosis: "The fact of the matter is that it remains the biggest problem with CTE. How do you make that diagnosis in someone's lifetime? An autopsy confirms the neuropathological basis for these diseases." Postmortem observations by forensic pathologists examining the death of NFL players have confirmed the serious nature of the disease. Dr. Wecht said, "These guys are dying within a few years [of developing CTE]. Muhammad Ali going back . . . thirty-five years since his last fight. That does not fit in with CTE, as far as we are aware."

Aspiring to greatness kept Ali in range of countless concussive blows for far too long. He played by the rules of the sport, which taught him to shake off the heavy daze from punishing blows in seconds. He had been dancing in the crosshairs of massive punches since age 12. Rigorous training in the ring prepared him to bounce back from a knockout blow before the referee counts to 10. Ali described the experience: "When I fight, I get in a half dream. Somebody hits you so hard that you don't know where you are. You see all these lights and your head is swimming and you can't think, and so you drop your hands. Sometimes, they hit me so hard that the alligators start playing the saxophone and the snakes start playing the drums and I don't know what happened. I'm in a half dream."

Research on boxers who experience brain injury from punches to the head prompted some medical organizations to call for banning the sport. The American Academy of Neurology and the American Medical Association argued that brain injury from boxing was an occupational hazard. Many wondered whether Ali's momentous achievements in the sport were worth the cost. Would he have developed Parkinson's had he chosen a different profession? Although the disease strikes a broad cross-section of people, studies on boxers have shown they exhibit higher degrees of brain atrophy than the general population. Researchers have also found that boxing substantially disrupts the chemistry of the brain, leading to a damaging autoimmune response with devastating effects on the central nervous system.

Observers suspected the cells that produce a neurotransmitter called dopamine were dying faster because of the time Ali spent in the prizefighting ring. The champ argued there were no other boxers who showed signs of Parkinson's, so there must have been some other contributing factor. Some fans thought the many blows to the head he endured changed Ali's personality. The public remembers the brash fight-talking prizefighter act, unaware that he was a mild-mannered man in real life: "They see me today as a quiet, soft-spoken, modest man. . . . The truth is, my personality really hasn't changed that much."

Three years after retiring from boxing, in 1984 Ali publicly announced that neurologist Dr. Stanley Fahn at New York University Medical Center had diagnosed him with Parkinson's syndrome. His personal physician, Dr. Dennis Cope, indicated that it was impossible to ignore the possibility that the physical symptoms were repercussions from repeated head trauma sustained in the ring, as chronic damage continues to mount for years after a boxer leaves the sport. Despite his increasing physical limitations from a progressive disease, Ali vigorously campaigned in the charitable fundraising arena without missing a round. Expanding his list of philanthropic causes, his fight plan now included lucrative Celebrity Fight Night fundraisers. Part of the money raised was used to advance Parkinson's research.

In the later years of his exceptional fight career, when Ali was no longer able to dance away from punches, he had to absorb them at a great physical price. Dr. Pacheco acknowledged that the champion's health was an afterthought and "He took some mammoth beatings." He also stated that walking away from the sport sooner, "wouldn't have stopped the Parkinson's. But I think it would not have compounded it as it has." Concussive and sub-concussive blows over the years contributed to chronic brain injury for the King of Heavyweights, who retired at age 39. He recalled, "When I get stunned, I'm not really conscious of exactly where I'm at or what's happening, but I always tell myself that I'm to dance, run, tie my man up, or hold my head way down." But as he told the public, "What I have suffered physically was worth what I've accomplished in life." Maya Angelou implied that we can prevail through the darkest of times in life's journey to reach new heights like the glorious butterfly. "We delight in the beauty of the butterfly, but rarely admit the changes it has gone through to achieve that beauty."

Since Ali was a cultural icon who commanded the world stage, when the truth about the serious symptoms he suffered from brutal physical damage surfaced, the dangers of competitive boxing advanced to the forefront of world attention. Hallmarks of Parkinson's disease began to appear, including worsening tremors, slurred speech, and impaired mobility. Dr. Fahn stated, "My assumption is that his physical condition resulted from repeated blows to the head over time. . . . It is anticipated that his symptoms can be reversed with medication, that he can lead a normal life. . . . Ali's mind is impressively alert and well-oriented."

His wife Lonnie shared a personal perspective on his condition: "it's scary for anybody to experience a physical decline. But when the whole world is watching and so much of your life has been defined by your physical skills, to lose that is very difficult."

Ali stayed on course despite his advancing physical challenges. He followed an extensive travel itinerary throughout most of the year, traveling to numerous countries and even entering war zones to champion humanitarian causes. He was reassured by his devout religious faith: "Every step of the way I believe that God has been with me. And, more than ever, I know that he's with me now." He said, "Every day is different, and some days are better than others, but no matter how challenging the day, I get up and live it. And it is the combination of will and faith that helps me do it."

During his worldwide journey for various causes, Ali traveled to Sudan to meet with President Jaafar Muhammad an-Nimeiry and revisited the country in 1988 to continue raising awareness about the tragic circumstances of famine victims. The challenging pace of his travel itinerary involved appearances in the political spotlight to deliver messages of peace that had a major impact on charitable causes and missionary work. He accepted prestigious honorary degrees, accolades for his statesmanship, and sports awards while spreading faith in Islam around the world. At the New York Stock Exchange, Ali rang the opening bell of the new millennium.

Ali became a powerful influence on the passage of federal laws designed to shake up the boxing establishment, in partnership with the late Arizona senator John McCain. McCain had boxed at the US Naval Academy and grew up worshiping the ring skills of Sugar Ray Robinson. He was responsible for the first boxing bill passed in 1996, the Professional Boxing Safety Act, which mandated state athletic commissions to participate in a national identification system to uniformly honor medical suspensions. He sought to address poor health and safety standards by corrupt promoters and to rein in governing bodies. The subsequent Muhammad Ali Reform Act, passed in 2000, was enacted to protect fighters from ruthless managers selling one-sided contracts that excluded access to affordable health care. After the legislative victory, major safeguards across all states would ensure a higher standard of care. However, on April 11, 1983, *Sports Illustrated* published an article by Robert H. Boyle that said what many in the boxing world believed: "Certainly reform is needed, but no amount of it will eliminate death in the ring."

Before the legislation endorsement, in 1976, Ali publicly disclosed that he would not encourage his children to take up the dangerous sport of professional boxing. He emphasized that the brain is delicate and advocated education over athletic achievement in the prizefighting ring. Dr. Pacheco drove home the point about the need for tighter oversight in the sport: "Almost all ring deaths are preventable. When a guy starts to take a beating, stop the fight. Put it on the scale and tell me which is more important: a thrilling, gruesome fight or a person's life?"

Accepting an invitation to be the final torchbearer for the 1996 Centennial Olympics in Atlanta, Ali astonished the world with star-quality courage in the face of debilitating Parkinson's, radiating with a blazing strength that ignited the night sky. Personal biographer Thomas Hauser observed, "In all likelihood there has never been a time in the history of the Earth when 3 billion people felt love at the same time. But Ali made it happen."

The torch relay for the Centennial XXVI Olympiad was the first to travel through the boundless reaches of space, aboard the Space Shuttle Columbia. The relay around the world involved more than 12,000 torchbearers lighting the way to the Games. Reigning world heavyweight champion and Atlantan Evander Holyfield carried the torch into Centennial Park stadium. The penultimate torchbearer was swimmer and four-time gold medalist Janet Evans, who would finally hand it to another secret athlete, after climbing the stairs to the top of the stage. In a stunning Olympic moment witnessed by some three billion people on the planet, Ali stepped out onto the world stage and Janet passed her flame to his Olympic torch held with trembling hands. Spectators roared, rocking the stadium with fervent cheers honoring the former gold medalist who became the Greatest of All Time. He sent the flickering flame high against the backdrop of the night sky to light the giant cauldron 116 feet overhead. At that moment, Ali ignited a new chapter in his life that inspired countless people, including those with debilitating conditions, by boldly stepping from the shadows. He embodied the spirit of reaching for your dreams with great fortitude despite adversity. Beyond the image of stellar heavyweight champion, he was celebrated around the world that night for his life as a great humanitarian. He believed, "I have never had a more powerful voice than I have now."

Janet Evans was only informed the night before the ceremony that she would transfer the flame to Muhammad Ali. She talked to the press about the emotional moment that was the most inspirational experience of her life. At first, she recalled, "I didn't understand the reverence. I didn't understand it until the stadium started shaking, like an earthquake." She expressed what many learned that night about a champion who had spent a lifetime carrying the torch for altruistic dreams beyond sports excellence: "Passing the Olympic torch to Muhammad to light the cauldron at the Atlanta Games in 1996 was the defining moment of my career, and a memory I will treasure forever, as much as any of the medals I won. As Olympians, our role is to inspire others to achieve their dreams, and no person has ever lived that role more than Muhammad Ali." She realized Ali was a powerful source of inspiration that transcended sports when he continued the fight for a better world beyond the ropes of the prizefighting ring.

Ali impressed many like sportswriter John Saracino, who later said "Parkinson's is no match for Ali." That night, billions witnessed his daring personality, which once enraged opponents with fight-talk, showmanship antics, and exceptional boxing talent. There was a new generation in the audience who had been unaware of Ali's fame more than three decades earlier, during the height of social justice movements in America. Many did not know that he had become a world-famous fighter for the people who promoted peace through a violent decade in the country when bloody battlefields converged from the Vietnam War to Kent State University during student antiwar protests. And that he was the reigning People's Champion when civil rights marches were under-way to the nation's capital and inner-city uprisings raged against oppressive racism across the nation. Spectators cheered for both the golden athletic achievements of a world-class champion and for the way he had demonstrated courage in the face of seemingly insurmountable odds. Two years after reigniting his dramatic impact on the world at the Centennial Games, Ali was named UN Messenger of Peace. He was committed to using his celebrity influence on the long road to achieve equality, peace, and freedom for all.

Award-winning author David Kindred spoke with me about the many facets of a rare superstar who enlightened our world while on the path to greatness in and out of the ring:

> I think he was the greatest athlete that I ever saw. That includes all of the great athletes . . . Michael Jordan, Jim Brown, whoever you want to name . . . and he was in the hardest sport that there is—boxing. It demands more of an athlete than any other game. You're on offense and defense all the time. . . . You have to be able to take punishment and give punishment. As an athlete, then he was beyond compare. As a person, I knew him to be a sweetheart. I think he was a chameleon. He could adapt to any situation. He was a great actor; he was a great storyteller. He could listen to everyone's story and then retell it better than they told it. So, he was a great improvisational comedian.
>
> All of this is in addition to the social justice stands . . . that were hard to take. He took them easily, he never wavered in his convictions on race, on politics, on religion. You knew where he stood . . . so there was great strength of will in that. . . . He was not only a great athlete, but he was a great person. He was a great man and there will never be another one like him. We're taught from a young age that we don't talk

about politics or religion or race, and he talked about all of that all of the time. He was a great teacher in that sense.

He was on the right side of history . . . of course, in the 1960s he was the most reviled man in America. By 1996, when he lit the flame for the Olympics in Atlanta, he was the most revered man in America. To go from reviled to revered was a trip that almost no one except Muhammad Ali could have made. . . . Nothing surprised me about Muhammad. . . .

I always say that the two best heavyweight fighters of all time were Cassius Clay and Muhammad Ali.

During a special ceremony in front of the US Olympic Dream Team III of basketball All-Stars, Ali was presented with a gold medal to replace the one from the 1960 Rome Olympics he had cast into the Ohio River, as the legend goes, to protest discrimination he experienced in Louisville. The moment spoke volumes about the enduring importance of a great champion to millions of people.

Sports Illustrated writer William Nack described Ali as "the most gifted and unforgettable athlete-performer of his time. . . . no stage was ever large enough for his range of expression." After the Games, the global interest in the legendary world champion was reignited, attracting a younger awe-inspired generation and cascading accolades that flowed from around the world. Ali launched a whirlwind travel schedule amidst an inundation of honors, commercial deals, and public appearances. At the Atlanta Games, he would say, "I realized that I had come full circle." In 2002, he lit the Olympic torch to start the 46-state relay involving thousands of people across the nation that ended in Salt Lake City for the Winter Olympics. Then in 2012, Ali was selected as an official flag bearer for the XXX Olympiad in London. His wife Lonnie helped him when he was physically incapable of standing in front of the flag alone at age 70. They had married in 1986, and her love would help him manage the serious challenges he would face in his life after boxing. Dr. Abraham Lieberman, then director of the Muhammad Ali Parkinson Center in Arizona, said, "His Parkinson's got worse, but he had a very devoted family who really treasured him and gave him as much quality of life as you could have." Ali's daughter Hana Yasmeen Ali described his compassion: "He has a kind and open heart and in spite of his physical limitations he continues to use his fame to inspire and uplift all people who cross his path, especially those on the down side of advantage."

12

JOURNEY OF THE HEART

The Daring Adventure

*Muhammad Ali on a Misty Morning Run Near His Dear Lake Training
Camp before the Championship Rematch with Leon Spinks in 1978.
Photograph by Keith Williams / Louisville Courier-Journal*

Muhammad Ali braved rough seas at critical crossroads in his life,
aware of the importance of core guiding principles to fulfill a higher
purpose. Mindful that his decisions would uplift others along the way, he
stated, "I set out on a journey of love, seeking truth, peace, and understanding." The controversial People's Champion made revolutionary choices
over his lifetime and stayed true to his convictions with self-sacrifice in the
face of extreme odds.

Ali gained prominence when the forces of change in America reached
critical mass, rallying greater support for advancing peace, equality, and

justice. He invested wholeheartedly in efforts to empower a spirit of global citizenship. As he achieved greatness in sports, Ali remained relentlessly outspoken about the harsh realities experienced by marginalized people, especially in the African American community. Once reviled for his religious beliefs and refusal to fight in the Vietnam War, over time Ali proved his ability to inspire worldwide alliances. Ali used his celebrity spotlight to advance the idea of self-determination, which would lift countless oppressed lives from the shadows cast by racism. In addition to elevating concerns over unjust inner-city conditions in the struggle for equality across America, he engaged in global peacekeeping missions. The champion was a compelling force behind broad initiatives that addressed critical needs for victims of injustice around the world. Acts of compassionate outreach touched many lives, especially where people suffered hardships from discrimination in American communities and devastation in warring conflict zones abroad. On the world stage, he continued to headline epic fights and bridge distances with understanding in a contentious global arena. The fortitude he demonstrated outside the ring promoting human rights would astound the world beyond his lifetime.

Transcending sports, Ali became a champion of hope for the infinite possibilities to advance our humanity. Both exploring diverse religions and extensive life lessons deepened his self-understanding. He said, "My soul has grown over the years, and some of my views have changed . . . I am still learning." While he expressed respect for different religions, he praised Allah as the almighty greatest, and strove to enlighten others with his message of faith in Islam. Like Mahatma Gandhi, Ali viewed different religions like "different roads converging to the same point." He distinguished between religion and spirituality: "Some things cannot be taught, but they can be awakened in the heart. Spirituality is recognizing the divine light that is within us all. Spirituality helps us achieve self-discipline, forgiveness, and love, which are so essential to a peaceful existence in living among others." Millions of people were drawn to his open spirit, especially in the Islamic world, where he was highly respected as a great humanitarian fighter. His wife Lonnie explained that his "spirituality extends beyond only Muslims in a concern for all people."

British author Norman Giller corresponded with me about Ali's concern for improving the lives of others. They first met in London for the 1963 fight against British champion Sir Henry Cooper. Giller described the rising contender as a mild-mannered young man who took time to see the quality of life experienced among black immigrants in the country:

Away from the cameras, he was quietly spoken, polite and wanted to know about you rather than talking about himself. He was very inquisitive about the way black immigrants were treated in the United Kingdom and requested to be taken to the poorer parts of London to see how they lived. We (fellow sportswriters) took him to Brixton in South London and he was impressed how they had merged with the white community.

In conversations with the immigrants (mostly West Indians) he called them "Brother" and he said how much better they were integrated compared to the worst ghettos in the United States. It was round about the time he was first being indoctrinated by the Black Muslims and within a year he had taken the world heavyweight title from Sonny Liston and had announced that in the future he would only answer to the name Muhammad Ali. By the time I met him in London again (for a world title defense against Henry Cooper at Highbury football stadium in 1966) he had become very political and was about to be put through the mill for refusing to join the U.S. Army. His interest in how the black community in London were treated had shifted from brotherhood to demanding equality. I remember him getting involved with a British civil rights campaigner called Paul Stephenson, and he used to go to schools, particularly in South London, and make impromptu speeches to the pupils about the importance of standing up for themselves and seeking equality.

Coming into the 1970s, when I worked with him as a publicist on several European fights (He needed a PR like Einstein needed a calculator), he had matured and always spoke wisely and with deep passion about how he was using his fame and platform as a boxer to put across his message of freedom, justice, and equality. They were not just empty words. He truly meant them. The Ali I met as a young man and then worked with into his 30s was inspirational and kindly, and spending time in his company made you walk taller and feel that you should follow his example and spread love, understanding and tolerance. The most motivational man to cross my path in many years of mixing with the world's major sports stars. He stood head and shoulders above them all.

The only pity was that he went to the well several times more than was sensible, but he always claimed even when Parkinson's had got hold of him that he was happy with his lot and at peace with his God. All he wanted to be remembered as was somebody who had made the world a better place. He transcended boxing and became more influential and popular than Popes, Kings, Queens and Presidents. For me Ali was and always will be The Greatest.

Throughout his lifetime, tributes seemingly from everywhere praised his tireless service for human rights. He was presented with a multitude of accolades for his worldwide influence beyond sports and his broad impact across cultures, races, and nationalities. He was among the exceptional humanitarians to receive the distinguished German gold Otto Hahn Peace Medal in honor of his courageous stand for peace and humanity.

Ali was present at The Longest Walk from San Francisco to Washington, DC, when Native American demonstrators traveled on foot thousands of miles in July 1978. The march was organized to protest the government threat of unjust legislative proposals that would terminate treaties in order to restrict fishing and hunting rights on traditional tribal lands. He joined forces with the indigenous peoples of America, walking with them into Washington, DC, presenting a powerful cross-cultural spirit of solidarity.

For decades, Ali voiced concerns over the struggles in the African American community, boldly promoting racial pride to encourage progress toward self-determination. A complex dynamic evolved from multiple lines of defense in this community as various groups—including Black Nationalists, the Student Nonviolent Coordinating Committee, the Black Panther Party, members of the civil rights movement, the Black Power movement, and the Organization for Afro-American Unity—organized against racial oppression as their efforts converged to end systemic racism. Through a wide-angle lens, Ali publicly identified the damage from social injustice where prevalent around the world. He kept the focus on our common ground, reinforcing the interrelated oneness of the human spirit that endeavors to prevail in a harmonious world, as expressed by Oglala Lakota Sioux holy man Black Elk:

> The first peace, which is the most important, is that which comes within the souls of people when they realize their relationship, their oneness with the universe and all its powers, and when they realize at the center of the universe dwells the Great Spirit, and that its center is really every-where, it is within each of us.

Ali explored a number of world religions, seeking deeper understanding through various perspectives on faith in God. He said, "There's truth in Hinduism. Christianity, Islam, all religions. And in just plain talkin'. . . . The only religion that matters is the real religion—love." He emphasized the importance of a formal education as an essential part of the lifelong process of attaining self-knowledge. He said, "A man who views the world the same at fifty as he did at twenty has wasted thirty years of his life." He learned broad viewpoints from the people and cultures he encountered during extensive international travels. He was recognized across every continent, from remote villages to urban metropolises. He became a poet laureate at Oxford and received honorary degrees from Ivy League universities. At age 23, lifelong friend Sister James Ellen sent him a letter that further enlightened him about a higher purpose in life: "You will note that Pope Paul prays and bids us all to dialogue with Hindus, Muslims, Buddhists— we are all God's children, and we must love and spread the gospel of love to the world. . . . God bless and protect you ever."

In the book *Soul of a Butterfly*, coauthored with his daughter Hana, Ali mentions the importance of interfaith discussions for deepening understanding about the divine wisdom of different religious traditions: "I understand that there are many paths to God, and I believe Islam is the correct path for me. . . . The day I met Islam, I found a power within myself that no man could destroy or take away. When I first walked into the mosque, I didn't find Islam; it found me." According to Lonnie, he has always been a very spiritual person. He was open to interfaith teachings that impart wisdom from different religious faiths. He believed that "Allah is the Light of the heavens and earth" (Holy Qur'an 24:35) and studied similar verses in the Bible passage, "I am the light of the world." (Holy Bible: John 8:12).

The People's Champion dared to convey a proud African American identity that challenged beliefs perpetuated by white supremacists for generations. Long before the Black Lives Matter movement, Ali refused the marginalized life of an invisible man lost in the fallout of systemic racism destroying lives in America. He defied racist attitudes with his statement, "I am America. I am the part you won't recognize, but get used to me. Black, confident, cocky. My name, not yours. My religion, not yours. My goals, my own. Get used to me."

He encouraged the African American community to believe that greatness is achievable by striving for excellence in all aspects of one's life. When confronting despair in struggling neighborhoods, he passionately promoted a vision of attainable dreams of gold to lift people and inspire a liberating worldview. Ali has been quoted about favoring a daring trajectory: "He who is not courageous enough to take risks will accomplish nothing in life." He offended upholders of the status quo who tried to keep him down. Senator Robert Kennedy shared the cause striving to reverse the destructive riptides of injustice originating from beliefs about racial inequality. Even after his astounding achievements as a world-class champion in the ring, persistent demeaning characterizations from racist viewpoints defined him as a second-class citizen in his own country. Ali fought fearlessly in the vanguard of revolutionary change in America and the world.

Once when reminiscing about the days of his youth, he said, "Every time I look in the mirror, I see that kid from Louisville, Kentucky, staring back at me. His name was Cassius Clay." He demonstrated early a lifelong commitment to caring for others, offering his help to improve circumstances for the less fortunate. After returning home at age 18 with a gold medal from the Olympics in Rome, his compassionate concern for other people was made public when he offered the prize winnings from his first professional fight against Tunney Hunsaker to Kosair Hospital for special needs children. The rising contender for the crown left lasting impressions when he embraced hospitalized children during many visits anywhere around the country. When appearing at medical centers to provide encouragement and empowering inspiration, he proved that the acts of kindness were part of his lifelong chosen path to "elevate souls." As he stunned critics and warmed hearts with his philanthropic efforts, his unwavering convictions, courage, and fortitude captured the most worldwide attention. When he faced harsh judgment, he disarmed the detractors by agreeing, "I'm not perfect . . . I still have things to work out, and I'm working on them."

After going the distance against the US government, during a courageous stand for religious freedom, he became the most famous conscientious objector in the world. His iconic image remained central to revolutionary thinkers rallying a spirit of solidarity during protest movements of the times demanding equal rights and justice. Millions witnessed his transformation into an international hero, who had survived the wrath of the American government for his defiance.

Ali left lasting impressions on many places around the world including his hometown of Louisville. Many of his friendships lasted a lifetime, particularly with Louisville librarian Sister James Ellen, who watched the teenager with great ambition shadowbox through the stacks of books when he worked at Spalding College (then known as Nazareth College) on his way to fulfilling his dreams. For 40 years, she saw his journey of faith bring him closer to God, as he spread the Word in a style that commanded world admiration. Even after his monumental boxing victories made him the most famous man in the world, he continued the relentless fight for human rights in this brilliant spotlight for the rest of his life. After his vast worldwide travels, Ali showed respect for the diverse peoples and cultures that make up our world stating, "I have come a long way since I started boxing. I've traveled all around the world and met all types of people. . . . The goal of our nations should be to work on understanding, respecting our differences, and celebrating our similarities. . . .We should appreciate the beauty in the diversity."

In his later years as a spiritual prizefighter, Ali proved he could go the distance with greater purpose, serving those in need with a sense of infinite possibilities. He had seen both immeasurable wealth and abysmal poverty during his journey to far corners of the world. As he followed his heart in pursuit of an idealistic plan for a better world, he left lasting impressions among millions of people in and out of the celebrity spotlight. His generous spirit touched countless lives from publicized goodwill missions to intimate moments, such as sharing his brand of life-sustaining willpower with a terminally ill child in a private hospital room without fanfare. Ali landed in Connecticut for the special visit after a long transatlantic flight from Zaire in 1974, when the championship fight against George Foreman was briefly postponed. His philanthropic focus and broad vision kept him involved in supporting charitable efforts concerned with health care, bullying, homelessness, old age homes, hunger and poverty, human trafficking, education, and literacy.

He championed causes worldwide, raising millions of dollars with universal impact. He unconditionally wrote personal checks for those in financial hardship regardless of race or nationality. Answering the call from Catholic Sisters during one of his missions around the world, Ali visited a children's polio hospital in Bogotá, Colombia, then supported a mission to deliver tons of humanitarian assistance to Liberian refugees in need of food, clothing, and medicine. Despite his struggles with Parkinson's, he continued his advocacy of humanitarian projects across all hemispheres for hundreds of days each year. He realized, "My greatest accomplishments in life were achieved outside the ring, and my greatest privilege in life was becoming a messenger of peace and love. Because there is nothing as great as working for God."

Ali revealed in *Soul of a Butterfly* that new paths were still unfolding moment by moment on the journey to fulfilling his evolving life purpose. In addition to involvement with goodwill missions and humanitarian aid, he became a powerful influence for the release of political hostages. Before the Gulf War, he traveled to Iraq in 1990 and negotiated the release of 15 American hostages, who safely boarded a flight with him back to the United States. During an interview, one of the hostages, Harry Brill-Edwards said, "I suppose what impressed me most about Ali was the way he cared for everyone. . . . I've always known that Ali was a super sportsman, but during those hours that we were together, inside that enormous body I saw an angel." After Ali's appeals to the Ayatollah Ali Khamenei for the release of Jason Rezaian, held hostage in Iran, the freed journalist said, the prison guards "started treating me in a better way, and I think it brought some doubt to them about the charges against me, and along with that my spirits were really lifted." Nelson Mandela was released from prison after 27 years and Ali met with him during a visit to South Africa in 1993.

The September 11th terrorist attacks shined the global spotlight on Ali once again, as he addressed the public about true Islam. He once expressed, "It hurts me to see what radical people are doing in the name of Islam . . . God is not behind assassins." For decades, he had been distributing autographed Islamic pamphlets, publicly spreading the faith around the world. Ali visited Ground Zero in New York and appeared as a champion for the people on a telethon that raised benefits for the victims of the devastating attacks. He had repeatedly asserted the true nature of Muslims, as America struggled to recover from the widespread damage that occurred in 2001: "There is nothing Islamic about killing innocent people in Paris, San Bernardino, or anywhere else in the world."

Ali was honored by his hometown when Walnut Street was renamed Muhammad Ali Boulevard in 1978. At the city's center, the boulevard will forever be treasured miles dedicated to the remarkable world-renowned champion. It commemorates the place where the glory days of young Olympian Cassius Clay were celebrated in a victory parade after his gold medal performance. Reverend King once marched down this historic street along the West End of town during the struggle for equal rights and justice. In a state known as the "gateway to the South," the street was a dividing line in segregated Louisville, where a seven-block music mecca attracted legends who electrified the nightlife during a vibrant jazz era. The nightclubs, banks, residences and prosperous African American–owned businesses declined before federal urban renewal projects leveled historic blocks, destroying the social dynamic of the community. Ali moved forward with his dream of building a cultural center in the area. In 2005, the Muhammad Ali Center opened its doors on the waterfront to the world, forever changing the city skyline. He observed that there were more rounds to go in the human rights arena to win the coveted prize—peace for the world. Ali expressed the important purpose of bridging understanding through the power of relationships that advance peace and spread love around the world: "As long as I'm alive, I will continue to try to understand more because the work of the heart is never done."

13

A HIGHER PURPOSE

True Riches of Life

*Muhammad Ali Holding Newborn
Daughter Laila, 1978. She Was the
Only Other Champion Boxer in the
Family, Who Became the Second to Win
the Super Middleweight Crown Three
Times and a Light Heavyweight Title.
Photograph by Michael Gaffney
© Michael Gaffney Photo*

Muhammad expressed deep gratitude to his fourth wife Lonnie for bringing together his nine children to celebrate the all-important love of family since their marriage in 1986 until the end of his life. He drew strength from his loved ones, who embraced the heart of this great champion at the center of their lives. He believed, "Material things lose their value over time, while matters of the heart deepen and strengthen with age and wisdom." Years of extensive travel taught him about the ways of the world, providing the insight that helped guide his children through life challenges with a caring father's perspective. Despite the demands of fame in the international spotlight, he was a proud parent who managed to focus his attention on the lives of his seven girls and two boys in different households. His children Maryum, Hana, Laila, Jamillah, Khaliah, Miya, Rasheda, Muhammad Jr., and youngest son Asaad were drawn together by the powerful love for their father. He taught them the virtues of his core guiding principles for living with a compassionate heart. They were encouraged to find purpose in life through good deeds that "pay it forward" in ways that make the world a better place. In passages from the book *Soul of a Butterfly*, he explained that spiritual fulfillment comes from reaching out to enrich others. He taught them that by keeping the needy and less fortunate close to their hearts, they would be closer to God.

When Muhammad's children shared sentiments publicly at the end of his life, it provided a rare intimate glimpse into his family life. The comments confirm that his relationships with his children drew strength from a conscious effort to bring an unlimited measure of love to parenting. His son Asaad with Lonnie expressed the powerful impact of having such a loving father in his life: "You've shown me how to love in ways I didn't know possible. You've shown me how to be brave and courageous in situations beyond my belief! You've taught me so much in the last 25 years—things that will forever be imprinted in my soul." Daughter Khaliah shared, "He was the greatest . . . as a family man, in those personal, intimate ways that only someone's child could know. We've been so incredibly blessed." Muhammad shared his contentment with the abundant love from the children in his life: "when it comes to love, compassion, and other feelings of the heart, I am rich."

Hana, his daughter with Veronica Porché Ali, expressed the depth of her gratitude for how his love helped her find inner peace and solace: "Daddy, you are my constant truth, my strength, my heaven on earth. Thank you for being there for me, thank you for believing in me, thank you for holding my hand in the dark and always standing by me." Hana revealed her feelings about the deep love her father shared with all his children: "His greatness lies in his ability to keep love in his heart through all of the upheavals of life. . . . In my eyes, he was even greater at being a loving father than he was at being a world champion."

Muhammad acknowledged, "It wasn't easy for them to make their own way with such a controversial and public father." His journey into fatherhood began with a family of four (Maryum, Jamillah, Rasheda, Muhammad Jr.) while married to his second wife, Khalilah Camacho Ali. This was a distressing time when government backlash sidelined his career after he admitted to being a conscientious objector against the Vietnam War. As a new father at age 26, Muhammad made a treasure trove of audiotapes that preserved loving memories from private family life. The conversations with his children at various times in their young lives were preserved among his cherished possessions.

He inspired his children to live in the spirit of God and taught them to show compassion, forgiveness, empathy, and openheartedness toward other people. He strongly believed, "The only true happiness comes from honoring God and treating people right." Along with playful jesting that brought joy to his children, serious lessons for living a fulfilling life were also captured on hundreds of recordings. His oldest child, daughter Maryum, shared cherished remembrances of her father, who played the good parent in the home by not being the disciplinarian. He wanted his children to enjoy the best in life. Although her father was often away traveling the world, she said that he effectively impressed upon her the importance of treating people with respect: "We were brought up to believe that God sees everything, and we're just more comfortable when we're doing right." He also taught her: "Honesty, integrity, kindness, and friendship are the true treasures we should be seeking." She added, "He wasn't a perfect person, but I admired how he was with his kids and what he wanted for us. . . ." Muhammad expressed love for his children in ways the 14th Dalai Lama believed should, "Give the ones you love wings to fly, roots to come back and reasons to stay."

The 2014 documentary *I Am Ali*, created by Carla Carter, featured several taped conversations with commentary by both Hana and Maryum about their father's caring touch. The collection of recorded phone conversations proved that a deep father-daughter connection with Maryum was not compromised by the demanding career that separated them during her childhood. At times, the recorder was on without them being aware that their young voices, expressing happy emotions at home, were being taped while he was away. As a parent, Muhammad believed, "It is our job to raise them, and guide them, not control them, and to love them no matter what." Among the many priceless audio diaries, his gentle guidance was captured during a phone conversation with his firstborn Maryum that kept the focus on nurturing a nascent life purpose at her tender age. He asked, "What's your purpose in life . . .?" and she replied, "To make people feel better. To fix people up." Muhammad praised her: "That's good. That's good, Maryum." He was known to travel with these tape recordings as precious cargo that he held in safekeeping until they could be passed on to his children. Author Paulo Coelho wrote, "Remember that wherever your heart is, there you will find your treasure."

Muhammad did his best to protect his children from the unpleasant aspects of negative news headline attention during tumultuous times in America. Maryum described an instance when her father's fame was brought into perspective for her while at school: ". . . there were three people mentioned in the lesson we were doing—Count Dracula, Ronald Reagan, and Muhammad Ali. I looked, and it hit me. . . . Like not long ago, we went to a basketball game at the Los Angeles Forum. And when we left, the whole crowd stood up and gave him an ovation. Or one time, we met Prince. I was excited; I was dying to meet Prince. We got there. Prince was looking at my dad, saying, 'Muhammad Ali, I love you so much!' And I said to myself, 'God this is incredible.'" She knew that people could relate to her father, drawn closer by seeing both his iconic invincible greatness and his relatable human vulnerability in the face of debilitating Parkinson's.

Soul of a Butterfly includes passages written about his greatest attribute, being a father who made his children feel unconditionally loved. He said, "Each of my children is unique and talented in his or her own way. God has blessed me. I'm a lucky man." He wrote about his perspectives on life, philosophy, religion, virtues, and about courageously living through challenges in life with devout religious faith.

The *Louisville Courier-Journal* featured an article by Katya Cengel entitled "Growing Up with The Greatest: Son of Ali," which explored Asaad's thoughts on his famous father. There was an exceptional list of impressive achievements that include Gold Medal Olympian, Sportsman of the Century, Presidential Medal of Honor, Messenger of Peace, and three-time world heavyweight champion. Asaad followed the example set by his father, showing a passion for high achievement in sports excellence with disregard for those who tried to discourage his dreams. He kept the spotlight on his legendary father with an arm tattoo adorned with boxing gloves and the three epic championship dates when The Greatest of All Time was crowned the world heavyweight king. Muhammad, however, stated he did not want his son to pursue a dangerous career in boxing. Instead, Asaad excelled in his own right on the baseball diamond and was drafted for the major leagues (amateur draft) by the Los Angeles Angels. He expressed great admiration for the strong positive attitude his father had shown through challenging difficulties in the fight against advancing Parkinson's.

Ali Entertained Visitors at His Fighter's Heaven Training Camp Built in Deer Lake, Pennsylvania. Daughter Hana Seems Intent on Redirecting the Focus on Herself. Photograph by Rex Larsen | Grand Rapids Press Photo

Asaad's sister Laila, daughter of Muhammad and Veronica, was a very public person who first attracted the celebrity spotlight with her winning athletic talent. Like her famous father, she became a professional prize-fighter who gravitated toward the celebrity limelight, also appearing in numerous media broadcasts in sports and entertainment as a reporter and host. She would not heed her concerned father's warning about the risks of the brutal sport, which damaged even the most gifted fighters. Despite his apprehension, he was poised ringside in support of Laila's athletic ambitions, offering cautious words of advice during her own dangerous ascent. Expected comparisons to her father prompted an acknowledgment that the natural aptitude for boxing runs in the family. However, she brought a unique style to her performance in the ring. At the 21-year-old's 1999 debut, she was welcomed by the town of Verona in New York and would set the record straight about the intense focus on her world-class skills in the fight ring. She said, "My dad never had this much attention on him when he was first fighting." The spotlight shined brightly on Laila's victory by decision over Joe Frazier's daughter, Jacqui Frazier-Lyde, in 2001. She was praised in the boxing world for her championship style, which had an extra special component of inherited DNA greatness proven by her WIBF and WBC super-middleweight belts. After eight years, Laila retired from boxing as an undefeated four-time champion with a record of 24 wins with 21 KOs/TKOs. Her protective father had stayed in her corner of the ring, supporting his daughter through stellar history-making victory rounds.

While raising his children Muhammad continuously remained in the world spotlight, as his growing legacy of love was reciprocated by millions of admirers who cheered for him. Sportswriter John Schulian praised his significance in the world: "He was important in the antiwar movement; he was important in matters of racial pride; he was important in teaching people how to love." His evolving Islamic faith provided a solid foundation as he aimed his sights on plans to spearhead unifying peace efforts around the world. He spoke about the religious conversion that was an awakening to a broader, more universal place of understanding: "When I was young, I followed a teaching that disrespected other people and said that white people were devils. I was wrong. Color doesn't make a man a devil. It's the heart and soul and mind that count." Later in his life, he would state that the most powerful religion that matters is love. The three-time world heavyweight champion had boldly entered retirement, becoming a spiritual prizefighter who promoted compassion and understanding in the world. Muhammad had conquered the prizefighting world, but discovered his true happiness comes from religious devotion and worshipping God. Aspiring for greatness in new arenas by courageously extending his reach in world affairs, he would always remind others it was guided by faith in God at the helm.

The love of family and winning the admiration of friends were among Muhammad's most important concerns in life, far surpassing the privileges afforded by his wealth or fame. Despite heavy odds, he persevered through tough seasons of change throughout his lifetime with a bold personality and all-embracing heart that disarmed his fiercest rivals and gained the respect of admirers in far corners of the world. Strong bonds of friendship, self-sacrifice, and unconditional acts of kindness when courageously sheltering others from dangerous political storms were major themes of his life. Muhammad's brother, Rahaman Ali said, "He was there for everyone. All walks of life. There wasn't anyone he wouldn't help . . . I am so proud to have been able to call him my brother."

One of those friendships was an unbreakable partnership with corner-man Angelo Dundee, which lasted over half a century from the start of their team debut in 1960. The bold-spirited young Cassius Clay celebrated a style that redefined standards in the professional prizefighting world. There were thousands of training hours spent together at the 5th Street Gym in Miami. Dundee braved the ascent with him through unprecedented rounds of achievement against the toughest class of professional heavyweight prizefighters. Muhammad was protective of Dundee, especially when fight promoters and vigilant Nation of Islam brethren challenged his place of importance beside the champion. The admired trainer was in Muhammad's corner until 1981, going the winning distance with the unique champion for two decades, across thousands of intercontinental miles to capture three world heavyweight crowns. Renowned as a great motivator with a penchant for psychological warfare, Dundee coached the talented 18-year-old through an astounding ascent to become the "Greatest of All Time." Dundee said, "When he started to go crazy, predicting the round in which he would score a knockout and all that, I realized that I had not only a great champ on my hands but also a fighter who was going to change history." In 1992, Dundee was applauded around the world for his impact on the sport of professional boxing when inducted into the International Boxing Hall of Fame. Since their final rounds by 1981, the most admired partnership in boxing has remained a hallmark in sports history, and a treasured relationship in the hearts of two lifelong friends. Angelo Dundee felt, "It would be nice if people remember me as Muhammad Ali's trainer, but it's more important to me to be Muhammad's friend."

Hometown Louisville friend and boxer Jimmy Ellis was the world heavyweight champion in 1968, a year after Muhammad was banned from the ring for refusing to be inducted into the army. His career had a tough start, and he often went without pay after competitive bouts. Muhammad always looked out for friends, and Ellis was one of the many fighters who benefited from his kindness. In the lonely, cruel fight business and long after, Ellis shared that Muhammad was a dear friend who helped him through tough times. As lifelong friends they were able to call on each other anywhere and any hour of the day or night.

Muhammad's professional relationship with trainer Drew "Bundini" Brown was another ray in the bright spotlight emanating from the champ's corner of the ring. Beginning in 1962, his voice amplified the fight action, shaking the rafters as he raised the roof with passionate emotions that echoed well past the final rounds of Muhammad's golden age. It was impossible to ignore the shoutouts heard during hundreds of sparring rounds and at fight venues around the world. Bundini accentuated the power of each stinging jab to reinforce Muhammad's winning mindset. From the opening bell, he cheered, pleaded, cried, praised, warned, proclaimed, prayed, and preached, as if hurling emotional lifelines in the ring to empower his warrior. When

Bundini was hospitalized in 1987, after a tragic accident left him near death, Muhammad came to his bedside at Good Samaritan Hospital in Los Angeles. They held hands, sharing their thoughts on meeting again on roads paved with gold in heaven. When Bundini said "I'm . . . so . . . sorry . . . champ," Muhammad placed a hand on his cheek and kissed his forehead, leaving no doubts about his place in the heart of the champion.

Ken Norton defeated Muhammad after throwing a jaw-breaking punch that led many to doubt the great champion would make it on the comeback trail to regain the title. In 1986 Norton suffered traumatic injuries from a car accident that left him lying unresponsive in the hospital. When Muhammad performed a levitation trick at his bedside, hospital staff noticed Norton's healthy physical reaction to the entertainment. In the documentary *Facing Ali*, Norton expressed gratitude to Muhammad for the chance to share one of the most brilliant spotlights in heavyweight boxing history. But for Norton, the impact went much deeper: "He saved my life, he saved my career. I can't thank him enough for the chance to fight him."

Muhammad first met freelance photojournalist Howard Bingham in Los Angeles when the 20-year-old faced George Logan for his 13th fight in April 1962. Bingham had never heard of undefeated prizefighter Cassius Clay, but began to closely follow the rising star from the first round of his victory match. Bingham's intimate photographic collection, which includes around 500,000 images taken over five decades, chronicles the extraordinary life of the legendary champion and his record-breaking achievements. He was with Muhammad during the years of his legal trouble with the government. Those images reveal a world champion in defeat, after devastating political backlash involving a draft evasion conviction followed his refusal to step forward at the induction ceremony. Each picture speaks a thousand words, and the collection captures many perspectives in the life of a freedom fighter, son, father, husband, friend, heroic humanitarian, crowned prizefighter, and compassionate People's Champion.

Back in Louisville, as an ambitious teenager reaching for the stars, Muhammad had spent time working in the college library with the Sisters of Charity of Nazareth. Sister James Ellen was the director of library services and curator of rare books at Spalding University (formerly Nazareth College). She hired him to work in the library at the start of what would become a 40-year friendship. She encouraged the soft-spoken sophomore from Central High School to learn by reading the books, as he shadow-boxed through the library stacks floating on dreams of glory. When he was discovered sleeping on the library table, she marked the spot with a sign stating "Cassius Slept Here." This honorable mention drew attention to a time from 1957 to 1958 when one of the greatest boxers of all time was already making memorable impressions. Sister James Ellen was later photographed in the June 19, 1963 *Louisville Courier-Journal* covering her eyes in dismay when she heard on the radio that Cassius was knocked to the canvas by Henry Cooper.

Another sister at the library read poetry to him, which inspired further interest in the art of rhyming verse that would characterize the promotional style of the rhapsodizing poetic prizefighter. Sister James Ellen recalled her perspective about the rising world champion saying, "I think he showed at that time the beginnings of what he was later to be—a world interest, who lived life to the fullest." The nuns displayed his early trophies at the college, then continued to follow his superstar career through decades to come. When he came back in town an Olympic champion, he made sure to show the sisters his gold medal, the ultimate prize from the games in Rome. These kindred spirits with compassionate hearts had an unbreakable bond over decades until her passing in February 2001 at age 96, after 70 years as a member of the Sisters of Charity of Nazareth. Sister James Ellen liked the title People's Champion, which she said perfectly defined his crowning achievement as "a spokesperson for the good of all people."

Shortly after he was diagnosed with Parkinson's, Muhammad's wife Lonnie joined him on travels as they took bold steps together in the humanitarian arena. The pace was vigorous, and she knew firsthand the challenges of his demanding schedule. She said, "There are times I'm not sure I'd survive without Howard (Bingham), particularly when Muhammad is traveling. Last year [1989], Muhammad went to Senegal, Yugoslavia, Saudi Arabia twice, Geneva, Pakistan, London, and India. Muhammad took sixty-seven trips inside the United States, and was on the road for 236 days." Bingham interviewed Muhammad for *Reader's Digest* in 2001, when the champ said he faced life's circumstances without regrets. When asked what Lonnie's devotion meant in his life, his answer was, "Everything." Bundini Brown felt that Muhammad would end up the lone survivor after killing everybody off with his hectic travel itinerary. Lonnie agreed to an extent saying, "I don't know about Muhammad living forever, but as far as killing the rest of us, Bundini might have been right." Worldwide travel would be scaled down in later years, when they enjoyed more serene private moments together at home.

Muhammad allowed only rare glimpses into his personal family life. He never felt compelled to discuss intimate details about the women in his life, including his four wives. However, during his last marriage to Lonnie, at a time when his demanding professional boxing career had ended, she

Library Director Sister James Ellen with Sisters of Charity of Nazareth and Cassius Clay. Photograph by James Drake 1963 / Getty Images

stepped into the spotlight to publicly express his thoughts, opinions, and feelings as it became more and more difficult for him to speak. While he continued to impress with new chapters of his life, advancing Parkinson's forced him into the toughest personal fight he ever faced. Lonnie went the distance by his side during the final years of his celebrated life as he pursued a higher purpose, including conflict resolution missions as a United Nations Messenger of Peace. The honor bestowed on him kept him apprised of troubling global events that raised real-time concerns necessitating urgent action. Together they traveled to conflict zones, wrote letters to world leaders recommending humanitarian solutions, and used the media spotlight to encourage compassionate dialogue for an effective diplomatic process.

During the breakup of his third marriage to Veronica in 1985, Muhammad went through a period of emotional and physical hardship, as health changes from the onset of Parkinson's syndrome brought new worries to the forefront. At his request, Lonnie played an important role in managing circumstances in the life of the iconic champion, first as a caring friend who always obtained his consent on final decisions. Sports journalists knew she was committed to preserving her husband's legacy. He and Lonnie shared a loving partnership and a commitment to becoming a powerful force for positive change in the world. This endeavor would come full circle with architectural plans to redirect sights on the Louisville skyline, where a young fighter's dreams of glory were born. Muhammad pursued his broader vision of greatness that ultimately encompassed humanitarian pursuits driven by a passionate concern for making lives better in a troubled world. He said, "Money and riches don't mean anything to me. I don't care about being a rich individual. I'm not living for glory or for fame. You have it today; tomorrow it's gone. I have bigger plans than that."

14

PRAYER FOR THE WORLD

The Muhammad Ali Center

*Visitors Walk by a Photograph of Muhammad Ali outside
the Muhammad Ali Center in Louisville, Kentucky.
Photograph by David Goldman / Associated Press*

Inspired by dreams of a better world, Muhammad and Lonnie Ali envisioned a cultural exchange center that would promote education programs, core life principles, and humanitarian endeavors. After working with Fortune 500 companies to fund the project and award-winning architects to design a blueprint, the monumental Muhammad Ali Center was created to celebrate the honored native son, making a bold statement on the skyline of Downtown Louisville. He expressed his all-important purpose in life: "It is my prayer that Muslims and all people who seek peace come together and work to make our world a better place for ourselves and our children."

Since his youth on training runs across the city's historic Walnut Street, Muhammad would have an indelible impact on the road to greatness that was renamed Muhammad Ali Boulevard. The location symbolizes miles of hard-won inroads to civil rights, where Reverend Martin Luther King Jr. led protests that challenged the unjust boundaries of the inner-city segregation line. This was the place where Cassius Clay later celebrated childhood dreams of glory during a victory parade that touched the hearts of many admirers after winning Olympic Gold. The soul of a community had been displaced when destructive urban renewal plans closed many African American businesses on old Walnut Street. After the world heavyweight champion reached the final crossroads of his career with his third title win in 1978, the landmark Muhammad Ali Boulevard signified the start for the revival of the district. The honor reflected his achievements beyond sports excellence as a champion of the greater humanitarian fight. Shortly before the Muhammad Ali Center opened to the public in November 2005, *Sports Illustrated* dedicated the Sportsman of the Year Legacy Award to Muhammad for his extraordinary sportsmanship, leadership, and humanity. The announcement was followed with the decision by President George W. Bush to present him with a Presidential Medal of Freedom, the highest civilian honor in the United States. *Sports Illustrated* had focused on the course of a phenomenal champion since the 1960 Olympic Games. As he became a global media sensation, they publicized his accomplishments in the world of boxing and beyond the ring. In 2015, the sports magazine paid tribute to him in the October 5 article by Tim Layden entitled, "The Legacy of the Greatest Still Grows," his 39th appearance on the cover.

At the Muhammad Ali Center, the heart of a champion beats through gallery exhibits highlighting important aspects of a remarkable life. The multicultural center preserves his legacy, enlightens the spirit, and inspires dreams that enrich lives. He fulfilled a special purpose stating: "For many years I have dreamed of creating a place to share, teach and inspire people to be their best and to pursue their dreams." Muhammad promoted an ideal vision that people could transcend differences to create unity around the world. Exhibits with the theme of six core principles (Confidence, Conviction, Dedication, Giving, Respect, and Spirituality) teach essential values to live by for a compassionate journey through life. They are designed to guide and encourage great achievements aligned with helping others. Visitors are invited to discover their best potential by attending seminars, roundtable discussions, and learning sessions that educate on an array of topics. Through community engagement, the Center shares Muhammad's legacy that emboldens people to discover a higher purpose in life. Interactive exhibits are intended to strengthen self-esteem and encourage visitors to strive for excellence. Videos replay the champ's epic record-breaking fights for visitors to experience the talent of an exceptional athlete.

The Center is committed to promoting Muhammad's vision of greatness for humanity, in the hope that it will rally others to go the distance to help advance the cause for creating a better world. He returned to his birthplace as a champion of peace to design a place that would become an international gateway to realizing groundbreaking dreams of gold for humanity. Muhammad's prayer to end devastating conflict in the world would be answered by empowering the next generation of leaders to find diplomatic solutions through open channels of communication supported by the Center.

The architectural design begins to tell the story of Muhammad's achievements in his remarkable lifetime. Preserving the Muhammad Ali legacy is the primary mission of the center, located at an urban riverfront location. At the highest level, View Pointe Hall shines brightly on the water with a night light that illuminates powerful currents of change surging with dreams of peace for humanity. Shining like a lighthouse that guides voyagers to safe passage, it leads us toward an endless horizon of possibilities on the journey to enrich our world.

The exterior facade is designed with terra cotta mosaic images of the three-time world champion shadowboxing in his prime. This powerful architectural element delivers a knockout punch on the eastern Louisville skyline, recalling the great achievements of the champion who conveyed the idea that nothing is beyond reach when pursuing your dreams. Adhering to six core principles, he charted the course toward life-changing goals with unwavering purpose motivated by the catchphrase, "Be Great: Do Great Things." A skylight illuminates an atrium surrounded by galleries, a library, a theater, and learning centers. The six-story building shines in the cityscape by night from the glass-enclosed summit, casting reflections on the waterfront from the heart of a champion.

Muhammad and his wife Lonnie conceived of architectural elements for the Center that light the way to downtown Museum Row. Private donors and blue-chip Fortune 500 companies invested in the building, and architectural teams from New York City to Louisville were involved with the $80 million design concept. Visible from the exterior, a three-story copper-colored cone represents the Olympic torch, enclosing an elliptical staircase

Celebrity Fight Night X on March 27, 2004. Lonnie and Muhammad Ali.
Photograph by Carlo Allegri / Getty Images

symbolic of the champion's ascent to sports excellence that began in 1960. Muhammad's six core principles have been featured on colorful sidewalk banners leading to the entrance. An open pavilion invites visitors to learn the story about his extraordinary life, and the skywalk over Sixth Street becomes a pathway to multicultural experiences when international visitors gather near the reflecting pool. With his world-renowned face on the mosaic-tiled wall to the west, Muhammad attracts people arriving at the epicenter of inspirational dreams. The exhibited archives reveal the heart, mind, soul, and dreams of a courageous champion, inviting us to boldly advance through a lifelong journey of self-discovery. The story of triumph unfolding from the main galleries inspires visitors to reach for astounding new heights.

Muhammad's life as portrayed at the Center inspires people to bridge distances and lift others by paying it forward in ways that can set a course toward world unity. Muhammad was aware that each act of kindness can advance momentous currents of change leading to the promise of a better day. The Center has promoted the cross-cultural exchange of ideas through educational forums that broaden awareness about our interrelated oneness, ensuring that Muhammad's mission has an impactful platform for the future. The Muhammad Ali Center makes us aware of the essential part we all play in the survival of our planet. As former UN assistant secretary-general Robert Muller said, "In the final battle for this planet between the forces of evil and good, no one can be neutral."

The exhibits celebrate the crowning accomplishments of a lifetime. As President Barack Obama acknowledged, "Muhammad Ali shook up the world. And the world is better for it. We are all better for it." Muhammad had ambitious plans for the Center, envisioning it as neutral territory, where global ambassadors could be invited to mediate contentious political issues in person or teleconference calls. In addition to museum exhibits there are seminars, workshops, and lectures by experts on various topics to enlighten and provide a basis for open discussions. The Center emphasizes the importance of international cooperation when dealing with critical situations that affect our lives on a worldwide scale. An overriding concern for the well-being of future generations keeps news headlines in focus on the Center's website, including progress on geopolitical decisions by world nations to avert a global warming disaster.

The Center's exhibits present Muhammad's achievements, courage of conviction, personal beliefs, and passionate concern for all people around the world. A key takeaway is the power of an individual daring voice to advance revolutionary ideals that ignite a spirit of unity and peace to enrich our world. Exhibit themes have included social justice, civil rights, the pursuit of excellence, and the impact of altruism. The Golden Rule, treating others as one would wish to be treated, emanates through the galleries from the compassionate heart of a renowned champion.

The Center upholds Muhammad's mission—a better world for future generations and discovering meaningful purpose in life—by preserving his legacy through events, programs, and projects that capture the imagination of young people. Thousands of children from different countries were invited to share personal messages that have been transferred onto square tiles placed prominently on a wall display. The children's Hopes and Dreams Wall encourages children to exchange imaginative thoughts expressed in pictures and words about the world we share. Spanning 55 feet in length, the 10-foot-high display was arranged with 5,000 3 x 3-inch wooden tiles that capture the spirit of young dreamers from 140 countries in 19 languages. Visitors experience a cross-cultural dreamscape that conveys promising hopes for our world.

The March 1964 issue of *Sports Illustrated* featured an enlightening exchange between Muhammad and children: "'Who's the greatest?' he asked the children, and they shouted his name. 'Who upset the world?' And they shouted his name. 'I am the champion.' He told them, 'and that means all of us are champions. I showed you now what we can do. We can do anything.'"

> Hold fast to dreams
> For if dreams die
> Life is a broken-winged bird
> That cannot fly. . .

Dreams by Langston Hughes

The Center also has outreach programs for inner-city communities. The Muhammad Ali Youth Association provides opportunities to discover a talent for sports, as just one avenue for achieving greatness. Workshops and lecture forums for personal growth address important topics to empower the youth and adults to achieve a better quality of life. Through the website, the Center's reach extends around the world on topics that promote understanding, service to others, compassion, and harmony. Programs target issues from health care and nutrition to protection of women and children from abuse, and they promote involvement with an international community in the fight for equality, justice, and freedom. In the first year of cultural exchange forums, the center arranged an international teleconference between local children and youth from overseas to discuss the problem of bullying.

A program sponsored by the Center called *Generation Ali* was created to inspire a youth movement of empowering voices around the world that encourage solidarity in the struggle for social justice. The cause focuses on the next generation of leaders who are young and "young at heart," encouraging them to spearhead efforts to advance human rights, civil liberties, and global citizenship. In addition, the Center awards education scholarships to those striving for personal excellence with strength of conviction to advance the ideal of world unity.

U-Give, a program in which young philanthropic advocates join forces and dedicate time to help others, is designed to encourage the youth across America to participate in volunteer community service opportunities. Special scholarship awards are given to students emulating Muhammad, who focus on peace initiatives from the perspective of global citizenship. Young people also receive awards for demonstrating a quality of life guided by the six core principles. In conjunction with the United Nations, the Center raises awareness about plans for humanitarian aid in places throughout the world ravaged by conflict and human suffering. Social reform, environmental protection, religious freedom, respect for the individual, and economic justice are all priority concerns. Education, so important to Muhammad, is emphasized in the provision of tutoring services to help the youth reach their best potential. The Center empowers visitors to believe they can achieve their dreams like Olympic gold medalist Wilma Rudolph who said, "Never underestimate the power of dreams and the influence of the human spirit. We are all the same in this notion: The potential for greatness lives within each of us."

Lifelong friend Howard Bingham was the honorary curator of photography and served as a board member until his passing on December 15, 2016. Having taken photographs of Muhammad around the world for decades, he was responsible for creating an extremely rich intimate photographic collection. It has been said that the size of the archived collection is so large that it could fill gallery walls on every continent. The images span a broad spectrum of moments in Muhammad's dynamic journey through life as a heavyweight champion, father, son, husband, humanitarian, messenger of peace, devout Muslim, freedom fighter, People's Champion, and citizen of the world. More than 50 years in the life of the spiritual prizefighter were brought into focus through Bingham's lens. He said, "I had the greatest of all blessings because my eye and my camera became the world's window to this magnificent life." Legendary images of a man, once called the most famous person in the world, continue to have a profound impact on millions of admirers to this day.

Video galleries capture his unrivaled athleticism in motion. The glory days of prizefighting are celebrated with historic footage of the world champion fighting the best heavyweights in a golden age of boxing. They also feature awe-inspiring interviews with opponents he faced in the ring, who honor his impact on the sport and on their lives in the spotlight of the three-time world champion. Sir Henry Cooper, George Chuvalo, Joe Frazier, Ernie Terrell, George Foreman, Ken Norton, Ron Lyle, Leon Spinks, and Larry Holmes among others have all shared their memories of facing Muhammad in the championship ring.

The Muhammad Ali Center reminds us that the power to connect with each act of kindness can overflow a reservoir of compassion that enriches the world. Muhammad believed, "Regardless of how small or how large the purpose, you were all born to accomplish a certain purpose. And it is knowing of that purpose that enables every soul to fulfill it."

The Center has a humanitarian exhibit with an interactive timeline charting important events that led Muhammad around the world. Videos, descriptive displays with photographs and articles document his worldwide endeavors in the humanitarian arena. Muhammad also embarked on daring global missions and joined forces with humanitarian groups to eliminate suffering and strife in the world. On one occasion, he personally delivered food and medical supplies to Cuba during the US embargo against the Fidel Castro regime. He was partnered with the Disarm Education Fund and Direct Relief International for this mission, when he took action to deliver over $1 million worth of medical supplies to Cuba in 1998. For a lifetime of service to others, he earned many honors and accolades including the Arthur Ashe Courage Award in 1997, given to Muhammad for courageously transcending sports after profound humanitarian contributions and demonstrating the strength of his convictions despite adversity.

As a freedom fighter who changed perceptions about the African American experience, he rebelled against a culture of racial subjugation that denied access to civil liberties and living the American Dream. He was included on the list of "100 Most Important People of the Century" by *Time* magazine in 1999, and President Bill Clinton presented him with the Presidential Citizens Medal in 2001. In 2012, he was the recipient of the Philadelphia Liberty Medal in honor of his lifetime dedication to humanitarianism, social activism, and selfless giving for philanthropic projects around the world.

In 2014, the Center inaugurated the Muhammad Ali Humanitarian Awards, recognizing influential politicians, celebrities, and private citizens awarded for their tireless lifetime advancement of altruistic initiatives. The event honors bold centers-of-influence responsible for having a crucial impact in the world. Honorees have included Eunice Kennedy Shriver, founder of the Special Olympics, and Harry Belafonte, a world-famous singer and celebrity activist involved for decades in promoting social justice. The awards drew international attention to Congolese national Rose Mapendo fighting for gender equality and Tanvi Girotra of India, who was recognized for leading an international organization fighting against human trafficking.

The humanitarian focus and ideals of Muhammad's legacy preserved by the Center bring together powerful humanitarians from around the world. Awards are presented to honor the greatness of these courageous global leaders who have demonstrated their commitment to continuing the Muhammad Ali legacy. The Humanitarian Awards evening hosted annually by the Center recognizes those who have profoundly embraced one of Muhammad's six core principles, which guide action plans that widen a circle of love and compassion around the world. The hand-blown glass awards are embossed with Muhammad's fingerprints to symbolize his widespread enduring mark on the world. The evening recognizes the efforts by individuals deeply committed to benefiting the lives of others within their communities and throughout the world. The awards recognize the accomplishments of individuals who have demonstrated altruistic acts of self-sacrifice and fortitude against obstacles they encounter while changing the world. In addition, the Center has a Lifetime Achievement Award for individuals making significant lifelong inroads toward peace, social and economic justice, human rights, freedom, and global citizenship. Former president Jimmy Carter was one recipient honored as a crusader in the struggle for peace.

The Humanitarian Awards are categorized according to the six core principles promoted by Muhammad Ali:

The Confidence Award honors individuals who possess self-assurance in their ability to undertake the cause to better the world.

The Conviction Award is granted to those taking an unwavering courageous stand to uphold their beliefs in the face of opposition.

The Dedication Award recognizes individuals who have been steadfast in their efforts to accomplish a humanitarian mission.

The Giving Award is for generous outreach without the expectation of anything in return.

The Respect Award gives tribute to those who encourage a sense of self-worth and self-esteem in the process of uplifting other people.

The Spirituality Award celebrates those who approach life with an open heart and sense of reverence for all creation that is greater than themselves.

From the landmark Center, Muhammad promoted interfaith understanding through festivals and high-profile visits with religious and spiritual leaders. This award-winning Center teaches us about Muhammad as well as ourselves through an experience that encourages us to pursue our dreams. Visitors explore galleries that guide them through a lifetime of groundbreaking events. The Center reinforces the idea that we all have an important role to play in creating a promising future for our planet.

Although he was a world heavyweight prizefighter in a violent sport, Muhammad demonstrated tender concern for children of the world, embracing their nascent dreams with compassion. According to Lonnie, Muhammad's true legacy evolved from a practice expressed by the commandment "Thou shalt Love thy neighbor as thyself." He ardently welcomed people into his heart with loving kindness and true concern for their well-being from the very start of his journey to greatness. He continues to inspire a worldview that unites people through an enlightened view of our essential interrelated oneness. As travelers arrive at the Muhammad Ali

Louisville International Airport, his impressive landmark presence and the global importance of his legacy are apparent at this international transportation hub even before reaching the Center.

His most important world title as the People's Champion was achieved through perseverance, conviction, kindness, patience, loving spirit, generosity, faith, and ability to make significant contributions in the quest to fulfill his Islamic duty. Lonnie explained that Muhammad was a generous soul with enormous heart whose "greatest present" to the world was the "Gift of Love." He raised millions and donated prizefighting winnings to philanthropic causes to support a host of organizations in his decades-long fight to change the world including:

Make-A-Wish Foundation
Athletes For Hope
BeatBullying
Boys & Girls Clubs of America
Buoniconti Fund To Cure Paralysis
Celebrity Fight Night Foundation
HELP USA
Human Rights Action Center
Jeff Gordon Children's Foundation
Keep Memory Alive
Michael J. Fox Foundation
Muhammad Ali Center
Muhammad Ali Parkinson Center
NAACP
Parkinson Society Maritime Region
Project A.L.S.
Save the Children
Special Olympics
The HollyRod Foundation
The Miami Project
UNICEF
Watering Seeds Organization

At the end of his life, a huge audience of mourners numbering an estimated billion people viewed his memorial service in hometown Louisville from all corners of the world, knowing his incomparable love of people, mission to end suffering in the world, and investments in the welfare of others around the globe. His high-profile fights brought world attention for the first time to developing world cities including Kinshasa, Manila, and Kuala Lumpur. His extensive work promoted service to others across vast continents at an astounding pace that would otherwise span several lifetimes. With strong religious faith, courage, and resilience, he lit a torch that continues to be held high, leading the way out of the dark despondency that plagues our world. With a heroic spirit, he followed his heart through life struggles, remaining undeterred by danger in the quest to change misfortunes and impart hope that humanity will prevail on the journey toward peaceful unity.

Since the doors to the Muhammad Ali Center opened, it has advanced strategic partnerships that regularly welcome young international visitors. It supports academic achievement through various international outreach initiatives and youth leadership development programs. The spotlight is directed on alleviating poverty and feeding the hungry, as well as honoring and empowering global humanitarian leaders striving to lift spirits and rebuild lives. The Center teaches principles of tolerance, advocates for social and economic justice for the poor, and promotes understanding across cultures, while preserving the legacy of a great champion in and out of the ring. Through the Muhammad Ali Center, the legendary Messenger of Peace endeavored to fulfill great dreams for the world: "I hope that one day all nations great and small will be able to stand up and say we lived in pursuit of peace for all. Maybe then there will come a day when instead of saying, 'God bless America' or, 'God bless some other country,' everyone will say, 'God bless the world.'"

15

UNIVERSAL IMPACT

The Legacy of Muhammad Ali

The Ali Universe: Aerial View of Ali vs. Liston II 1965
Photograph by Neil Leifer / Getty Images

When Muhammad Ali embarked on a journey of peace and love, the expanding universe seemed to embrace a bold new star, who brightened many lives. As a child, he gazed at the infinite sky with innocent wonder, feeling he was destined for a special purpose in life. The young man became the most recognized celebrity on the planet by turning the boxing ring into a world stage with his commanding winning spirit. Fans around the world shouted, "Muhammad Ali is the greatest!", praising the extraordinary fighter who electrified the sport of professional heavyweight kings with unprecedented impact. The compassionate heart of this champion held a deep concern for the well-being of all people. He followed a spiritually enlightened path with unwavering faith, teaching others that the indivisible oneness of the human journey lived with compassion would lead to a brighter tomorrow. Beyond the spotlight of the brutal championship ring, he continued to shake up the world with spiritual prizefighting in new arenas. Inspired by a vision of greatness with a higher purpose beyond sports, his humanitarian missions have enriched lives in a troubled world. He said, "Boxing was just a means to introduce me to the world."

Muhammad's legendary fame and great compassion had universal impact. It transcended race, politics, religion, and opened doors to welcoming hearts on every continent. Maya Angelou observed, "His impact recognizes no continent, no language, no color, no ocean. . . . Muhammad Ali belongs to all of us." The champion defined his stature in the world: "I just don't think another fighter will ever be followed by people in every country on the planet. You can go to Japan, China, all of the European, African, Arab and South American countries, and, man, they know me."

As an outspoken advocate for self-determination, he inspired the pursuit of great personal achievements, reaching especially deep into the heart of the African American community. Many agreed with biographer Thomas Hauser: "He wasn't just a standard-bearer for black Americans. He stood up for everyone." The wide impact of his life's mission reflected great courage and fortitude in the face of seemingly impossible odds. Muhammad was celebrated by many as the most transcendent American sportsman of any era. The world admired his persevering strength and sacrifice for his religious beliefs to an extent beyond compare. He was a multifaceted icon who achieved greatness by breaking through fiercely enforced racial barriers to living the American Dream.

Muhammad had a tremendous love for people and remained approachable in a world community that honored the greatest sports figure of the 20th century. As the People's Champion, his compassionate commitment to end suffering in the world led him to accomplish more than seemed possible in a single lifetime. Despite the progressive effects of Parkinson's, his worsening condition did not interfere with an extensive travel itinerary to fulfill his mission. He continued to visit many countries throughout the course of many months each year. People could relate to a vulnerability revealed by his health struggles in ways that brought them closer to this remarkable man. Muhammad battled Parkinson's until his passing on June 3, 2016, in Scottsdale, Arizona, from septic shock complications at age 74. Michael J. Fox praised Muhammad as more than a boxing champion: "Muhammad was a true legend—a champion in the boxing ring, and a champion for millions of Parkinson's families. We looked up to him as an example of grace and courage in the face of great challenges. He will be missed."

During his lifetime, before the advent of social media networks that broadcast news instantaneously to millions, Muhammad became a superstar. His world-class boxing record was only the start of a legendary lifetime of accomplishments in and out of the fight ring spotlight. Belgian boxer Jean-Pierre Coopman described what many who faced him in the ring experienced. He said, "Everybody forgets I was the European heavyweight champion. Nobody talks about that. But everybody asks me questions about the Ali fight, wherever I go in Belgium. . . . It was a defining moment not only of my career but of my life." British champion Sir Henry Cooper told anyone who was listening that his proudest moment was sharing the ring with Muhammad Ali.

Still, there are people who believe he was far from an exemplary hero, including *Ghosts of Manila* author Mark Kram, who said that "Ali was no more a social force than Frank Sinatra." The perspective overlooks the extent of Muhammad's impactful humanitarian outreach. Biographer Thomas Hauser responded, "I disagree with Mark Kram's thesis that Ali was not an important social or political figure." Kram had a different tone when expressing his thoughts about the heart of the People's Champion: "But peer closer and there is much more . . . his genuine humanity that is felt more than heard, his caring about what happens to us all." Paul Fichtenbaum, *Sports Illustrated* group editor, described the incomparable champion: "Muhammad Ali was a singular force of athletics, humanitarianism and social equality unlike anyone in our history. He was a fighter and a champion, yet many of his most important victories came outside the ring."

American social activist and former Georgia state senator Julian Bond observed, "It's hard to imagine that a sports figure could have so much political influence on so many people." Impressions from President Barack Obama were profound: "I grew up having my identity shaped by what he accomplished." Muhammad's far-reaching impact is ever unfolding as essays written by new generations of young scholars, poets, and authors power the sails of a legendary story about this daring champion for peace.

Challengers in the ring respected the legend known for his compassionate heart, whose promotional fight-talk matched the devastating sting of his lightning-quick jabs. However, Muhammad put his talents in perspective: "I'm quite honored that so many still consider me 'The Greatest.' However, there were many who went before me who paved the way, and my idol will always be Sugar Ray Robinson, who was, and remains, one of the best pound-for-pound fighters to have ever lived in this century." More importantly his vision of greatness prevailed, as he challenged the status quo in the fight arena for justice. Boxing champion Sugar Ray Leonard said, "what he stood up for, what he believed in, what he sacrificed for—gave every minority hope."

After already leaving a tremendous impact on the world from the prizefighting ring, Muhammad continued to influence the momentum of change with a vision that placed people in need first. He covered different territories visiting universities for lectures on race relations, meeting with international dignitaries, and spending time with people on inner-city streets just shooting the breeze. During his vast world travels, he witnessed the cruel disparity between astronomical wealth of the privileged few and unspeakable poverty among subjugated people. The world took notice as he braved the ascent to conquer mountains of injustice and descended to dangerous racist strongholds of the Deep South taking on more than seemed humanly possible. He engaged in many undisclosed good deeds, avoiding unwanted fanfare. Despite all the accolades, he never claimed to be perfect. Instead, he struck a balance when facing his critics, stating that he was just like everyone else. He impressed people from all walks of life, extending a helping hand wherever the need arose, and invited the world to join him. He set the record straight about his intentions all along by stating, "I'm not looking to be idolized." Award-winning actor Dustin Hoffman, who learned the true nature of the champion, said, "fighting was his profession, peace was his passion and grace is his essence." Muhammad described his lifelong purpose in straightforward terms, "Fighting injustice, fighting racism, fighting crime, fighting illiteracy, fighting poverty, using this face the world knows so well, and going out and fighting for truth and different causes." Muhammad expressed his accomplishments in a down-to-earth manner explaining, "Maybe I was great in the ring, but outside of boxing, I'm just a brother like other people."

Sports Illustrated editor Paul Fichtenbaum said, "His legacy defines the very best of who we aspire to be." Football star Jim Brown described his importance: "He represented what a man should be in an America that's free because he made people accept him as a man, as an equal and he was not afraid to represent himself in that way." Former UN ambassador Andrew Young explained the impact of the unique international icon who, in his words, encouraged young African American men "to respect themselves and express their rebellion constructively. . . ." American Blues musician B. B. King was also inspired by the People's Champion: "By Ali standing up as he did, that gave many of us much more courage. That gave us much more hope than we'd ever had before."

Muhammad continued to be honored decades after his retirement from the ring when he received the Amnesty International Lifetime Achievement Award. During a ceremony at the Muhammad Ali Center the year before his death, *Sports Illustrated* announced the decision to rename the Legacy Award after Muhammad, which is given to athletes who uphold the ideals of sports excellence, human rights activism, and philanthropy. The honor is now called the "Sports Illustrated Muhammad Ali Legacy Award" in honor of a treasured legend. Muhammad said, "When I was featured on my first *Sports Illustrated* cover in 1963, it was a huge turning point in my career. Ever since, *Sports Illustrated* has been there documenting the great moments of my life, a relationship that has been integral to both my boxing career and now, the mission and legacy of the Muhammad Ali Center. It's a relationship for which I will always be grateful." He also received an honorary doctorate of humanities from Princeton University, honorary degree from Columbia University, Hollywood Walk of Fame Star, and was named *La Gazzetta Dello Sport* Athlete of the Century for its 120th anniversary issue in Italy. Twenty years into retirement, the Oscar-winning film *When We Were Kings*, directed by Leon Gast, documented his epic victory over world champion George Foreman when he regained the heavyweight crown. In addition to the inundation of honors for his involvement with missions that deliver humanitarian aid to hundreds of thousands around the world, a species of rose was even named after him.

Alex Wallau, former ABC Sports president, described the life of the champion lived to the fullest: "He's done more in his first forty-nine years than most people could do in forty-nine lifetimes. He's reached heights that almost anyone would envy." In 2016, Muhammad passed away leaving the brilliant light of his fighting spirit shining worldwide. Media featured the powerful icon of freedom during weeks of honored remembrances. His first professional opponent, Tunney Hunsaker, once expressed feelings about the rising star in the sport voiced by many who followed: "I'm honored, highly honored, to have been the first person Muhammad Ali fought in his professional career . . . it was an honor for me to have been in the ring with him. . . ." His impact would resonate with people from many other arenas in the world. Kareem Abdul-Jabbar said admiringly, "I may be 7'2" tall but I never felt taller than when standing in his shadow." President Obama described the essence of an astounding life when he said, "This is the Muhammad Ali who inspires us today—the man who believes real success comes when we rise after we fall; who has shown us that through undying faith and steadfast love, each of us can make the world a better place. He is, and always will be, the champ."

As he traveled the world, Muhammad was aware that every opportunity for a meaningful personal connection could advance understanding around the globe. Indigenous rights activists Chief Sidney Hill (Chief spiritual leader of the Haudenosaunee, Iroquois Confederacy), and Oren R. Lyons (Faithkeeper of the Turtle Clan for the Onondaga Nation) both spoke with deep respect at his memorial service. Chief Hill said Muhammad was "a man of compassion who used his great gifts for the common good. His spirit has a clear path to the creator." Chief Lyons comforted mourners: "He brought a light into this world—my world, our world. And that light will shine a long, long time."

When the tragic news of his death was announced, social media lit up with instant messages from all over the world revealing the enormous impact of losing the legendary champion. On June 5 after his passing, 15,000 to 20,000 bees swarmed a tree outside the Muhammad Ali Center. The *Louisville Courier-Journal* article mentioned that the bees were directly across from a billboard photograph of Muhammad with the world-renowned mantra, "Float like a butterfly, sting like a bee," leading many to believe his spirit had returned to the iconic landmark.

Muhammad's passing united millions of people from diverse faiths and nationalities as they tuned in to the seemingly endless tributes for the life of the Greatest of All Time, including extended around-the-clock coverage by the ESPN American Sports Network. In several interviews, his children publicly shared the deeply emotional experience of watching the final breaths of their father's life. Daughter Hana publicly revealed the final moments with her father and son Asaad shared faith in a divine homecoming: She said, "All of us were around him hugging and kissing him and holding his hand, chanting Islamic prayer. All of his organs failed, but his HEART wouldn't stop beating. For 30 minutes . . . his heart just

Ali Visits a Children's Play Group in Notting Hill, London.
Photograph by R. McPhedran / Getty Images

kept beating. No one had ever seen anything like it. A true testament to the strength of his Spirit and Will." His son Asaad said, "No one will ever touch this earth the way you did. God . . . took back one of his kings!"

Muhammad's dynamic life was a brilliant beacon of inspiration, casting light on bold humanitarian dreams for a peacefully united world. Robert Muller believed, "In the end it is those who have dreamed and loved the strongest who will survive the longest in the memory of humanity." Many times, he defied long-held unjust attitudes with a compassionate devotion to following an enlightened spiritual path. Biographer Thomas Hauser said, "His true legacy is that we're better people in a better world because he has been here." Bob Dylan, whose songs publicized the injustice prevalent throughout the 1960s, described Muhammad's awe-inspiring impact: "He instilled courage and fear in the hearts of men, and remains the firelight of strength and independence." The powerful force of his humanitarian impact left deep impressions, moving millions of people around the world who mourned the death of an unforgettable champion. Caesars Palace Las Vegas and Madison Square Garden in New York were among the famous American sports arenas that paid tribute to the world-class heavyweight champion on their marquees. Social media networks displayed heartfelt condolences from around the world that expressed gratitude for a beloved champion who promoted a bold spirit of compassion throughout his lifetime:

Thomas Meeker, president and CEO of Churchill Downs, Inc., said, "Today, football may have its Namaths and other stars; basketball has its Chamberlains, Birds and Jordans; baseball has its Babe Ruths. And boxing has Cassius Clay. But humanity has Muhammad Ali."

Basketball All-Star Kareem Abdul-Jabbar said, "Today we bow our heads at the loss of a man who did so much for America. Tomorrow we will raise our heads again remembering that his bravery, his outspokenness, and his sacrifice for the sake of his community and country lives on in the best part of each of us."

Former welterweight Champion and senator Manny Pacquiao said, "We lost a giant today. Boxing benefited from Muhammad Ali's talents but not nearly as much as mankind benefited from his humanity."

Major League Baseball star Henry "Hank" Aaron said, "For a guy to be that big and move the way he did; it was like music, poetry, no question about it. And for what he did outside the ring, Ali will always be remembered. When you start talking about sports, when you start talking about history; you can't do it unless you mention Ali. We've lost a giant in Muhammad Ali."

Dr. Ferdie Pacheco from Team Ali said, "Some people leave no mark on the world, some leave life changing legacies. Ali was one of those—the best. We live in a much darker place for his passing."

Lennox Lewis, three-time world heavyweight champion, said that Muhammad was, "a giant among men. Ali displayed greatness in talent, courage, and conviction that most of us will never be able to truly comprehend."

America's Olympic and Paralympic athletes from Team USA posted, "#TheGreatest."

On June 10, 2016, Ambassador Attallah Shabazz delivered a eulogy expressing the deep unbreakable bond of brotherhood between Muhammad and her father Malcolm X: "Muhammad Ali was the last of a fraternity of amazing men bequeathed to me directly by my dad . . . who my dad loved as a little brother 16 years his junior, and his entrusted friend." She closed with a quote from her father, "May we meet again in the light of understanding."

Muhammad's widow, Yolanda "Lonnie" Ali, eulogized the spirit of the cherished humanitarian champion: "Muhammad was not one to give up on the power of understanding, the boundless possibilities of love and the strength of our diversity. He counted among his friends people of all political persuasions, saw truth in all faiths and the nobility of all races. . . ."

His daughter Rasheda Ali-Walsh also memorialized her father, speaking at his funeral in Louisville: "May you live in paradise free from suffering. You shook up the world in life, now you are shaking up the world in death. No one compares to you Daddy. You once said, 'I know where I'm going and I know the truth. And I don't have to be who you want me to be. I am free to be who I am.' Now you are free to be with your creator. We love you so much Daddy. Until we meet again . . . fly, butterfly . . . fly."

Muhammad wanted the world to know:

> I would like to be remembered as a man who won the heavyweight title three times, who was humorous and who treated everyone right. As a man who never looked down on those who looked up to him, and who helped as many people as he could. As a man who stood up for his beliefs no matter what. As a man who tried to unite all humankind through faith and love. And if all that's too much, then I guess I'd settle for being remembered only as a great boxer who became a leader and a champion of his people. And I wouldn't even mind if folks forgot how pretty I was.

A Bicycle Hangs in Tribute to Muhammad Ali.
Photograph by Jessica Able June 2016 / The Record

A red and white bike hangs at the entrance of Spalding University
Columbia Gym in tribute to the ambitious 12-year-old Cassius Clay,
whose journey to greatness began with a bike ride to town. He shadowboxed
with dreams of Olympic gold at the gym and would become the greatest
heavyweight champion of all time named Muhammad Ali.

NOTES

FOREWORD

1. Norman Giller is a renowned, British-based sports historian who has more than 100 published books. He became firm friends with Muhammad Ali after they met in 1963 during a prizefighting venue in London. As his publicist for several European fights, he knew that Muhammad also fought to make the world a better place.

CHAPTER 1

Page 3 Before I won . . .
Muhammad Ali with Hana Yasmeen Ali, *Soul of a Butterfly: Reflections on Life's Journey* (New York: Simon & Schuster, 2004), 94.

Page 4 His mind . . .
Thomas Hauser, *Muhammad Ali: His Life and Times* (New York: Open Road Integrated Media, 1992), 10–11.

Page 5 You want to be . . .
Muhammad Ali and Richard Durham, *The Greatest: My Own Story* (New York: Random House, 1975), 46.

Page 5 My mother . . .
Ali with Ali, *Soul of a Butterfly*, 26.

Page 5 Although, at times . . .
Ibid., 24.

Page 6 popping off . . .
Thomas Hauser, *Muhammad Ali: A Tribute to the Greatest* (New York: Pegasus Books, 2016), 146.

Page 6 I encouraged him . . .
Bob Waters, *Miami Herald Sunday Magazine*, June 4, 1967.

Page 6 Once I found . . .
Ibid.

Page 6 it has been characteristic . . .
Mark Collings, ed., *Muhammad Ali: Through the Eyes of the World* (New York: Sky-horse Publishing, 2007), 358.

Page 6 Hi, my name is . . .
Jon Saraceno, "Ali-Dundee Duo," *USA Today* Sports, *Ali 1942–2016: Remembering a Champion, Civil Rights Activist, American Legend*, June 27, 2016, 17.

Page 7 He was a very energetic . . .
Bucktin, Christopher, "Muhammad Ali's Childhood Best Friend Reveals What a True Legend He Really Was," mirror.co.uk, June 5, 2016, https://www.mirror.co.uk/sport/boxing/muhammad-alis-childhood-best-friend-8120926.

Page 8 white devils
Hauser, *Muhammad Ali: His Life and Times*, 91.

Page 8 irredeemable racism
Marqusee, Mark. *Redemption Song: Muhammad Ali and the Spirit of the Sixties* (New York: Verso, 2005), 57.

Page 9 He was different . . .
William Nack, "Young Cassius Clay," *Sports Illustrated*, June 19, 1992, www.si.com/boxing/2015/09/23/muhammad-ali-childhood-cassius-clay-louisville-si-vault.

Page 10 the best American . . .
Hauser, *Muhammad Ali: His Life and Times*, 18.

Page 10 Louisville Lip
Ibid., 43.

Page 11 he was so shy . . .
Ibid., 20–22.

Page 11 I knew . . .
Evan Fanning, "50 Stunning Olympic Moments No. 17: Cassius Clay Wins Gold in 1960," *The Guardian*, March 7, 2012, www.theguardian.com/sport/london-2012-olympics-blog/2012/mar/07/stunning-olympic-moments-cassius-clay.

Page 12 Tell your readers . . .
David Kindred, "TSN Archives: Muhammad Ali Will Always Be the Greatest," sportingnews.com, September 19, 2021, www.sportingnews.com/us/boxing/news/

tsn-archives-muhammad-ali-will-always-be-the-greatest/2kgiryrasg4u183j6g0p7g
6ko.

Page 12 La Perle Noire

Naomi Wilcox-Lee, "Wilma Rudolph—'The Fastest Woman on Earth'," April 17, 2014, https://sheroesofhistory.wordpress.com/2014/04/17/wilma-rudolph-the -fastest-woman-on-earth/sheroesofhistory.wordpress.com.

Page 12 I would be . . .

Barbara Summers, ed., "Wilma Rudolph," in *I Dream a World: Portraits of Black Women Who Changed America* (New York: Stewart, Tabori and Chang, 1989), 140.

Page 14 He was good . . .

A. J. Liebling, "Poet and Pedagogue," *New Yorker*, March 3, 1962, www.newyorker .com/magazine/1962/03/03/poet-and-pedagogue.

Page 14 the loudmouth from Louisville....

Stefan Fatsis, "The Sports Writer Who Hated Muhammad Ali," Slate.com, June 6, 2016, https://slate.com/culture/2016/06/the-new-york-times-arthur-daley-never -stopped-hating-muhammad-ali.html.

Page 14 Some of us . . .

Huston Horn, "Eleven Men Behind Cassius Clay," *Sports Illustrated*, March 11, 1963, https://vault.si.com/vault/1963/03/11/the-eleven-men-behind-cassius-clay.

Page 15 Age of Cassius Clay

Angelo Dundee and Bert Randolph Sugar, *My View from the Corner: A Life in Boxing* (New York: McGraw-Hill, 2008), 92.

CHAPTER 2

Page 17 I'm young . . .

Hauser, *Muhammad Ali: His Life and Times*, 54.

Page 17 heir apparent . . .

Huston Horn, "Eleven Men Behind Cassius Clay," *Sports Illustrated*, March 11, 1963, https://vault.si.com/vault/1963/03/11/the-eleven-men-behind-cassius-clay.

Page 18 the king . . .

Sugar Ray Robinson and Dave Anderson, *Sugar Ray* (New York: Viking Press, 1970), 348.

Page 18 Robinson could deliver . . .

Ron Flatter, "The Sugar in the Sweet Science," Special to espn.com, www.espn .com/classic/biography/s/Robinson_ Sugar_ Ray.html (March 14, 2022).

Page 18 Robinson can always . . .
  "Sport: Businessman Boxer," *Time*, Vol. LVII, no. 26, 60, June 25, 1951, https://time.com/vault/issue/1951-06-25/.

Page 18 You don't think . . .
  Thomas Hauser, *The Black Lights: Inside the World of Professional Boxing* (Fayetteville: University of Arkansas Press, 2000), 29.

Page 18 He didn't bend . . .
  Hauser, *Muhammad Ali: His Life and Times*, 460.

Page 19 It's very hard . . .
  Jahanzeb Tahir Aziz, "Muhammad Ali, the Greatest Boxer of All Time . . . Now On Twitter!," tribune.com.pk, March 2, 2014, https://tribune.com.pk/article/20870/muhammad-ali-the-greatest-boxer-of-all-time-now-on-twitter.

Page 19 See how pretty . . .
  Ali and Durham, *The Greatest: My Own Story*, 412.

Page 20 butterfly . . . with busy . . .
  Jonathan Eig, *Ali: A Life* (New York: Houghton Mifflin Harcourt, 2017), 115.

Page 20 Float like . . .
  Hauser, *Muhammad Ali: His Life and Times*, 63.

Page 20 Dance! . . .
  Ali and Durham, *The Greatest: My Own Story*, 282.

Page 21 no prizefighter . . .
  Martin Kane, "The Art of Ali," *Sports Illustrated*, May 5, 1969, https://vault.si.com/vault/1969/05/05/muhammad-ali-art-boxing-strategy.

Page 21 The Greatest
  Norman Giller, *The Ali Files: His Fights, His Foes, His Fees, His Feats, His Fate* (Sussex: Pitch Publishing, 2015), 10.

Page 21 My wife . . .
  David Remnick, *King of the World: Muhammad Ali and the Rise of an American Hero* (New York: Vintage Books, 1999), 113.

Page 21 heavyweight Sugar Ray
  Ibid., 112.

Page 21 he could hit . . .
  Sean Gregory, "Why Muhammad Ali Matters to Everyone," TIME.com, June 4, 2016, https://time.com/3646214/muhammad-ali-dead-obituary/.

Page 22 . . . he'd be the first . . .
  Angelo Dundee Interview by Helmut Sorge, "The Best Ali Is the One We Never Saw," in Benedikt Taschen, ed., *Greatest of All Time: A Tribute to Muhammad Ali*, 150.

Page 22 Those experts . . .
Giller, *The Ali Files*, 55.

Page 22 I smoothed Clay . . .
Nick Thimmesch and Charles Parmiter, "Muhammad Ali: The Dream," TIME. com, March 22, 1963, https://time.com/3537815/muhammad-ali-dead-the -dream/.

Page 22 I got him . . .
Ibid.

Page 22 Dundee gave me . . .
Ibid.

Page 23 Champions aren't made . . .
Karl Evanzz, *I Am the Greatest: Best Quotations from Muhammad Ali* (Kansas City, MO: Andrews McMeel Publishing, 2002), 11–12.

Page 23 Float like . . .
Hauser, *Muhammad Ali: His Life and Times*, 131.

Page 23 I worked with him . . .
Shirley Povich, "Clay to Be Champ for Long Time Pastrano Says," *Louisville Courier-Journal*, March 7, 1964.

Page 23 Cassius was one . . .
Dundee and Sugar, *My View from the Corner*, 79.

Page 24 He taught me . . .
Hauser, *Muhammad Ali: His Life and Times*, 463.

Page 24 is the most important . . .
Dundee and Sugar, *My View from the Corner*, 78.

Page 24 great natural talent
Hauser, *Muhammad Ali: His Life and Times,* 463.

Page 24 he would have been . . .
Ibid.

Page 24 It's the repetition . . .
Jeff Johnson, "Muhammad Ali in His Own Words: Six of His Best Quotes to Live," nbcnews.com, June 4, 2016, www.nbcnews.com/news/nbcblk/remembering-muhammad-ali-six-quotes-pack-punch-n585571.

Page 25 You were born . . .
James Baldwin, *The Fire Next Time* (New York: Vintage, 1992), 7.

Page 25 Clark will fall . . .
Giller, *The Ali Files*, 27.

Page 26 I showed tonight . . .
  Ibid., 36.

Page 26 Besmanoff must . . .
  Bob Velin, "Fight by Fight: Muhammad Ali's Legendary Career," usatoday.com, June 4, 2016, www.usatoday.com/story/sports/2016/06/04/muhammad-ali-fight -by-fight career/85341622/.

Page 26 I showed . . .
  Giller, *The Ali Files*, 33.

Page 26 I have the fastest . . .
  Ibid., 39.

Page 26 Letter from Cassius Clay to Sr. James Ellen Huff in 1961.
  Spalding University Library Archives.

Page 27 Letter from Sr. James Ellen Huff to Cassius Clay on October 11, 1961.
  Spalding University Library Archives.

Page 28 Hold your right . . .
  Giller, *The Ali Files*, 42.

Page 28 I've refereed the best...
  Ibid, 42–43.

Page 28 Now everybody's . . .
  Ibid., 57.

Page 28 Sonny Banks . . .
  Ibid., 43.

Page 28 My strategy . . .
  Ali with Ali, *Soul of a Butterfly*, 119.

Page 29 This kid is something . . .
  Giller, *The Ali Files*, 18.

Page 29 Now I want Fraud . . .
  Ibid., 54.

Page 29 I know what it takes . . .
  Ibid., 49.

Page 29 He's brainier . . .
  Giller, *The Ali Files*, 58.

Page 29 He won't last . . .
  Ibid., 57.

Page 30 If he stands . . .
Dean Walter Myers, *The Greatest: Muhammad Ali* (New York: Scholastic Paperbacks, 2001), 46.

Page 30 He throws punches . . .
Giller, *The Ali Files*, 61.

Page 30 Hello tomato red . . . Goodbye Mr. Jones!
Ibid., 63.

Page 30 a marksman
Hauser, *Muhammad Ali: His Life and Times*, 37.

Page 31 moral responsibility . . .
Martin Luther King Jr. "Letter from Birmingham Jail," April 16, 1963, https://lib eralarts.utexas.edu/coretexts/_files/resources/texts/1963_MLK_Letter_Abridged .pdf.

Page 31 Justice too long . . .
Ibid.

Page 31 moral issue
Mark K. Updegrove, "Why JFK Decided to Embrace Civil Rights as a 'Moral Issue' in 1963," abcnews.go.com, June 11, 2020, https://abcnews.go.com/Politics/ jfk-decided-embrace-civil-rights-moral issue1963/story?id=71172778.

Page 32 If they put . . .
Giller, *The Ali Files*, 64.

Page 32 Now for that big . . .
Ibid., 69.

Page 32 People tell me . . .
"C. Marcellus Clay Esq.," sportsillustrated.com, October 6, 1963, www.si.com/ boxing/2015/09/24/cassius-clay-henry-cooper-london-vault-jun-10-1963.

Page 32 I'm not even . . .
"Muhammad Ali vs. Henry Cooper (First Meeting)," BoxRec.com, https:// boxrec.com/media/index.php/Muhammad_ Ali_ vs._ Henry_ Cooper_(1st_ meet ing) (March 14, 2022).

Page 32 It ain't no jive . . .
"'E Said 'E Would And 'E Did," sportsillustrated.com, July 1, 1963, https://vault .si.com/vault/1963/07/01/e-said-e-would-and-e-did.

Page 32 jab and move!
Giller, *The Ali Files*, 67.

Page 33 sleight of hand
Stephen Brunt, *Facing Ali, 15 Writers, 15 Stories* (Guilford, CT: Lyons Press, 2004), 40.

Page 33 gamesmanship
Dundee and Sugar, *My View from the Corner*, 97.

Page 33 people said I cut . . .
Mark Collings, ed., *Muhammad Ali*, 121.

Page 33 dream street
Hauser, *Muhammad Ali: His Life and Times*, 49.

Page 33 Clay was out . . .
Giller, *The Ali Files*, 70.

Page 33 hit me harder . . .
Robert Edwards, *Henry Cooper—The Authorised Biography* (London: John Blake Publishing, 2012), 179.

Page 33 the fastest . . .
Collings, ed., *Muhammad Ali*, 78.

Page 33 the exception . . .
Ibid., 78.

Page 33 Ali rode the crest . . .
Hauser, *Muhammad Ali: His Life and Times*, 156.

Page 34 Tell them . . .
"Mahalia Jackson Prompts Martin Luther King, Jr. to Improvise 'I Have a Dream' Speech," www.history.com, August 28, 1963, www.history.com/this-day-in-history/mahalia-jackson-the-queen-of-gospel-puts-her-stamp-on-the-march-on-washington (March 14, 2022).

Page 34 will one day . . .
King, "'I Have a Dream' Speech, in Its Entirety," Npr.org, January 18, 2010, www.npr.org/2010/01/18/122701268/i-have-a-dream-speech-in-its-entirety.

Page 34 I have a dream . . .
Ibid.

CHAPTER 3

Page 36 He should be . . .
Nick Tosches, *The Devil and Sonny Liston* (New York: Little, Brown and Company, 2000), 165.

Page 36 I didn't have . . .
Dundee and Sugar, *My View from the Corner*, 105.

Page 36 The only way . . .
Bob Mee, *Ali and Liston: The Boy Who Would Be King and the Ugly Bear* (New York: Skyhorse Publishing, 2011), 170.

Page 36 You big ugly bear . . .
Giller, *The Ali Files*, 72.

Page 36 The punches . . .
Hauser, *Muhammad Ali: His Life and Times*, 67.

Page 36 Do you think . . .
Alex Haley, *The Autobiography of Malcolm X* (New York: Random House, 1964), 354.

Page 36 when you get . . .
Hauser, *Muhammad Ali: His Life and Times*, 67.

Page 36 I'm always nervous . . .
David Kindred, *Sound and Fury: Two Powerful Lives, One Fateful Friendship* (New York: Free Press, 2006), 70.

Page 37 You can't punch . . .
Hauser, *Muhammad Ali: His Life and Times*, 463.

Page 37 I am the greatest . . .
Darren Rovell, "Muhammad Ali's 10 Best Quotes," espn.com, June 3, 2016, www.espn.com/boxing/story/_/id/15930888/muhammad-ali-10-best-quotes.

Page 37 too ugly . . .
Giller, *The Ali Files*, 76.

Page 38 The biggest thing . . .
Mee, *Ali and Liston*, 173.

Page 38 I'll hit Liston . . .
Hauser, *Muhammad Ali: His Life and Times*, 51.

Page 39 I've been telling . . .
Mee, *Ali and Liston*, 196.

Page 39 I feel . . .
Miami Daily News, February 24, 1964.

Page 39 Float like a butterfly . . .
Hauser, *Muhammad Ali: His Life and Times*, 63.

Page 39 Blabber Mouth will . . .
David Remnick, "American Hunger: The Invention of Muhammad Ali," *New Yorker*, October 12, 1998.

Page 40 I can't see . . .
Dundee and Sugar, *My View from the Corner*, 117.

Page 40 I want the world to know there's dirty work afoot!
Ibid., 118.

Page 40 Forget the bullshit
Hauser, *Muhammad Ali: His Life and Times*, 69.

Page 40 This is for the big one, son . . .
Dundee and Sugar, *My View from the Corner*, 118.

Page 40 like a little kid . . .
Ibid., 119.

Page 40 could hit you . . .
Ibid.

Page 40 I'm gonna upset . . .
Ibid., 120.

Page 40 Wait a minute! . . .
Hauser, *Muhammad Ali: His Life and Times*, 71.

Page 41 I must be the greatest . . .
Ibid., 72.

Page 41 Sister James Ellen Huff Congratulation Letter to Cassius, February 26, 1964
Spalding College Library Archives.

Page 41 Cassius Clay is a . . .
Alicia Coleman, "What's in a Name: Meet the Original Cassius Clay," TIME.com, June 10, 2016, https://time.com/4363225/original-cassius-clay-muhammad-ali/.

Page 41 I know where . . .
Hauser, *Muhammad Ali: His Life and Times*, 75.

Page 42 Any upheaval . . .
Baldwin, *The Fire Next Time*, 9.

Page 43 worthy of all praises . . . most high
"The Life of the Greatest," June 5, 2016, cbsnews.com, www.cbsnews.com/news/the-life-of-the-greatest/.

Page 44 on this pilgrimage . . .
"Racial Equality and Islam," February 9, 2018, https://imam-us.org/racial-equality-in-islam.

Page 44 as a result . . .
George Breitman, ed. Malcolm X, *Malcolm X Speaks: Selected Speeches and Statements* (New York: Grove Press, 1965), 58.

Page 44 But always I must . . .
Alex Haley and Malcolm X, *The Autobiography of Malcolm X*, 349.

Page 45 I still say the kid . . .
Giller, *The Ali Files*, 76.

Page 45 he thought that Ali . . .
Collings, ed., *Muhammad Ali*, 85.

Page 45 There is nothing . . .
Karl Evanzz, *I Am the Greatest*, 28.

Page 46 How long . . .
Martin Luther King Jr., "Our God Is Marching On!", Montgomery, Alabama, March 25, 1965, The Martin Luther King, Jr. Research and Education Institute, Stanford University, kinginstitute.stanford.edu, https://kinginstitute.stanford.edu/our-god-marching (March 14, 2022).

Page 48 I believe . . .
Malcolm X, *By Any Means Necessary (Malcolm X Speeches & Writings)* (New York: Pathfinder Press, 1992), 190.

Page 48 It is a time . . .
Lori Grisham, "Quotes: Half a Century After His Death, Malcolm X Speaks," usatoday.com, February 19, 1965, www.usatoday.com/story/news/nation-now/2015/02/21/malcolm-x-anniversary-death/23764967/.

Page 48 unconquered . . .
"Eulogy Delivered by Ossie Davis at the Funeral of Malcolm X," February 27, 1965, www.malcolmx.com/eulogy/ (March 14, 2022).

Page 48 Many will ask . . .
Ibid.

Page 49 Turning my back . . .
Ali with Ali, *Soul of a Butterfly*, 93.

Page 49 It is most unfortunate . . .
Sister James Ellen Huff Letter to Mrs. Clay, May 18, 1965, Spalding College Library Archives.

Page 49 Your contribution has made inroads . . .
Ibid.

Page 50 Phantom Punch
Dundee and Sugar, *My View from the Corner*, 129.

Page 50 Anchor Punch
Wallace Mathews, "The Punch Missed 'Round the World," *New York Post* Sports, nypost.com, May 25, 2001, https://nypost.com/2001/05/25/the-punch-missed -round-the-world.

Page 50 a perfect right-hand . . .
Collings, ed., *Muhammad Ali*, 416–17.

Page 50 It didn't make . . .
Giller, *The Ali Files*, 79.

Page 51 I have nothing but contempt . . .
Myers, *The Greatest*, 54.

Page 51 No contest . . .
Stephen Koepp and Neil Fine, eds., *Ali: The Greatest 1942–2016* by Robert Lipsyte (New York: Time Inc. Books, 2016), 72.

Page 51 Floyd would be smart . . .
Gilbert Rogin, "Rabbit Hunt in Vegas," *Sports Illustrated*, November 22, 1965, www.si.com/boxing/2015/09/24/muhammad-ali-floyd-patterson-las-vegas.

Page 51 a lot of people . . .
Collings, ed., *Muhammad Ali*, 126.

Page 51 I never fought . . .
Hauser, *Muhammad Ali: His Life and Times*, 135.

Page 51 They're all afraid
Greenfeld, ed., "Sports Illustrated Tribute to Muhammad Ali 1942–2016," Back Cover.

CHAPTER 4

Page 53 I have nothing . . .
Caroline Linton, "Muhammad Ali Quotes on Justice, War and Racism," splin-ternews.com, June 4, 2016, https://splinternews.com/muhammad-ali-quotes-on -justice-war-and-racism-1793857266.

Page 54 Sister James Ellen Huff Letter to Muhammad, March 22, 1966
Spalding College Library Archives.

Page 55 damn fast . . .
Hauser, *Muhammad Ali: His Life and Times*, 143.

Page 55 The greatest Ali . . .
Ibid., 155.

Page 55 You have disgraced . . .
Ali and Durham, *The Greatest: My Own Story*, 313.

Page 55 What's my name?
Myers, *The Greatest*, 58.

Page 55 wonderful demonstration . . .
Hauser, *Muhammad Ali: His Life and Times*, 159.

Page 55 using my slave . . .
Ibid., 157.

Page 56 There is no one . . .
Murray Rose, "Floored in 4th, Zora Folley Kayoed in 7th by Flashy Champion," *Gettysburg Times*, March 22, 1967.

Page 56 He's smart . . .
"Zora Folley ranks Muhammad Ali as No. 1," *Sports Illustrated* (Staff), April 10, 1967, https://vault.si.com/vault/1967/04/10/zora-folley-ranks-muhammad-ali-as -no-1.

Page 56 As Muhammad Ali puts . . .
Andrew Wolfson, "Muhammad Ali Lost Everything in Opposing the Vietnam War. But in 1968, He Triumphed," *Louisville Courier-Journal*, February 19, 2018, www.usatoday.com/story/news/2018/02/19/1968-project-muhammad-ali -vietnam-war/334759002/.

Page 57 Why should they . . .
Marqusee, *Redemption Song*, 214.

Page 57 In your struggle . . .
Ibid., 213.

Page 57 No matter what . . .
Erin Blakemore, "Martin Luther King, Jr. and Muhammad Ali's Surprising Secret Friendship," biography.com, January 29, 2021, www.biography.com/news/martin -luther-king-jr-muhammad-ali-friendship.

Page 57 I am proud . . .
Marqusee, *Redemption Song*, 219–20.

Page 58 He has an absolute . . .
Greenfeld, ed., "'I Am Not Worried About Ali'" by Bill Russell with Tex Maule, June 19, 1967, *Sports Illustrated, Muhammad Ali: A Tribute 1942–2016*, 103.

Page 58 I ain't got . . .
Hauser, *Muhammad Ali: His Life and Times*, 139.

Page 58 The price I paid . . .
Ali with Ali, *Soul of a Butterfly*, 100.

Page 58 even the Nation . . .
   Ibid., 95.

Page 59 Sister James Ellen Huff Letter to Muhammad, August 25, 1966,
Spalding College Library Archives.

Page 59 There'd been . . .
   Hauser, *Muhammad Ali: His Life and Times*, 168.

Page 59 Who's the heavyweight . . .
   Howard L. Bingham and Max Wallace, *Muhammad Ali's Greatest Fight: Cassius
Clay vs. the United States of America* (New York: M. Evans & Company, 2012), 189.

Page 59 They will try . . .
   Ali and Durham, *The Greatest: My Own Story*, 126.

Page 59 My new job . . .
   "The Black Scholar Interviews: Muhammad Ali," thefreelibrary.com, March 5,
2022, www.thefreelibrary.com/The+Black+Scholar+interviews%3A+Muhammad
+Ali.-a0307917840.

Page 60 one of history's . . .
   Martin Luther King Jr. Speech, "The Black Freedom Movement: The Casualties
of the War in Vietnam," The Nation Institute, Los Angeles, investigatinghistory.cuny
.edu, February 25, 1967, https://investigatinghistory.ashp.cuny.edu/module11D.
php.

Page 60 the greatest purveyor . . .
   Martin Luther King Jr. Speech, "Beyond Vietnam: A Time to Break Silence,"
americanrhetoric.com, April 4, 1967, www.americanrhetoric.com/speeches/mlk-
atimetobreaksilence.htm (March 14, 2022).

Page 60 cruel irony
   Ibid.

Page 61 We've been too often . . . We've been too . . .
   "Final Words: Cronkite's Vietnam Commentary," npr.com, July 18, 2009, www
.npr.org/templates/story/story.php?storyId=106775685.

Page 61 If I've lost . . .
   Kenneth T. Walsh, "50 Years Ago, Walter Cronkite Changed a Nation: TV Star
Led a Country Against the Vietnam War," usnews.com, February 27, 2018, www
.usnews.com/news/ken-walshs-washington/articles/2018-02-27/50-years-ago
-walter-cronkite-changed-a-nation.

Page 61 I just want . . .
   Martin Luther King Jr., "I've Been to the Mountaintop," April 3, 1968, www
.americanrhetoric.com/speeches/mlkivebeentothemountaintop.htm (March 14,
2022).

Page 62 Even in our sleep . . .
"Echoes of 1968: Robert F. Kennedy Delivering News of King's Death," NPR.
org, April 4, 2008, https://www.npr.org/transcripts/89365887.

Page 62 We Tell . . .
Kindred, *Sound and Fury*, 152.

Page 62 My prayers . . .
Hauser, *Muhammad Ali: His Life and Times*, 162.

Page 62 We Believe . . .
Bingham and Wallace, "Muhammad Ali's Greatest Fight," 215.

Page 63 a champion of justice . . .
The March on Washington in 2 Fists, Kartemquin Films, Vimeo.com, 1970, https://
vimeo.com/73307920.

Page 63 March on Washington all in two fists
The March on Washington in 2 Fists, Kartemquin Films, Vimeo.com, 1970, https://
vimeo.com/73307920.

Page 64 Declared Unfair
Craig Whitney, "3-Year Ring Ban Declared Unfair," *New York Times*, September 15, 1970, https://www.nytimes.com/1970/09/15/archives/3year-ring-ban
-declared-unfair-commissions-action-called-abitrary.html.

Page 64 He'll be mine . . .
Associated Press, "Scores TKO: Clay Takes 15 Rounds," *Times Daily*, December 8,
1970.

Page 64 I want Joe Frazier
"Ali Says Frazier Can't Move Fast," *New York Times*, November 19, 1970,
www.nytimes.com/1970/11/19/archives/ali-says-frazier-cant-move-fast-derides
-victory-over-foster-after.html.

Page 64 Nobody has to tell . . .
"Muhammad Ali—In His Own Words," bbc.com, June 4, 2016, http://news.bbc
.co.uk/sport2/hi/boxing/6267397.stm.

CHAPTER 5

Page 65 Most people would . . .
Bernie Yuman, "The First Time I Met Muhammad Ali," LasVegasSun.com,
February 17, 2012, https://lasvegassun.com/news/2012/feb/17/first-time-i-met
-muhammad-ali/.

Page 66 Everything changes . . .
Mark Kram, "He Moves Like Silk, Hits Like a Ton," *Sports Illustrated*, October 26, 1970.

Page 66 I never thought . . .
Ibid.

Page 67 They identify . . .
Hauser, *Muhammad Ali: His Life and Times*, 217.

Page 67 superman to extraordinary . . .
Dundee and Sugar, *My View from the Corner*, 164.

Page 68 He destroyed a generation . . .
"Muhammad Ali: What They Said," bbc.com, June 4, 2016, https://www.bbc.com/sport/boxing/16289663.

Page 68 There's not a man . . .
Jorge Rivas, "15 of Muhammad Ali's Greatest Quotes," Colorlines.com, January 17, 2012, https://www.colorlines.com/articles/15-muhammad-alis-greatest-quotes.

Page 68 He's not disrespecting . . .
William Nack, "Twenty-Five Years Later, Ali and Frazier Are Still Slugging It Out," *Sports Illustrated,* September 24, 2015, www.si.com/boxing/2015/09/24/muhammad-ali-joe-frazier-william-nack-si-vault.

Page 69 was just a nice . . .
Kyle Almond, "Muhammad Ali, Like You've Never Seen Him Before," cnn.com, quote by Keith William, *Louisville Courier-Journal* photographer, July 2019, www.cnn.com/interactive/2019/07/us/muhammad-ali-courier-journal-cnnphotos/.

Page 69 If there is anything . . .
Rex Bellamy, "Soul Music in Frazier's Workshop," *The Times* (London), February 16, 1971.

Page 69 I'm gonna kill . . .
Felix Dennis and Don Atyeo, *Muhammad Ali: The Glory Years 2002* (London: Ebury Press, 2003), 188.

Page 70 Most guys . . .
Hauser, *Muhammad Ali: His Life and Times*, 339.

Page 70 He's out!
Dave Anderson, "Joe Frazier Beats Muhammad Ali in 'Fight of Century,'" nytimes.com, June 10, 2016, https://www.nytimes.com/2016/06/11/sports/joe-frazier-beats-muhammad-ali-in-fight-of-century.html.

Page 70 get back on . . .
Dundee and Sugar, *My View from the Corner*, 169.

Page 70 You got God . . .
Mark Kram, "At the Bell . . . ," *Sports Illustrated*, March 8, 1971, *Sports Illustrated Muhammad Ali: The Tribute 1942–2016* (New York: Time Inc., 2006), 148.

Page 71 I was surprised . . .
Ibid., 149.

Page 71 That punch blew . . .
Taschen, ed., *Greatest of All Time*, 383.

Page 71 I was trying . . .
Neil Allen, "Bundini Brown, The Witch Doctor at the Court of Ali," *The Times* (London), October 25, 1974.

Page 71 incredible left hook . . .
Collings, ed., *Muhammad Ali*, 416.

Page 71 Just lost a fight . . .
Koepp and Fine, ed., *Ali: The Greatest* by Robert Lipsyte, 91.

Page 71 Joe said he . . .
Hauser, *Muhammad Ali: His Life and Times*, 230.

Page 71 I never thought . . .
Koepp and Fine, ed. *Ali: The Greatest* by Robert Lipsyte, 24.

Page 72 No man ever beat me twice
Ibid., 91.

Page 72 For the record . . .
Barbara L. Tischler, *Muhammad Ali: A Man of Many Voices* (London: Routledge, 2015), 200.

Page 72 integrity of character
Malcolm Mitchell, "Cassius Clay at Yale," November 17, 2016, https://www.easthamptonstar.com/archive/cassius-clay-yale-malcolm-mitchell easthamptonstar.com.

Page 72 At a time . . .
Hauser, *Muhammad Ali: His Life and Times*, 194.

Page 73 We were wrong . . .
Robert S. McNamara, *In Retrospect: The Tragedy and Lessons of Vietnam* (New York: Vintage Books, 1996), 373.

Page 73 Success is not . . .
Ali with Ali, *Soul of a Butterfly*, 121.

CHAPTER 6

Page 75 If you sign to fight . . .
   "Farewell Muhammad Ali—Most Memorable Quotes from 'The Greatest of All Time,'" May 31, 2019, www.freepressjournal.in/headlines/farewell-muhammad-ali -most-memorable-quotes-from-the-greatest-of-all-time.

Page 76 Ellis is ugly . . .
   Tex Maule, "He Has Heavy Things on His Mind," *Sports Illustrated*, July 26, 1971, https://www.si.com/boxing/2015/09/25/muhammad-ali-jimmy-ellis.

Page 76 I don't care . . .
   Ibid.

Page 76 I was just waiting . . .
   Giller, *The Ali Files*, 119.

Page 77 I felt exalted . . .
   Ali Khaled, "How Muhammad Ali Became a Sporting Hero to the Arab World," English.alarabiya.net, May 20, 2020, https://english.alarabiya.net/ sports/2016/06/04/How-Muhammad-Ali-became-a-sporting-hero-to-the-Arab -world.

Page 77 Agony Hill
   Ali with Ali, *Soul of a Butterfly*, 139.

Page 78 I called him . . .
   Hauser, *Muhammad Ali: His Life and Times*, 136.

Page 78 When we talked . . .
   Ibid.

Page 78 Now people . . .
   Joe Ryan, *Boxing in the 1970s: The Great Fighters and Rivalries* (Jefferson, NC: McFarland & Company, 2013), 109.

Page 78 I don't want . . .
   Collings, ed., *Muhammad Ali*, 330.

Page 78 People's Choice
   Kevin Dettmann, "When Muhammad Ali Called Elvis Presley 'The Greatest,'" elvisbiography.net, June 1, 2020, https://elvisbiography.net/2019/01/15/when -muhammad-ali-called-elvis-presley-the-greatest.

Page 78 I tried to fight . . .
   Neil Allen, *The Times* (London), February 16, 1973.

Page 79 I was thinking . . .

Thomas Hauser, "Ali's Role in Boxing, Society and Beyond," espn.com, November 25, 2005, https://www.espn.com/sports/boxing/ali/news/story?id=2236756.

Page 79 Imagine you have . . .

Kevin Mitchell, "Ken Norton: a Jaw-Breakingly Good Fighter and Myth Buster," *The Guardian*, September 19, 2013, https://www.theguardian.com/sport/blog/2013/sep/19/ken-norton-jaw-breaking-fighter.

Page 79 Losing to Norton . . .

Hauser, *Muhammad Ali: His Life and Times*, 251.

Page 80 I know it was close . . .

Giller, *The Ali Files*, 153.

Page 80 I'll get out of boxing . . .

Ibid., 147.

Page 82 Float like . . .

January Makamba, Tread Reader Clip, November 11, 2019, YouTube, https://threadreaderapp.com/thread/1193878521011167232.html (March 14, 2022).

Page 82 Stay there, Baby . . .

Levi Johansen, "Muhammad Ali vs Joe Frazier II—Jan 28, 1974—Entire Fight—Rounds 1–12 & Interviews," December 18, 2010, YouTube, www.youtube.com/watch?v=JMOIWWyNHJs.

Page 82 I left him . . .

Giller, *The Ali Files*, 159.

Page 82 The fight is won . . .

Koepp and Fine, eds., *Ali: The Greatest* by Robert Lipsyte, 20.

CHAPTER 7

Page 83 Float like a butterfly . . .

Hauser, *Muhammad Ali: His Life and Times*, 267 (Howard Bingham Tape Collection).

Page 84 I've never felt so free . . .

Daniel Marans, "Watch Muhammad Ali Explain Why He Feels More Free in Africa Than the U.S.," huffpost.com, June 4, 2016, https://www.huffpost.com/entry/muhammad-ali-africa_ n_57534e51e4b0ed593f14a767.

Page 84 He changed my life . . .
Don Lomena, "Muhammad Ali Received Liberty Medal," *Los Angeles Times,*
September 4, 2012, www.latimes.com/sports/la-xpm-2012-sep-14-la-sp-sn
-muhammad-ali-liberty-medal-20120914-story.html.

Page 84 a 50-carat . . .
Mark Kram, "The Fight's Lone Arranger," *Sports Illustrated,* September 2, 1974,
https://vault.si.com/vault/1974/09/02/the-fights-lone-arranger.

Page 85 I loved the people . . .
Ali with Ali, *Soul of a Butterfly,* 129.

Page 85 *féticheurs* . . .
Greenfeld, ed., "Breaking a Date for the Dance" by George Plimpton, in *Sports
Illustrated: The Tribute, 1942–2016,* November 11, 1974 (New York: Time, Inc.,
2016), 172.

Page 85 I've had appointments . . .
Koepp and Fine, eds., *Ali: The Greatest* by Robert Lipsyte, 95.

Page 85 Ali, bomaye . . .
Giller, *The Ali Files,* 161.

Page 85 Ali, kill him!
Ibid.

Page 85 Of course, I did not want to kill . . .
Ali with Ali, *Soul of a Butterfly,* 129.

Page 85 I'm gonna dance!
Myers, *The Greatest,* 120.

Page 85 The time may . . .
Jonathan Snowden, "Muhammad Ali's Greatest Fight: George Foreman and the
Rumble in the Jungle," June 4, 2016, https://bleacherreport.com/articles/1919959
-muhammad-alis-greatest-fight-george-foreman-and-the-rumble-in-the-jungle.

Page 85 What am I . . .
Lilian Thuram, *My Black Stars: From Lucy to Barack Obama* (Liverpool: Liverpool
University Press, 2001), 234.

Page 86 I thought George . . .
Hauser, *Muhammad Ali: His Life and Times,* 274.

Page 86 I've wrestled . . .
Myran Sinclair, October 17, 2021, Muhammad Ali, "I'm So Fast I Can Run
Through a Hurricane and Don't Get Wet," YouTube Video, https://www.youtube
.com/watch?v=DuDja8lsWe4.

Page 86 when George gets . . .
Hauser, *Muhammad Ali: His Life and Times*, 269.

Page 87 The Mummy
Ibid., 264.

Page 87 I've seen Foreman . . .
Mike Johnston, "The Louisville Lip: Best Muhammad Ali Quotes," sportsnet
.com, June 4, 2016, www.sportsnet.ca/more/best-muhammad-ali-quotes-of-all
-time-on-life-boxing-joe-frazier-george-foreman-sonny-liston/.

Page 87 The King . . .
Hauser, *Muhammad Ali: His Life and Times*, 266.

Page 87 He's playing with fire . . .
Giller, *The Ali Files*, 161.

Page 87 You're gonna meet . . .
"Playboy Interview: Muhammad Ali" (Second Interview, 1975), November 1,
1975, https://genius.com/Playboy-playboy-interview-muhammad-ali-second
-interview-1975-annotated.

Page 87 I'm so fast . . .
Myran Sinclair, Muhammad Ali "I'm so fast I can run through a hurricane
and don't get wet," October 17, 2021, YouTube Video, www.youtube.com/
watch?v=DuDja8lsWe4

Page 87 The best way . . .
Greenfeld, ed., "Breaking a Date for the Dance," 90.

Page 88 Move, Ali! Move!
Ali and Durham, *The Greatest: My Own Story*, 406.

Page 88 You are just . . .
Koepp and Fine, eds., *Ali: The Greatest* by Robert Lipsyte, 96.

Page 88 oppressive, as the closing . . .
Norman Mailer, *The Fight* (New York: Random House, 2013), 176.

Page 88 Dance, champ; dance! . . .
Hauser, *Muhammad Ali: His Life and Times*, 274.

Page 88 Is that all . . .
Jonathan Snowden, "Muhammad Ali's Greatest Fight: George Foreman and the
Rumble in the Jungle," June 4, 2016, https://bleacherreport.com/articles/1919959
-muhammad-alis-greatest-fight-george-foreman-and-the-rumble-.

Page 88 I was world . . .
Taschen, ed., "Greater Than the Greatest: An Interview with George Foreman,"
588.

Page 89 I started throwing . . .
  "Playboy Interview" (Second Interview, 1975).

Page 89 What did I tell you?
  Koepp and Fine, eds., *Ali: The Greatest* by Robert Lipsyte, 98.

Page 89 Man, this is the wrong . . .
  Mohamed Ali, "Muhammad Ali: Joe Frazier's the Only Guy That Talked Back,"
  Michael Parkinson Interview, YouTube Video, March 20, 2014, www.youtube.com/
  watch?v=pfej5XI9v7A.

Page 89 George just didn't . . .
  "Playboy Interview" (Second Interview, 1975).

Page 89 There was George trying . . .
  Ibid.

Page 89 I purposely left him . . .
  Ibid.

Page 89 This guy can't hit at all . . . I'm going to knock him out this round
  Jon Saraceno, "Q&A with Ferdie Pacheco, Muhammad Ali's Longtime Doctor and Corner Man," Special for *USA Today* Sports, www.Khou.com, June 4,
  2016, www.khou.com/article/features/qa-with-ferdie-pacheco-muhammad-alis
  -longtime-doctor-and corner-man/285-231391259.

Page 89 Well, hurry up . . .
  Ibid.

Page 91 after the fight . . .
  Giller, *The Ali Files*, 163.

Page 91 It's never been . . .
  Greenfeld, ed., "Breaking a Date for the Dance," 95.

Page 91 I was going down . . .
  Mikal Gilmore, "The Greatest of All Time," *Rolling Stone: The Greatest of All Time
  1942–2016*, 40.

Page 91 Impossible is just . . .
  ESPN the Magazine, "I Shook Up the World! The Meaning of Muhammad Ali,"
  June 27, 2016, 96.

Page 92 believed the sky had fallen
  George Foreman and Joel Engel, *By George: The Autobiography of George Foreman*
  (New York: Simon & Schuster, 2000), 116.

Page 92 I'd become a boxer . . .
  Hauser, *Muhammad Ali: His Life and Times*, 265.

Page 92 Wallace taught us . . .
   Ibid., 292.

Page 92 the time of our struggle . . .
   Thomas Hauser, "The Importance of Muhammad Ali," espn.com, June 2, 2016, https://www.espn.com/sports/boxing/ali/news/story?id=2236712.

CHAPTER 8

Page 96 If you even dream . . .
   ESPN the Magazine, "I Shook Up the World! The Meaning of Muhammad Ali," 84.

Page 96 He wouldn't hit . . .
   Hauser, *Muhammad Ali: His Life and Times*, 296.

Page 96 I'm gettin' old . . .
   Giller, *The Ali Files*, 165.

Page 96 It was obvious . . .
   Ibid., 168.

Page 97 Got some unfinished . . .
   Ibid., 171.

Page 98 Being a fighter . . .
   Hauser, *Muhammad Ali: His Life and Times*, 213.

Page 98 Ali is a master . . .
   Ferdie Pacheco, "'Fight Doctor' Fond of the 'Greatest,'" *USA Today* Sports, *Ali 1942– 2016 Remembering a Champion, Civil Rights Activist, American Legend*, 19.

Page 99 he had what . . .
   Hauser, *Muhammad Ali: His Life and Times*, 228.

Page 99 He's still trying . . .
   Thomas Hauser, *Boxing Is . . . : Reflections on the Sweet Science* (Fayetteville: University of Arkansas Press, 2010), 92.

Page 99 He has all . . .
   Jennifer Frey, "Mark Kram, Pulling No Punches," washingtonpost.com, May 29, 2001, www.washingtonpost.com/archive/lifestyle/2001/05/29/mark-kram-pulling-no-punches/b495fd01-85b0-4d7d-9589-bfe384c9d17c/.

Page 99 Because he is
   Ibid.

Page 99 Muhammad's under Joe's . . .
Taschen, ed., *Greatest of All Time*, 475.

Page 99 Showmanship is a large . . .
Ali with Ali, *Soul of a Butterfly*, 119–20.

Page 99 I was no philosopher . . .
Taschen, ed., "'What's Keepin' Him Up?': An Interview with Joe Frazier by Helmut Sorge," 586.

Page 100 Nineteen seventy-one . . .
Brunt, *Facing Ali*, 117.

Page 100 I want to hurt him . . .
Hauser, *Muhammad Ali: His Life and Times*, 313.

Page 100 He won't call . . .
Greenfeld, ed., "The Epic Battle Between Joe Frazier and Muhammad Ali" by Mark Kram, 109.

Page 101 Jack be nimble . . .
John Dower, *Thrilla in Manila*, TV Movie, HBO Documentary Films, 2008.

Page 101 Stay mean . . .
Greenfeld, ed., "The Epic Battle Between Joe Frazier and Muhammad Ali," 110.

Page 101 We blew those . . .
Dundee and Sugar, *My View from the Corner*, 212.

Page 102 Old Joe Frazier . . .
Ibid.

Page 102 They lied, pretty boy.
Ibid.

Page 102 This is the closest . . .
Brunt, *Facing Ali*, 122.

Page 102 Go down . . .
Greenfeld, ed., "Lawdy, Lawdy, He's Great" by Mark Kram, 110.

Page 102 no man could take this punishment
David West, ed., "Thrilla in Manila" by Ferdie Pacheco, 352.

Page 102 Every fight hurts . . .
Myers, *The Greatest*, 79.

Page 103 The fight's over, Joe . . .
Greenfeld, ed., "The Fight's Over, Joe," by William Nack, 254.

Page 103 The world . . .
Ferdie Pacheco, *The 12 Greatest Rounds of Boxing: The Untold Stories* (New York: Total Sports, 2000), 159.

Page 104 only one fellow . . .
"Muhammad Ali: Joe Frazier's the Only Guy That Talked Back," Muhammad Ali Interview with Michael Parkinson, March 20, 2014, YouTube, www.youtube.com/watch?v=pfej5XI9v7Ar.

Page 104 Joe Frazier is the greatest fighter
Giller, *The Ali Files*, 177.

Page 104 Man, I hit him . . .
Mark Kram, "The Epic Battle Between Joe Frazier and Muhammad Ali," *Sports Illustrated*, October 13, 1975, https://www.si.com/boxing/2015/09/24/muhammad -ali-joe-frazier-epic-battle-1975 (March 14, 2022).

Page 104 That fight . . .
Hauser, *Muhammad Ali: His Life and Times*, 326.

Page 104 I never back down and . . .
Taschen, ed., *Muhammad Ali: Greatest of All Time*, 586.

Page 105 This has been going on . . .
Richard Sandomir, "BOXING; No Floating, No Stinging: Ali Extends Hand to Frazier," www.nytimes.com, March 15, 2001, www.nytimes.com/2001/03/15/sports/boxing-no-floating-no-stinging-ali-extends-hand-to-frazier.html.

Page 105 The world has lost . . .
"The world lost a great champion—Ali," www.irishtimes.com, November 8, 2011, https://www.irishtimes.com/news/the-world-has-lost-a-great-champion-ali -1.1285653.

Page 106 I knew the punishment . . .
Christopher Bucktin, "Muhammad Ali's Doctor Begged Him to Quit Boxing After the Thrilla in Manila," Mirror.co.uk, June 4, 2016, www.mirror.co.uk/sport/boxing/muhammad-alis-doctor-begged-him-8116534~Dr. Ferdie Pacheco, Fight Doctor.

CHAPTER 9

Page 107 the dangerous mental point . . .
Koepp and Fine, eds., *Ali: The Greatest* by Robert Lipsyte, 100.

Page 107 It's just a job . . .
"Muhammad Ali—In His Own Words," bbc.com, June 4, 2016, www.bbc.com/sport/boxing/16146367.

Page 108 Rhythm is everything . . .
Robinson and Anderson, *Sugar Ray*, 75.

Page 108 he was still . . .
Hauser, *Muhammad Ali: His Life and Times*, 339.

Page 109 He was the best . . .
Ibid., 339.

Page 109 I remember looking . . .
Ibid., 341.

Page 109 So I don't . . .
Ibid.

Page 109 You saw a miracle . . .
Giller, *The Ali Files*, 194.

Page 109 Acorns fall in September!
Ibid., 197.

Page 109 I don't think . . .
Hauser, *Muhammad Ali*, 29.

Page 110 I was young . . .
Pat Putnam, "He's the Greatest, I'm the Best," *Sports Illustrated*, February 27, 1978, https://vault.si.com/vault/1978/02/27/hes-the-greatest-im-the-best-ali-was-his-man-then-and-ali-is-his-man-now-but-when-24-year-old-leon-spinks-attacked-both-idol-and-the-heavyweight-title-came-tumbling-down.

Page 110 You've proven . . .
Hauser, *Muhammad Ali: His Life and Times*, 349.

Page 111 You've got to . . .
Pat Putnam, "He's the Greatest, I'm the Best," sportsillustrated.com, February 27, 1978, https://vault.si.com/vault/1978/02/27/hes-the-greatest-im-the-best-ali-was-his-man-then-and-ali-is-his-man-now-but-when-24-year-old-leon-spinks-attacked-both-idol-and-the-heavyweight-title-came-tumbling-down.

Page 111 reckless generosity
Ibid.

Page 111 He was fighting . . .
"Spinks Takes Ali's Crown: 'Underestimated' Foe, Loser Claims . . . ," *Chicago Tribune*, February 16, 1978.

Page 111 I'm the latest . . .
Giller, *The Ali Files*, 201.

Page 111 Leon Spinks borrowed . . .
Hauser, *Muhammad Ali: His Life and Times*, 356.

Page 113 I suffered . . .
"Ali vs Spinks (second meeting)," BoxRec.com, https://boxrec.com/media/index.php/Leon_ Spinks_ vs._ Muhammad_ Ali_(2nd_ meeting).

Page 114 Where did he go . . .
Pat Putnam, "One More Time to the Top," *Sports Illustrated,* September 25, 1978.

Page 114 Against Spinks the second . . .
Hauser, *Muhammad Ali: His Life and Times*, 360.

Page 114 Goodbye, Leon
Dundee and Sugar, *My View from the Corner*, 226.

Page 114 It was beautifully . . .
Pat Putnam, "One More Time to the Top," *Sports Illustrated,* September 25, 1978.

Page 114 . . . my greatest fight . . .
Bob Markus, *I'll Play These: A Sports Writer's Life* (Bloomington, IN: Xlibris, 2011), 309.

Page 114 I want to be . . .
Harry Mullan, "Long Read Chasing Muhammad Ali," *Boxing News*, 1986, www.boxingnewsonline.net/long-read-chasing-muhammad-ali.

Page 115 We had traveled . . .
Dundee and Sugar, *My View from the Corner*, 228.

Page 115 I've been doing . . .
Pat Putnam, "One More Time to the Top," *Sports Illustrated,* September 25, 1978.

Page 115 A champion doesn't . . .
Collings, ed., *Muhammad Ali*, 352.

CHAPTER 10

Page 118 Ali's mind made . . .
Pete Dexter, "Seven Scenes from the Life of a Quiet Champ," thestacksreader.com, June 1980, www.thestacksreader.com/seven-scenes-from-the-life-of-a-quiet-champ/.

Page 118 He was a great . . .
Hugh McIlvanney, *Hugh McIlvanney on Boxing* (New York: Beaufort Books, 1982), 179.

Page 118 Mountains can't . . .
Mark Kram, *Ghosts of Manila: The Fateful Blood Feud Between Muhammad Ali and Joe Frazier* (New York: HarperCollins, 2001), 9.

Page 119 refuses to see . . .
Taschen, ed., *Greatest of All Time*, 551.

Page 119 Herbert has been . . .
Hauser, *Muhammad Ali: His Life and Times*, 383.

Page 119 There was an old . . .
George Vecsey, "At 39, Ali Has More Points to Prove," archive.nytimes.com, November 29, 1981, https://archive.nytimes.com/www.nytimes.com/books/98/10/25/specials/ali-39.html.

Page 119 Angelo thinks . . .
McIlvanney, *Hugh McIlvanney on Boxing*, 183.

Page 119 I never let anyone talk me . . .
Ali with Ali, *Soul of a Butterfly*, 122.

Page 120 Ali was a walking time bomb . . .
Hauser, *Muhammad Ali: His Life and Times*, 418.

Page 120 I may have placed him in jeopardy inadvertently
Ibid., 415.

Page 121 All I could think . . .
Pat Putnam, "Doom in the Desert," *Sports Illustrated*, October 13, 1980, https://www.si.com/boxing/2015/09/24/muhammad-ali-larry-holmes-fight-si-vault.

Page 122 It is sad . . .
Mark Ribowsky, *Howard Cosell: The Man, the Myth, and the Transformation of American Sports* (New York: W.W. Norton & Company, 2011), 385.

Page 122 In my youth, I set out . . .
Ali with Ali, *Soul of a Butterfly*, 127.

Page 122 This is your . . .
Pat Putnam, "Doom in the Desert."

Page 123 I'm the boss . . .
Pat Putnam, "Doom in the Desert."

Page 123 When the tenth . . .
McIlvanney, *Hugh McIlvanney on Boxing*, 178.

Page 123 They're saying . . .
  Ibid.

Page 123 I love the man . . .
  Thomas Hauser, "The Night When Ali Screamed in Pain," www.theguardian
.com, January 6, 2007, www.theguardian.com/sport/2007/jan/07/boxing.features.

Page 123 Boxing owes . . .
  Ibid., 180.

Page 123 I didn't like . . .
  Ibid., 177.

Page 123 Psychologically . . .
  Ibid., 179.

Page 123 I spent three . . .
  Pat Putnam, "Better Not Sell the Old Man Short," sportsillustrated.com, September 29, 1980, https://vault.si.com/vault/1980/09/29/muhammad-ali-larry-holmes
-fight.

Page 123 scandalous
  Hauser, *Muhammad Ali: His Life and Times*, 404.

Page 123 Just because a man can pass . . .
  Ibid., 404–5.

Page 124 You dream . . .
  Ibid., 412.

Page 124 I shall return.
  Giller, *The Ali Files*, 208.

Page 124 All my life . . .
  Ali and Ali, *Soul of a Butterfly*, 133.

Page 124 Before the fight . . .
  Ibid.

Page 125 Time makes more . . .
  Chris Walker, "A Look Back at Thomas Paine, and Why Impeachment Makes
'Common' Sense (Even If You Think It's a Losing Cause)," hillreporter.com, September 25, 2019, https://hillreporter.com/a-look-back-paine-and-why-impeachment
-makes-sense-even-if-you-think-its-a-losing-cause-opinion-46555.

Page 125 This is number 5! . . .
  Coachstrout's Classic Fights, "Muhammad Ali vs Trevor Berbick," March 23,
2018, YouTube, www.youtube.com/watch?v=cRVixOr3irw.

Page 125 I love you . . .
  Ibid.

Page 125 In everyone's heart . . .
  Ibid.

Page 125 Great men . . .
  Dundee and Sugar, *My View from the Corner*, 232.

Page 125 Father Time caught . . .
  Hauser, *Muhammad Ali: His Life and Times*, 431.

Page 125 I thought I . . .
  Ibid., 427.

Page 126 His life was . . .
  Taschen, ed., "The Best Ali Is the One We Never Saw: An Interview with Angelo Dundee by Helmut Sorge," 150.

Page 126 Muhammad had it . . .
  "Angelo Dundee: The Best I've Trained," ringtv.com, September 23, 2010, www .ringtv.com/124373-angelo-dundee-the-best-ive-trained/.

Page 126 In the history . . .
  Khalid Hussain, "Ali: The Alpha and the Omega," thenews.com.pk, June 5, 2016, www.thenews.com.pk/tns/detail/561096-ali-alpha-omega.

Page 126 concussive blows . . .
  Hauser, *Muhammad Ali: His Life and Times*, 349.

Page 127 people still wonder . . .
  Pacheco, *The 12 Greatest Rounds of Boxing*, 167.

Page 127 deceived himself, massively
  Hauser, *Muhammad Ali: His Life and Times*, 419.

Page 127 takes some blows . . .
  McIlvanney, *Hugh McIlvanney on Boxing*, 174.

Page 127 seems to have learned . . .
  Ibid., 174.

Page 128 I've never seen . . .
  Taschen, ed., *Greatest of All Time: A Tribute to Muhammad Ali*, 593.

Page 129 The Real Fight Ring
  Ali with Ali, *Soul of a Butterfly*, 75.

Page 129 Even Muhammad Ali is human . . .
  Hauser, *Muhammad Ali: His Life and Times*, 404.

CHAPTER 11

Page 132 It is after . . .
Ali with Ali, *Soul of a Butterfly*, 12.

Page 132 Now I dream . . .
Hauser, *Muhammad Ali: A Tribute to the Greatest*, 183–84.

Page 132 I have learned . . .
Ali with Ali, *Soul of a Butterfly*, 16.

Page 132 Few cared . . .
Enrique Encinosa, "The Life and Times of Luis Sarria," cyberboxingzone.com, August 2004, www.cyberboxingzone.com/boxing/w0804-sarria.html.

Page 132 To tell a boxer . . .
Gary Smith, "Ali and His Entourage: Life After the End of the Greatest Show on Earth," *Sports Illustrated*, October 10, 2014, www.si.com/boxing/2014/10/10/muhammad-ali-entourage.

Page 132 people who didn't care . . .
Hauser, *Muhammad Ali: His Life and Times*, 423.

Page 133 You didn't have . . .
Ibid., 422.

Page 133 There's absolutely no evidence . . .
Lee Groves, "Muhammad Ali-Trevor Berbick: The Greatest Takes His Final in the Bahamas," ringtv.com, December 11, 1981, www.ringtv.com/632052-muhammad-ali-trevor-berbick-the-greatest-takes-his-final-bows-in-the-bahamas/.

Page 133 caused by injuries . . .
Associated Press, "Ali Suffered Too Many Blows to the Head," *Ocala Star Banner*, July 16, 1987.

Page 134 Nobody to my knowledge . . .
Dr. Cyril H. Wecht, Exclusive Interview on March 27, 2016.

Page 135 When I fight . . .
Collings, ed., *Muhammad Ali*, 196–97.

Page 135 They see me today . . .
Ali with Ali, *Soul of a Butterfly*, 79.

Page 136 He took some . . .
Robert H. Boyle, "Too Many Punches, Too Little Concern," sportsillustrated.com, April 11, 1983, https://vault.si.com/vault/1983/04/11/too-many-punches-too-little-concern.

Page 136 wouldn't have stopped . . .
Bucktin, "Muhammad Ali's Doctor Begged Him to Quit Boxing After the Thrilla in Manila."

Page 136 When I get stunned . . .
"Playboy Interview" (Second Interview, 1975).

Page 136 What I have suffered physically . . .
Taschen, ed., *Greatest of All Time*, 568.

Page 136 We delight . . .
"Maya Angelou Quotes: 15 of the Best," TheGuardian.com, May 29, 2014, www .theguardian.com/books/2014/may/28/maya-angelou-in-fifteen-quotes.

Page 136 My assumption . . .
Hauser, *Muhammad Ali: His Life and Times*, 494.

Page 136 It is anticipated . . .
Ibid., 433

Page 136 it's scary for . . .
Ibid., 496.

Page 137 Every step of the way . . .
Ali with Ali, *Soul of a Butterfly*, 16.

Page 137 Every day is different . . .
Ali with Ali, *Soul of a Butterfly*, 151.

Page 137 Certainly reform . . .
Boyle, "Too Many Punches."

Page 137 Almost all ring . . .
"We Must Learn from Senseless Boxing Death," Denverpost.com, September 24, 2005, https://www.denverpost.com/2005/09/24/we-must-learn-from-senseless -boxing-death/.

Page 138 In all likelihood . . .
"The Life and Times of Muhammad Ali, 'The Greatest,'" *Louisville Courier-Journal*, usatoday.com, June 4, 2016, www.usatoday.com/story/sports/boxing/2016/06/04/ muhammad-ali-life-timeline/1780707/.

Page 138 I have never . . .
Ali with Ali, *Soul of a Butterfly: Reflections on Life's Journey*, simonandschuster.com, https://www.simonandschuster.com/books/The-Soul-of-a-Butterfly/Muhammad -Ali/9781476747378/.

Page 138 I didn't understand . . .
Tim Layden, "The Legacy of the Greatest Still Grows," *Sports Illustrated*, October 5, 2015.

Page 138 Passing the Olympic . . .
Nick Zaccardi, "World Mourns Death of Muhammad Ali," olympics.nbcsports
.com, June 4, 2016, https://olympics.nbcsports.com/2016/06/04/muhammad-ali
-dies-world-mourns/.

Page 139 Parkinson's is no . . .
Collings, ed., *Muhammad Ali*, 24.

Page 139 I think he was . . .
Interview with author David Kindred on September 15, 2021.

Page 140 the most gifted . . .
William Nack, "Greatest Sports Figures of Last 40 Years No.1: Muhammad Ali,"
sportsillustrated.com, September 19, 1994, https://vault.si.com/vault/1994/09/19/
muhammad-ali-greatest-sports-figure.

Page 140 I realized . . .
"I Am Still the Greatest," Heard on *All Things Considered*, Read by Lonnie Ali, npr
.org, April 6, 2009, www.npr.org/2009/04/06/102649267/i-am-still-the-greatest.

Page 140 His Parkinson's . . .
"Muhammad Ali 'Had a Tough Time for a Year' Before Death—Doctor," bbc
.com, June 5, 2016, https://www.bbc.com/sport/boxing/36454654.

Page 140 He has a kind . . .
Michael Gaffney, *The Champ: My Year with Muhammad Ali* (New York: Diversion
Books, 2012), 4.

CHAPTER 12

Page 141 I set out on a journey . . .
Ali with Ali, *Soul of a Butterfly*, 16.

Page 142 My soul has grown . . .
Ibid., 16

Page 142 different roads . . .
A. Jayabalan, CMF, "Mahatma Gandhi's Discovery of Religion," 1998, www
.mkgandhi.org/articles/discovery.htm.

Page 142 Some things cannot be taught . . .
Ali with Ali, *Soul of a Butterfly*, 12.

Page 142 Spirituality helps us . . .
Ibid., 195.

Page 142 spirituality extends . . .
Muhammad Ali, www.muftisays.com, September 24, 2010, www.muftisays.com/blog/abu+mohammed/417_24-09-2010/muhammad-ali.html.

Page 143 Away from the . . .
Correspondence with author Norman Giller on September 23, 2021.

Page 144 The first peace . . .
Joseph Epes Brown, *The Sacred Pipe: Black Elk's Account of the Seven Rites of the Oglala Sioux* (Norman: University of Oklahoma Press, 1953), 115.

Page 144 There's truth . . .
Taschen, ed., *Greatest of All Time*, 652.

Page 144 A man who views . . .
"Muhammad Ali—in His Own Words," bbc.com, June 4, 2016, www.bbc.com/sport/boxing/16146367.

Page 145 You will note . . .
Letter from Sr. James Ellen Huff to Cassius Clay, May 18, 1965, Spalding University Library Archives.

Page 145 I understand that there are many . . .
Ali with Ali, *Soul of a Butterfly*, 195.

Page 145 The day I met Islam . . .
Ibid., 74.

Page 145 According to Lonnie . . .
Jon Saraceno, "Caring for The Greatest, Muhammad Ali," *AARP Bulletin*, June 2014, https://www.aarp.org/home-family/caregiving/info-2014/caregiving-muhammad-lonnie-ali-parkinsons.html.

Page 145 I am America . . . get used to me.
Koepp and Fine, eds., "Ali: The Greatest" by Robert Lipsyte, 8.

Page 145 He who is not . . .
Jennifer Leigh Selig, ed., *What Now? Words of Wisdom for Life after Graduation* (Kansas City, MO: Andrews McMeel Publishing, 1999), 241.

Page 146 Every time I look . . .
Ali with Ali, *Soul of a Butterfly*, 136.

Page 146 elevate souls . . .
Ibid., 100.

Page 146 I'm not perfect . . .
Ibid., 13.

Page 146 I have come . . .
  Ibid., 15.

Page 147 My greatest accomplishments . . .
  Ibid., 204.

Page 147 I suppose what impressed . . .
  Evanzz, *I Am the Greatest*, 32.

Page 148 started treating me . . .
  Eugene Scott, "The Political Fights of Muhammad Ali," cnn.com, June 4, 2016, https://www.cnn.com/2016/06/04/politics/muhammad-ali-political-moments/index.html.

Page 148 It hurts me to see . . .
  Ali with Ali, *Soul of a Butterfly*, 186.

Page 148 There is nothing Islamic . . .
  Gilmore, "The Greatest of All Time," *Rolling Stone*, 41.

Page 148 As long as I live . . .
  Ali with Ali, *Soul of a Butterfly*, 16.

CHAPTER 13

Page 149 Material things lose . . .
  Ali with Ali, *Soul of a Butterfly*, 106.

Page 150 You've shown me . . .
  Melissa Chan, "How Muhammad Ali's Children Mourned His Death," Yahoofinance.com, June 5, 2016, https://finance.yahoo.com/news/muhammad-ali-children-mourned-death-135858921.html.

Page 150 He was the greatest . . .
  Lance Knickerbocker, "Muhammad Ali's Daughter and Main Line Resident: 'He Was the Greatest,'" vista.today.com, June 10, 2016, https://vista.today/2016/06/muhammad-alis-daughter-main-line-resident-greatest/.

Page 150 When it comes . . .
  Ali with Ali, *Soul of a Butterfly*, 16.

Page 150 Daddy, you are . . .
  Ibid., 10.

Page 150 His greatness lies . . .
  Ibid., 209.

Page 150 It wasn't easy . . .
Ibid., 170.

Page 151 The only true . . .
Ibid., 201.

Page 151 We were brought . . .
Gregory Allen Howard, "How Does It Feel Being a Child of the Most Famous Man in the World," in *Greatest of All Time,* Taschen, ed., 604.

Page 151 Honesty, integrity, kindness . . .
Ali with Ali, *Soul of a Butterfly*, 162.

Page 151 He wasn't a perfect . . .
Claire Lewins, *I Am Ali: The Man Behind the Legend—An Intimate Portrait,* Video Documentary, 2014.

Page 151 Give the ones . . .
Dalai Lama, *Dalai Lama's Little Book of Selected Quotes: on Love, Life, and Compassion* (Toronto: Lumière Publishing, 2021).

Page 151 What's your purpose?
W Claire Lewins, *I Am Ali: The Man Behind the Legend—An Intimate Portrait,* Video Documentary, 2014.

Page 152 Make people feel...
Ibid.

Page 152 That's good. That's good, Maryum.
Ibid.

Page 152 It is our job . . .
Ali with Ali, *Soul of a Butterfly*, 165.

Page 152 Remember that wherever your heart . . .
Paulo Coelho, *The Alchemist* (New York: HarperOne, 1993), 122.

Page 152 . . . there were three . . .
Hauser, *Muhammad Ali: His Life and Times*, 365.

Page 152 Like not long ago . . .
Ibid., 366.

Page 152 Each of my children . . .
Ali with Ali, *Soul of a Butterfly*, 168.

Page 153 My dad never . . .
Nathan Aaseng, *African American Athletes* (New York: Facts on File, Inc., 2003), 7.

Page 154 He was important . . .
Hauser, *Muhammad Ali: His Life and Times*, 455.

Page 154 When I was young . . .
Hauser, *Muhammad Ali: A Tribute*, 201–2.

Page 154 He was there . . .
Keir Mudie and Christopher Bucktin, "Muhammad Ali's Final Hours—Daughters Whispered 'You Can Go Now' as Legend Passes Away," Mirror.uk.com, June 4, 2016, https://www.mirror.co.uk/news/world-news/muhammad-alis-final-hours-daughters-8116602.

Page 155 I am so proud . . .
Christopher Bucktin, "Muhammad Ali's Brother Reveals He Knew He Would Become World's Greatest Boxer Aged Just 12," June 4, 2016, www.mirror.co.uk/sport/boxing/muhammad-alis-brother-reveals-knew-8116486.

Page 155 When he started . . .
Carols Irusta, "Dundee: Ali Was, Still Is 'The Greatest,'" espn.com, January 17, 2012, www.espn.com/boxing/story/_/id/7470417/muhammad-ali-was-continues-greatest.

Page 155 It would be nice . . .
Hauser, *Muhammad Ali: His Life and Times*, 464.

Page 156 I'm . . . so . . . sorry . . .champ
Eig, *Ali: A Life*, 512.

Page 156 He saved my life . . .
Justin Tate, "The 50 Greatest Boxing Quotes of All Time," bleacherreport.com, January 24, 2011, https://bleacherreport.com/articles/575189-50-greatest-boxing-quotes-of-all-time.

Page 157 I think he showed . . .
Lauren Yates, "Cassius Clay Slept Here," *Spalding University News*, Fall 1997.

Page 157 a spokesperson . . .
Ibid.

Page 157 There are times . . .
Hauser, *Muhammad Ali: His Life and Times*, 479.

Page 157 Everything
Howard Bingham, "Face to Face with Muhmmad Ali," *Reader's Digest*, December 2001, 96.

Page 157 I don't know . . .
Hauser, *Muhammad Ali: His Life and Times*, 479.

Page 159 Money and riches
Taschen, ed., *Greatest of All Time*, 271.

CHAPTER 14

Page 161 It is my prayer . . .
Ali with Ali, *Soul of a Butterfly*, 188.

Page 162 For many years . . .
"The Newsroom, 'The Greatest' Muhammad Ali Dies Aged 74," scotsman.com, June 5, 2016, www.scotsman.com/sport/boxing/greatest-muhammad-ali-dies-aged -74-1475069.

Page 163 six core principles
https://alicenter.org/muhammad-alis-principles-are-a-guide-for-the-athlete -humanitarian-athlete-mentor-and-athlete-activist/.

Page 163 Be Great: Do Great Things
Muhammad Ali Center, "Ali Center Launches New Digital Museum and Archives as Part of Ali Festival," prnewswire.com, June 8, 2011, www.prnewswire .com/news-releases/ali-center-launches-new-digital-museum-and-archives-as-part -of-ali-festival-301308327.html.

Page 165 In the final battle . . .
Robert Muller, *Planet of Hope* (New York: Amity House, 1985), 93.

Page 165 Muhammad Ali shook . . .
"Statement from President Barack Obama and First Lady Michelle Obama on the Passing of Muhammad Ali," The White House Office of the Press Secretary, ObamaWhiteHouse.archives.gov, June 4, 2016, https://obamawhitehouse.archives .gov/the-press-office/2016/06/04/statement-president-barack-obama-and-first -lady-michelle-obama-passing.

Page 165 'Who's the greatest?'
Houston Horn, "The First Days in the New Life of the Champion of the World," *Sports Illustrated*, March 9, 1964, https://vault.si.com/vault/1964/03/09/the-first -days-in-the-new-life-of-the-champion-of-the-world.

Page 166 Hold fast to dreams . . .
Rampersad and Roessel, eds., *The Collected Poems of Langston Hughes*, 32.

Page 166 young and young at heart leaders
Muhammad Ali Center Website, https://alicenter.org/generation-ali/.

Page 167 Never underestimate . . .
Jone Johnson Lewis, "Wilma Rudolph—Wilma Rudolph Quotes," July 3, 2019, www.thoughtco.com/wilma-rudolph-quotes-3530190.

Page 167 I had the greatest
Howard Bingham, "What Ali Means to Me, by Howard Bingham," *USA Today Sports, Remembering a Champion, Civil Rights Activist, American Legend*, 24.

Page 167 Regardless of how . . .
Taschen, ed., *Greatest of All Time*, 318.

Page 170 greatest present . . . Gift of Love
Ibid., 284.

Page 171 I hope . . .
Ali with Ali, *Soul of a Butterfly*, 17.

CHAPTER 15

Page 174 Boxing was just . . .
Ali and Durham, *The Greatest: My Own Story*, 5.

Page 174 His impact recognizes . . .
Collings, ed., *Muhammad Ali*, 46.

Page 174 I just don't . . .
Gerald Early, ed., *The Muhammad Ali Reader* (New York: HarperCollins, 1998), 154.

Page 174 He wasn't just . . .
Hauser, "The Importance of Muhammad Ali."

Page 175 Muhammad was a true . . .
Michael J. Fox Foundation for Parkinson's Research, "Saying Goodbye to a True Legend: Muhammad Ali (1942–2016)," June 4, 2016, www.michaeljfox.org/news/saying-goodbye-true-legend-muhammad-ali-1942-2016.

Page 175 Everybody forgets . . .
Brunt, *Facing Ali*, 246–47.

Page 175 Ali was no . . .
Michael Ellison, "Ali Danced Like Butterfly but Had Feet of Clay Says Author," theguardian.com, June 12, 2001, https://www.theguardian.com/world/2001/jun/12/sport.boxing.

Page 175 I disagree . . .
Jennifer Frey, "Pulling No Punches," Washingtonpost.com, May 29, 2001, www.washingtonpost.com/archive/lifestyle/2001/05/29/mark-kram-pulling-punches/b495fd01-85b0-4d7d-9589-bfe384c9d17c/.

Page 175 But peer closer . . .

Mark Kram, "One Nighter in San Juan," sportsillustrated.com, March 1, 1976, https://vault.si.com/vault/1976/03/01/muhammad-ali-fight-san-juan-puerto -rico.

Page 175 Muhammad Ali was a singular . . .

Gentry Estes, "Ali to Grace a New Sports Illustrated Cover," Courier-Journal.com, June 4, 2016, www.courier-journal.com/story/sports/boxing/muhammad-ali/2016/06/04/muhamamd-ali-to-grace-new-sports-illustrated -cover/85398898/.

Page 175 It's hard . . .
Hauser, "The Importance of Muhammad Ali."

Page 175 I grew up . . .

"Emotional Farewell for 'The Greatest,'" thedailystar.net, June 11, 2016, www .thedailystar.net/sports/emotional-farewell-the-greatest-1237921.

Page 176 I'm quite honored

"Sugar Ray Robinson Wins Split Decision from Ali," espn.com, September 6, 2010, www.espn.com/boxing/fnf/981202topten.html.

Page 176 what he stood . . .

Jon Saraceno, "Appreciation: Muhammad Ali Was a Champion In and Out of the Boxing Ring," usatoday.com, June 4, 2016, www.usatoday.com/story/sports/box-ing/2016/06/04/muhammad-ali-appreciation/1635243/.

Page 176 I'm not looking . . .
Hauser, *Muhammad Ali*, 517.

Page 176 fighting was his profession . . .
Collings, ed., *Muhammad Ali*, 189.

Page 176 Fighting injustice . . .
Hauser, *Muhammad Ali: His Life and Times*, 516.

Page 176 Maybe I . . .
Ibid., 517.

Page 177 His legacy . . .

Paul Fichtenbaum, ed. "Muhammad Ali Will Grace the Cover of *Sports Illustrated* This Week for the 40th Time," sportsillustrated.com, June 4, 2016, www.si.com/boxing/2016/06/05/muhammad-ali-death-sports-illustrated-cover.

Page 177 He represented . . .

Tom Withers, Associated Press Sportswriter, "Brotherly Bond: Ali and Jim Brown Shared Passion, Purpose," *Hartford Courant*, Courant.com, June 5, 2016, https://www .courant.com/sdut-brotherly-bond-ali-and-jim-brown-shared-passion-2016jun04 -story.html.

Page 177 to respect themselves . . .
Hauser, *Muhammad Ali: His Life and Times*, 513.

Page 177 By Ali standing . . .
Collings, ed., *Muhammad Ali*, 228.

Page 177 When I was featured . . .
"Sports Illustrated Dedicates Sportsman of the Year Legacy Award to Muhammad Ali," sportsillustrated.com, September 25, 2015, https://www.si.com/boxing/2015/09/25/sports-illustrated-sportsman-year-legacy-award-renamed-for-muhammad-ali.

Page 177 He's done more . . .
Hauser, *Muhammad Ali: His Life and Times*, 500.

Page 178 I'm honored . . .
Ibid., 26.

Page 178 I may be 7'2" . . .
Kareem Abdul-Jabbar, "I Never Felt Taller Than When Standing in Muhammad Ali's Shadow," Huffpost.com, June 4, 2016, https://www.huffpost.com/entry/i-never-felt-taller-than-_b_10296792.

Page 178 This is the Muhammad Ali . . .
President Barack Obama, "What Muhammad Ali Means to Me," *USA Today Sports: Ali 1942–2016: Remembering a Champion, Civil Rights Activist, American Legend*, 9.

Page 178 a man of compassion . . .
Muhammad Ali Memorial: Chief Sidney Hill and Chief Oren Lyons June 10, 2016, WLKY, YouTube, 8:15, www.youtube.com/watch?v=CdLzviYQh70.
He brought a light . . .
Ibid.

Page 178 Float like a butterfly . . .
Hauser, *Muhammad Ali: His Life and Times*, 63–64.

Page 178 All of us were around . . .
The Greatest, Sports Illustrated, June 13, 2016, 49.

Page 179 No one will ever . . .
Melissa Chan, "How Muhammad Ali's Children Mourned His Death," yahoo finance.com, June 6, 2016, https://finance.yahoo.com/news/muhammad-ali-children-mourned-death-135858921.html.

Page 179 In the end . . .
Muller, *A Planet of Hope*, 42.

Page 179 His true legacy is . . .
Hauser, *Muhammad Ali: His Life and Times*, 509.

Page 179 He instilled courage . . .
Ibid.

Page 180 Today, football may . . .
Collings, ed., *Muhammad Ali*, 12.

Page 180 Today we bow . . .
Alysha Tsuji, "Kareem Abdul-Jabbar on Muhammad Ali's Most Important Lesson: 'Stay True to What You Believe In,'" ftw.usatoday.com, June 4, 2016, https://ftw .usatoday.com/2016/06/kareem-abdul-jabbar-muhammad-ali-life-lesson-stay-true -belief-tribute.

Page 180 We lost a giant . . .
"Sport and Showbiz Stars Pay Tribute To 'King,'" news.sky.com, June 4, 2016, https://news.sky.com/story/sport-and-showbiz-stars-pay-tribute-to-king -10303692.

Page 180 For a guy . . .
Hauser, *Muhammad Ali: His Life and Times*, 450.

Page 180 Some people . . .
Bucktin, "Muhammad Ali's Doctor Begged Him to Quit Boxing After Thrilla in Manila."

Page 180 a giant among . . .
"Sport and Showbiz Stars Pay Tribute To 'King,'" news.sky.com, June 4, 2016.

Page 180 #TheGreatest
"Athletes, Celebrities React to Muhammad Ali's Death," US Olympic and Paralympic Team, USA Team @ TeamUSA, sportsillustrated.com, June 4, 2016, www.si.com/boxing/2016/06/04/muhammad-ali-dead-athletes-celebrities-tribute -reaction.

Page 180 Muhammad Ali was . . .
Dave Zirin, "Another Side of the Champ Revealed," June 28, 2016, https:// socialistworker.org/2016/06/28/another-side-of-the-champ-revealed.

Page 181 May we meet . . .
Ibid.

Page 181 Muhammad was not . . .
"In Their Own Words: Eulogies for Muhammad Ali," nytimes.com, June 10, 2016, https://www.nytimes.com/2016/06/11/sports/lonnie-billy-crystal-bill -clinton-eulogies-for-muhammad-ali.html.

Page 181 May you live . . .

"Muhammad Ali Memorial: Rasheda Ali-Walsh," WLKY News Louisville, June 10, 2016, YouTube, www.youtube.com/watch?v=8h8ieYV2J1k.

Page 181 I would like to be remembered . . .

Ali with Ali, *Soul of a Butterfly*, 200.

BIBLIOGRAPHY

BOOKS

Ali, Muhammad with Hana Yasmeen Ali. *Soul of a Butterfly: Reflections on Life's Journey*. New York, NY: Simon and Schuster, 2004.

Ali, Muhammad and Herbert Muhammad with Richard Durham. Edited by Toni Morrison. *The Greatest: My Won Story*. New York: Random House, 1975.

Ali, Muhammad, Thomas Hauser, and Richard Dominick. *Healing: A Journal of Tolerance and Understanding*. New York: HarperCollins, 1996.

Baldwin, James. *The Fire Next Time*. New York: Dial Press, 1963.

Brunt, Stephen. *Facing Ali, 15 Writers, 15 Stories: The Opposition Weighs In*. Guilford, Connecticut: Lyons Press, 2002.

Dundee, Angelo and Burt Randolph Sugar. *My View from the Corner: A Life in Boxing*. New York: McGraw-Hill, 2009.

Early, Gerald, Editor. *The Muhammad Ali Reader*. Hopewell, New Jersey: The Ecco Press, 1998.

Eig, Jonathan. *Ali: A Life*. New York: Houghton Mifflin Harcourt, 2017.

Ellison, Ralph: *Invisible Man*. Norwalk, CT: First Edition Library, 1980.

Evanzz, Karl. *I am the Greatest: The Best Quotations from Muhammad Ali*. Kansas City, MO: Andrew McMeel, 2002.

Ezra, Michael. *Muhammad Ali: The Making of an Icon*. Philadelphia: Temple University Press, 2009.

Giller, Norman. *The Ali Files: His Fights, His Foes, His Fees, His Feet, His Fate*. United Kingdom: Pitch Publishing, 2015.

Hauser, Thomas. *Muhammad Ali: A Tribute to the Greatest*. New York, NY: Pegasus Books, 2016.

Hauser, Thomas. *Muhammad Ali: His Life and Times*. New York, NY: Open Road Integrated Media, 1991.

Jenkins, Mark Collings. *Muhammad Ali: Through the Eyes of the World*. New York: Skyhorse Publishing, 2007.

Kindred, David. *Sound and Fury: Two Powerful Lives, One Fateful Friendship*. New York, NY: Free Press, 2006.

Kram, Mark. *Ghosts of Manila: The Fateful Blood Freud Between Muhammad Ali and Joe Frazier*. New York, NY: Perennial, 2001.

Lanker, Brian and Barbara Summers. *I Dream of World: Portraits of Black Women Who Changed America*. New York: Stewart, Tabori & Chang, 1989.

Marable, Manning. *Malcolm X: A Life of Reinvention*. New York: Penguin Books, 2011.

Marqusee, Mark. *Redemption Song: Muhammad Ali and the Spirit of the Sixties*. New York, NY: Verso, 1999.

McNamara, Robert S. *In Retrospect: The Tragedy and Lessons of Vietnam*. New York: Vintage Books, 1996.

Montville, Leigh. *Sting Like a Bee: Muhammad Ali vs. the United States of America, 1966–1971*. New York: Doubleday, 2017.

Muhammad, Elijah. *Message to the Black Man in America*. Phoenix, AZ: Secretarius Memps Publication, 2006.

Muller, Robert. *A Planet of Hope*. New York: Amity House, 1986.

Myers, Walter Dean. *The Greatest: Mohammad Ali*. New York: Scholastic, 2001.

Rampersad, Arnold, editor and David Roessel, associate editor. *The Collected Poems of Langston Hughes*. New York: Alfred A. Knopf, 1995.

Remnick, David. *King of the World: Muhammad Ali and the Rise of an American Hero*. New York, NY: Picador, 1998.

Robinson, Sugar Ray and David Anderson. *Sugar Ray*. New York: Viking Press, 1970.

Taschen, Benedikt, ed. *Greatest of All Time: A Tribute to Muhammad Ali*. Germany: Taschen, 2010.

West, David, editor. *The Mammoth Book of Muhammad Ali*. Philadelphia: Running Press, 2012.

X, Malcolm. *Malcolm X Speaks: Selected Speeches and Statements*. New York: Grove Press, 1965.

X, Malcolm, with Alex Haley. *The Autobiography of Malcolm X*. New York: Penguin Books, 1965.

MAGAZINE ARTICLES

"Ali Does 'Roadwork' on 'Freedom Road': Retired Heavyweight Champ Makes TV Acting Debut in Four-Hour Drama," *Ebony Magazine*, October 1979.

Bingham, Howard. "Unforgettable Courage: These Heroes Lifted a Nation." *Reader's Digest*, December 2001.

Boyle, Robert H. "Too Many Punches, Too Little Concern: With Boxing Ills Under Fresh Public Scrutiny, New Research on Brain Damage in Experienced Fighters Suggests a Road to Medical Reform," *Sports Illustrated*, April 11, 1983.

Clancy, Frank. "The Bitter Science: Head Blows from Boxing Can Cause Dementia and Alzheimer's. Can the Same Chronic Brain Injury Also Lead to Parkinson's?" *Neurology Now*, Vol. 2, no. 2 (March/April 2006), 24–25.

Clay, Cassius. "My $1,000,000 Getaway." *Sports Illustrated,* February 24, 1964.

Editors of *Sports Illustrated*. "Muhammad Ali: The Tribute." New York: *Sports Illustrated*, June 14, 2016.

Felsenthal, Edward, editor. "Woodstock, the Moon and Manson: The Turbulent End of the '60s." *Time*, 2019.

Goodell, Jeff. "Obama Takes on Climate Control." *Rolling Stone*, October 8, 2015, 36–45.

Hoffer, Richard. "A Lot More Than Lip Service on February 25, 1964: Cassius Clay Beats Sonny Liston." *Sports Illustrated*, November 29, 1999.

Hoffer, Richard. "The Tribute: Muhammad Ali 1942 to 2016." *Sports Illustrated*, June 13, 2016.

Horn, Huston. "The Eleven Men Behind Cassius Clay." *Sports Illustrated,* March 11, 1963. https://www.si.com/vault/1963/03/11/606229/the-eleven-men-behind-cassius-clay.

Horn, Huston. "'E Said 'E Would 'E Did." *Sports Illustrated*, July 1, 1963.

Horn, Huston. "His Fight and His Future: The First Days in the New Life of the Champion of the World." *Sports Illustrated*, March 9, 1964.

Jackson, Jimmy. "FOCUS: Of Books and Boxers, Cabbages and Kings." *Fellowship of Catholic University Students*. Sisters of Charity of Nazareth Archives, Louisville, Kentucky.

Jones, Robert. "The Negro in Viet Nam Sgt. Clide Brown, Jr." *Time*, May 26, 1967.

Kane, Martin. "Ali-Clay: The Once and Future King? The Art of Ali." *Sports Illustrated*, May 5, 1969, 48–56.

Kram, Mark. "The Epic Battle Between Joe Frazier and Muhammad Ali: Lawdy, Lawdy, He's Great." *Sports Illustrated*, October 13, 1975.

Layden, Tim. "The Legacy of the Greatest Still Grows, Ali: The Legacy." *Sports Illustrated*, October 5, 2015.

Lipsyte, Robert. *"Time Commemorative Edition: Muhammad Ali The Greatest 1942–2016."* New York: *Time*, June 6, 2016.

Maule, Tex. "His Fight and His Future: Yes, It Was Good and Honest." *Sports Illustrated*, March 9, 1964.

Maule, Tex. "Cassius Clay vs. Sonny Liston: Cassius to Win a Thriller." *Sports Illustrated*, May 24, 1965.

Maule, Tex. "The Fight You Didn't See: A Quick, Hard Right and a Needless Storm of Protest." *Sports Illustrated*, June 7, 1965, 22–25.

Maule, Tex. "The Big Fight: Clay vs. Terrell: The Left That Was." *Sports Illustrated*, February 6, 1967.

Maule, Tex. 'The Scramble for Ali's Title: Once and Future King." *Sports Illustrated*, July 10, 1967.

Maule, Tex. "When Right Made Might: Of All the Stuff Ali Showed Lyle, Only the Right Hand Was Telling" *Sports Illustrated*, May 26, 1975.

Nack, William. "Not with a Bang but a Whisper" *Sports Illustrated*, December 21, 1981.

Nack, William. "Once and Forever: Young Cassius Clay at 50 Mohammad Ali Is Much-Admired Figure, Just to See Was in His Formative Years as a Fun-Loving but Purposeful Youth in Louisville." *Sports Illustrated*, January 13, 1992.

Nack, William. "The Fight Is over Joe: More Than Two Decades after They First Met in the Ring, Joe Frazier is Still Taking Shots at Muhammad Ali, But It's a War of Words." *Sports Illustrated*, September 30, 1996.

Olsen, Jack. "Cassius Clay: the Man, the Muslim, the Mystery: A Case of Conscience." *Sports Illustrated*, April 11, 1966.

Omalu, Bennet, et al. "Chronic Traumatic Encephalopathy in the National Football League Player." *Neurosurgery*, 57: 128–134, 2005.

Patterson, Floyd. "In Defense of Cassius Clay." *Esquire*, August 1, 1966.

Putnam, Pat. "Ali's Desperate Hour: Once More to the Well." *Sports Illustrated*, October 4, 1977.

Putnam, Pat. "Doom in the Desert." *Sports Illustrated*, October 13, 1980.

Remnick, David. "The Sporting Scene, American Hunger." *New Yorker*, October 12, 1998 (Gleason quote).

Rogin, Gilbert. "The Big Fight: Can Clay Do It Again?: Still Hurt and Lost." *Sports Illustrated*, November 16, 1964.

Rogin, Gilbert. "The Big Fight: Clay vs. Patterson: Rabbit Hunt in Vegas." *Sports Illustrated*, November 22, 1965.

Shecter, Leonard. "The Passion of Muhammad Ali." *Esquire*, April 1, 1968.

Sisters of Charity of Nazareth. "Special Tribute: Sister James Ellen Huff, SCN '38." SCN Archives, Louisville, Kentucky.

Smith, Gary. "Ali and His Entourage: Life After the End of the Greatest Show on Earth." *Sports Illustrated*, April 25, 1988.

White, Theodore H. "Bell of Decision Rings Out in Vietnam: Approaching Elections Challenge a Nation's History and Offer Hope for the Future." *Life*, September 1, 1967.

Yates, Lauren. *"Cassius Clay Sleep Here" Spalding University News*, Louisville, Kentucky, 1997.

NEWSPAPERS

Associated Press. "Frazier Hits Canvas 6 Times; George Foreman Wanted It Stopped." *Toledo Blade*, January 23, 1973.

Associated Press. "Tough Fight: Ali Suffered from Too Many Blows to the Head, Former Boxer Faces Ordeal of Parkinson's" *Ocala Star Banner*, July 16, 1987.

Batchelor, Matt. "Muhammad Ali; Children; Education Is Crucial Part of Center's Goals." *Courier-Journal*, November 19, 2005, K10.

Beecher, William. "Raids in Cambodia by U.S. Unprotested," *New York Times*, May 9, 1969, 1.

Cengel, Katya. "Growing up with the Greatest: Son of Ali Talks about His Famous Dad." *Courier-Journal*, June 21, 2010.

Coomes, Mark. "Muhammad Ali; Lonnie Ali; Dream Realized, 13 Years in the Making. Muhammad Ali Center." *Courier-Journal,* November 19, 2005, K3.

de Vise, Daniel. "Morgan State Honors Its Civil Rights Sit-in Pioneers." *Washington Post*, November 11, 2011.

Hale, Ray. "A Golden Moment: 1960 Olympic Victory Launched Muhammad Ali into the Spotlight." *Courier-Journal*, August 30, 2010.

Jan, Tracy. "Racial Economic Gap Unchanged Since 1968: 50 Years after Major Study on Inequality, No Gains Seen for Blacks." *Washington Post–Express Newspaper*, February 28, 2018.

Kamen, Jeff. "The Day I Secretly Watched Muhammad Ali Coach Peace to Chicago Gang Members." *Chicago Tribune*, June 7, 2016.

Kaufman, Sarah L. "Muhammad Ali's Grace Broke the Mold of a Heavyweight Champion," *Washington Post*, June 4, 2016.

"Muhammad Ali's Decision: What People Think. How the People React to Muhammad Ali's Decision: Looks Are Deceiving." *New York Amsterdam News*, May 6, 1967, 1.

Shafer, Sheldon S. "Muhammad Ali: Beyond the Museum: 'Center Will Revolve Around Ideas.'" *Courier-Journal*, November 19, 2005, C2.

Shafer, Sheldon S. "Muhammad Ali: Center of Inspiration." *Courier-Journal,* January 5, 2012.

Tompkins, Wayne. "Unforgiving: Muhammad Ali; A Polarizing Legacy; Ali's Refusal to Serve Still Rankles Some." *Courier Journal,* November 19, 2005, K8.

Ungar, Laura. "Muhammad Ali: The Battle with Parkinson's" *Courier-Journal,* January 5, 2012.

Vecsey, George. "At 39, Ali has More Points to Prove." *The New York Times*, November 29, 1981.

Whiney, Craig R. "3-Year Ring Ban Declared Unfair: Commissions Action Call 'Arbitrary.'" *New York Times*, September 15, 1970, 56.

Young, Dick. "Judges 'Rally' Decisive" *St. Petersburg Independent*, September 30, 1976, p16.

ONLINE ARTICLES

Able, Jessica. "'The Greatest' Served Alongside Sisters of Charity of Nazareth." *Record/Archdiocesan News*, June 8, 2016, https://therecordnewspaper.org/greatest-served-alongside-sisters-charity-nazareth/.

Astridge, Elizabeth. "A Lifelong Friendship: Muhammed Ali and Sr. James Ellen Huff, SCN." *FAMVIN,* June 14, 2016, https://famvin.org/en/2016/06/14/lifelong-friendship-muhammad-ali-sr-james-ellen-huff-scn/.

Bagchi, Rob. "50 Stunning Olympic Moments No. 35: Wilma Rudolph's Triple Gold in 1960." *Guardian,* June 1, 2012, https://www.theguardian.com/sport/blog/2012/jun/01/50-stunning-olympic-moments-wilma-rudolph.

Bai, Bo. "Ali's Meeting with Deng Xiaoping Revived Boxing in China." June 4, 2016, www.espn.com/boxing/ali/story/_/id/15948776/boxing-muhammad-ali-visits-china-meets-deng-xiao-ping.

Bennett Jr., James. "Remembering Muhammad Ali's Surprise Visit to All-Black High School in Winter Haven." *The Ledger,* June 9, 2016, https://www.theledger.com/story/news/2016/06/09/remembering-muhammad-alis-surprise-visit-to-all-black-high-school-in-winter-haven/27148846007/.

Bhatia, Sidharth. "When Muhammad Ali Came to Bombay and Floored the City." The Wire, June 4, 2016, https://thewire.in/culture/when-muhammad-ali-came-to-bombay-and-floored-the-city.

Boniface, Russell, associate editor. "Muhammad Ali Center Is a Knockout." *AIArchitect,* February 2006, http://info.aia.org/aiarchitect/thisweek06/0203/0203pw_ali.htm.

Bucktin, Christopher. "Muhammad Ali's Doctor Begged Him to Quit Boxing after the Thrilla in Manila." *Mirror,* June 4, 2016, https://www.mirror.co.uk/sport/boxing/muhammad-alis-doctor-begged-him-8116534.

Bynon, Daffydd. "Sport Picture of the Day Muhammad Ali's Bike Started It All." *Guardian,* June 7, 2016, https://www.theguardian.com/sport/picture/2016/jun/07/sport-picture-of-the-day-muhammad-alis-red-bike-started-it-all.

Callahan, Maureen. "How Muhammad Ali Secured the Release of 15 U.S. Hostages in Iraq." NewYorkPost.com, November 29, 2015, https://nypost.com/2015/11/29/the-tale-of-muhammad-alis-goodwill-trip-to-iraq-that-freed-us-hostages/.

Clark, Peter Allen. "Muhammad Ali Had a Lifelong Mission to Help Those in Need." Mashable, June 4, 2016, https://mashable.com/article/muhammad-ali-charity-legacy.

Eisenband, Jeff. "Muhammad Ali Sent This Supportive Telegram to a Jailed Mating Luther King, Jr. in 1967." thepostgame.com, January 16, 2017, http://www.thepostgame.com/muhammad-alis-telegram-martin-luther-king-jr.

Ellsberg, Daniel. "Lying about Vietnam." *New York Times* Opinion, June 29, 2001, https://www.nytimes.com/2001/06/29/opinion/lying-about-vietnam.html.

Fanning, Evan. "50 Stunning Olympic Moments No. 17: Cassius Clay Wins Gold in 1960." *Guardian,* March 7, 2012, https://www.theguardian.com/sport/london-2012-olympics-blog/2012/mar/07/stunning-olympic-moments-cassius-clay.

"Final Words: Cronkite's Vietnam Commentary." *NPR,* July 18, 2009, https://www.npr.org/templates/story/story.php?storyId=106775685.

"Former Heavyweight Champion George Foreman on Muhammad Ali." *Tokyo Journal,* https://www.tokyojournal.com/component/k2/item/838-george -foreman-278.html.

Gildea, William. "Before He Became Muhammad Ali, Cassius Clay Was a Kid Who Got His Bike Stolen." *Washington Post,* June 7, 2016, https://www.wash-ingtonpost.com/sports/boxing-mma-wrestling/before-he-became-muhammad -ali-cassius-clay-was-a-kid-who-got-his-bike-stolen/2016/06/07/809b769a -2cd7-11e6-9de3-6e6e7a14000c_story.html?utm_term=.b0ff656266a6.

Gilmore, Mikal. "How Muhammad Ali Conquered Fear and Changed the World." Mensjournal.com, November 2011, www.mensjournal.com/features/ how-muhammad-ali-conquered-fear-and-changed-the-world-20130205.

Gregory, Sean. "Why Ali Matters to Everyone." *Time.com.* June 4, 2016, http:// time.com/3646214/muhammad-ali-dead-obituary/?xid=homepage.

Irusta, Carlos. "Dundee: Ali Was, Still Is 'The Greatest.'" ESPN.com. January 17, 2012, http://www.espn.com/boxing/story/_/id/7470417/muhammad-ali-was -continues-greatest.

Jerving, Sarah. "Global Warming—What Exxon Knew about the Earth's Melting Arctic." *Wall Street Journal,* November 8, 2015, https://graphics.latimes.com/ exxon-arctic/.

Kelly, Ned. "This Day in History: When Muhammad Ali Came to China." May 20, 2021, www.thatsmags.com/shanghai/post/5349/history-when-muhammad-ali -came-to-china.

Khaled, Ali. "How Muhammad Ali Became a Sporting Hero to the Arab World." *Alarabiya News,* https://english.alarabiya.net/sports/2016/06/04/How -Muhammad-Ali-became-a-sporting-hero-to-the-Arab-world.

Levin, Jordan. "Bygone Days: The Sweet Music of Miami's Overtown." *Miami Herald,* February 1, 2009, https://www.miamiherald.com/entertainment/ent -columns-blogs/jordan-levin/article1931267.html.

LewAllen, Dave. "Muhammad Ali Visit Propelled Rainbow Connection." June 6, 2016, https://www.wxyz.com/news/region/oakland-county/boxing -great-muhammad-alis-visit-to-local-teenager-marked-beginning-of-wishes-for -michigan-kids.

Lipsyte, Robert. "Not the Greatest: Joe Frazier Was a True Gladiator, but He'll Always Be Remembered as Muhammad Ali's Foil." Slate, November 9, 2011, www.slate.com/articles/sports/sports_nut/2011/11/joe_frazier_dead_he_was_a _true_gladiator_but_he_ll_always_be_remembered_as_muhammad_ali_s_foil_ .html.

Mailer, Norman. "Ego," *Life* Magazine, March 19, 1971, https://books.google .com/books?id=iVMEAAAAMBAJ&pg=PA19-IA15#v=onepage&q&f=false.

Martinez, Michael. "Obama Honors Girls Killed in 1963 Church Bombing." cnn .com, May 24, 2013, www.cnn.com/2013/05/24/politics/obama-birmingham -medals/index.html.

Mather, Victor. "Ali's Least Memorable Fight." *New York Times*, June 26, 1976, https://www.nytimes.com/2016/06/06/sports/who-lost-when-muhammad-ali -fought-a-pro-wrestler-the-fans.html.

"Muhammad Ali." American Civil Liberties Union, https://www.aclu.org/ muhammad-ali.

"Muhammad Ali." Wikipedia. https://en.wikipedia.org/wiki/Muhammad_Ali.

Muhammad Ali Center. AliCenter.Org. https://alicenter.org/about-us/.

"Muhammad Ali Center." Beyer Blinder Beller, http://www.beyerblinderbelle .com/projects/18_muhammad_ali_center.

"Muhammad Ali Delivers Aid to Liberian Refugees." August 20, 1997, https:// apnews.com/article/8b230c6b31cefd5851ab22645be0f62c.

"Muhammad Ali Eulogized as Transcending Sports and Culture." *Newsweek*, June 4, 2016, https://www.newsweek.com/muhammad-ali-transcended-sports -culture-466533.

"Muhammad Ali Fought for America to Understand Islam, Not Fear It." The Undefeated. Andscape, 2017, https://theundefeated.com/features/muhammad -ali-fought-for-america-to-understand-islam-not-fear-it/.

"Muhammad Ali in India." Wikipedia, https://en.wikipedia.org/wiki/Muham mad_Ali_in_India.

"Muhammad Ali's Pilgrimage to Makkah: The Journey of a Butterfly." *Emel Magazine*, Issue 17, December 30, 2018, https://www.emel.com/article?id=& a_id=1722.

"Muhammad Ali: A Transcendent Life: Humanitarian and Peace Advocate." University of Louisville Libraries, https://library.louisville.edu/c.php?g=1105926 &p=8063585.

"Muhammad Ali Visits Children's Hospital," muhammadalisaved.com, March 17, 2022, http://muhammadalisaved.com/muhammad-ali-visits-childrens-hospital/.

Pope, Derrick Alexander. "Leroy Johnson: In the Center Ring of Change." *Georgia Bar Journal*, Vol. 22, no. 5 (February 2017), www.gabar.org/newsandpublica tions/georgiabarjournal/upload/217GBJ_web.pdf.

Powell, Azizi. "19th Century African American Spiritual/Ring Shout 'You Got a Right to the Tree of Life' (also known as 'Run, Mary Run'), Part I: Information & Lyrics." Pancocojams, April 4, 2020, http://pancocojams.blogspot .com/2020/04/19th-century-african-american.html.

Remnick, David. "American Hunger: As an ambitious, searching young man, Cassius Clay invented himself, and became the most original and magnetic athlete of the century—Muhammad Ali." *New Yorker*, October 12, 1998, https://www .newyorker.com/magazine/1998/10/12/american-hunger.

Romeo, Marissa. "The Betsy to Host 10th Annual Overture to Overtown Jazz Festival." Broadwayworld.com, March 4, 2022, www.broadwayworld.com/ miami/article/The-Betsy-to-Host-10th-Annual-Overture-To-Overtown-Jazz -Festival-20220304.

Saraceno, Jon. "Caring for The Greatest, Muhammad Ali." *AARP Bulletin*, June 2014, https://www.aarp.org/home-family/caregiving/info-2014/caregiving -muhammad-lonnie-ali-parkinsons.html.

Saraceno, Jon. "Muhammad Ali–Angelo Dundee Partnership Helped Create a Boxing Legend." usatoday.com, June 4, 2016, www.usatoday.com/story/sports/ boxing/2016/06/04/muhammad-ali-angelo-dundee-bond/85357044/.

Saraceno, Jon. "Q&A with Ferdie Pacheco, Muhammad Ali's Longtime Doctor and Corner Man." usatoday.com, June 4, 2016, https://www.usatoday .com/story/sports/boxing/2016/06/04/muhammad-ali-ferdie-pacheco -interview/85352836/.

Sayers, Justine. "Bees Swarm in Tree Near the Famous Quote Mural." CourierJournal.com, June 5, 2016, https://www.courier-journal.com/story/sports/ boxing/muhammad-ali/2016/06/05/bees-swarm-tree-near-famous-ali-quote -mural/85447810/.

Schmitt, Rick. "Birmingham Church Bombing: 50 Years On." *Washington Lawyer*, DC Bar.org, September 2013, https://www.dcbar.org/bar-resources/publica tions/washington-lawyer/articles/september-2013-birmingham-bomb.cfm.

Scruggs, Afi-Odelia. "Beyond Vietnam: The MLK Speech That Caused an Uproar." *USA Today*, January 13, 2017, https://www.usatoday.com/story/news/nation -now/2017/01/13/martin-luther-king-jr-beyond-vietnam-speech/96501636/.

Sharma, Amol, and Matthew Futterman. "McCain Champions Boxing Regulations in Lonely Fight." wallstreetjournal.com, October 16, 2008, www.wsj .com/articles/SB122418182528041339.

"16th Street Baptist Church Bombing." Wikipedia, https://en.wikipedia.org/ wiki/16th_Street_Baptist_Church_bombing.

Smith, Peter. "Muhammad Ali Appeals to Ayatollah Khamenei to Release U.S. Hikers." *Courier Journal*, June 13, 2014, www.courier-journal.com/story/sports/ boxing/muhammad-ali/2014/06/13/ali-iran-hikers/9866789/.

Snowden, Jonathan. "The Brutal Power of Pride: Ali and Frazier's Final Act, 40 Years Later." Bleacher Report, October 1, 2015, https://bleacherreport.com/ articles/2572862-the-brutal-power-of-pride-ali-and-fraziers-final-act-40-years -later.

"UCLA Anderson School of Management. 2015 John E. Anderson Distinguished Alumni Award Recipient: Lonnie Ali '82, Vice Chairman, The Muhammad Ali Center." anderson.ucla.edu, http://www.anderson.ucla.edu/alumni/alumni -awards/lonnie-ali-86.

"UN Peace Messenger Muhammad Ali Encourages Afghan Children to Prepare for Future." November 19, 2002, https://news.un.org/en/story/2002/11/51882 -un-peace-messenger-muhammad-ali-encourages-afghan-children-prepare -future.

Verigan, Bill. "Larry Holmes Fights Like a Champ to KO Mohammad Ali in 1980 Las Vegas Bout." *New York Daily News,* October 3, 1980, https://www.nydaily news.com/sports/ali-takes-lot-blows-loss-holmes-1980-article-1.2373364.

"Watts Rebellion (Los Angeles): August 11, 1965, to August 16, 1965." Sanford University, Martin Luther King, Jr. Research and Education Institute. https://kinginstitute.stanford.edu/encyclopedia/watts-rebellion-los-angeles.

Whitney, Craig, "3-Year Ring Ban Declared Unfair." *New York Times*, September 15, 1970, https://www.nytimes.com/1970/09/15/archives/3year-ring-ban-declared-unfair-commissions-action-called-abitrary.html.

Wolff, Eli A., and Mary A. Hurns. "Muhammad Ali's Principles Are a Guide for the Athlete Humanitarian, Athlete Mentor and Athlete Activist." Alicenter.org, June 18, 2020, https://alicenter.org/muhammad-alis-principles-are-a-guide-for-the-athlete-humanitarian-athlete-mentor-and-athlete-activist/.

DVDS, TV AND YOUTUBE.COM

"The BoxingRUs: Boxing and the Mafia Video." October 11, 2012, https://www.youtube.com/watch?v=YYjg2p7k7Y0.

Coalition for Clean Air. "Muhammad Ali and the Fight for Clean Air," June 6, 2016, YouTube, www.ccair.org/bill-burke-muhammad-ali-and-the-fight-for-clean-air/.

Gast, Leon, director. *When We Were Kings*. Polygram USA Video, 2003. The BoxinRUs. "Boxing and the Mafia." YouTube, https://www.youtube.com/watch?v=YYjg2p7k7Y0.

"In Their Own Words: Muhammad Ali Episode 2," WETA, September 8, 2015, https://www.pbs.org/video/their-own-words-muhammad-ali-introduction/.

Lewens, Clare, director. *I AM ALI: The Man Behind the Legend:* Universal Pictures Home Entertainment. November 11, 2014.

"Louisville, KY: Heavyweight Champion Muhammad Ali Got Together with Civil Rights Leader Martin Luther King for a Friendly Chat." Youtube, https://www.youtube.com/watch?v=XOhvupjhS3U.

McCormack, Pete, director. *Facing Ali*. Lions Gate Entertainment, December 29, 2009.

Muhammad Ali vs. Trevor Berbick: The Last Hurrah, "Drama in the Bahamas," Rhino, February 12, 2002.

"Planet Earth: The Future." Discovery Communications, April 24, 2007.

INDEX

Page numbers in italics indicate photographs.

ABOUT THE AUTHOR

Margueritte Shelton earned undergraduate and graduate degrees from New York University. She developed an interest in diverse peoples and cultures of the world through her studies in anthropology. She is a member of the Muhammad Ali Center in Louisville, Kentucky. Raised in New York City, Shelton now resides in Virginia with her family. *Muhammad Ali: A Humanitarian Life* is her first book.

CPSIA information can be obtained
at www.ICGtesting.com
Printed in the USA
BVHW041017081222
653666BV00002B/2